Local Politics and the Dynamics of Property in Africa

Access to land and property is vital to people's livelihoods in rural, peri-urban, and urban areas in Africa. Through recourse to a variety of political, administrative, and legal institutions, people exert tremendous energy and imagination to have their land claims recognized as rights. This book provides a detailed analysis of how public authority and the state are formed through debates and struggles over property in the Upper East Region of Ghana. Although scarcity may indeed promote exclusivity, the evidence from Ghana shows that when many institutions contend for the right to authorize claims to land, the result of an effort to unify and clarify the law is to intensify competition among these institutions and to weaken their legitimacy. The book explores particularly how state divestiture of land in 1979 encouraged competition between customary authorities and how, as a result, the institution of the earthpriest was revived. Such processes are key to understanding property and authority in Africa.

Christian Lund has worked on issues concerning land and politics in West Africa for almost twenty years. He is the author of *Law, Power, and Politics in Niger: Land Struggles and the Rural Code* (1998) and the editor and coeditor, respectively, of *Twilight Institutions: Public Authority and Local Politics in Africa* (2007) and *Negotiating Property in Africa* (2002). In addition, he has published in *Africa, Development and Change, Journal of Modern African Studies*, and *World Development*. Lund is a member of the Social Science Research Council in Denmark and director of the Graduate School in International Development Studies at Roskilde University. Lund was also editor of *European Journal of Development Research* from 2000 to 2004.

Local Politics and the Dynamics of Property in Africa

Christian Lund

Roskilde University, Denmark

CAMBRIDGE
UNIVERSITY PRESS

CAMBRIDGE UNIVERSITY PRESS
Cambridge, New York, Melbourne, Madrid, Cape Town, Singapore,
São Paulo, Delhi, Dubai, Tokyo

Cambridge University Press
32 Avenue of the Americas, New York, NY 10013-2473, USA

www.cambridge.org
Information on this title: www.cambridge.org/9780521148511

First published 2008
First paperback edition 2010

A catalog record for this publication is available from the British Library.

Library of Congress Cataloging in Publication Data

Lund, Christian.
Local politics and the dynamics of property in Africa / Christian Lund.
p. cm.
Includes bibliographical references and index.
ISBN 978-0-521-88654-3 (hardback)
1. Land tenure – Ghana. 2. Right of property – Ghana. 3. Local government – Ghana. I. Title.
HD1022.Z63L86   2008
333.309667–dc22   2007038690

ISBN   978-0-521-88654-3 Hardback
ISBN   978-0-521-14851-1 Paperback

Contents

Maps, Figures, and Tables

Maps

Figures

Tables

Acknowledgments

The debts I incurred in completing this book are many. Generous support from the Danish Social Science Research Council enabled me to take a full sabbatical and to travel to Ghana. I believe that ample time to focus on my research at the beginning of the project has been crucial to its completion. Support for travel was also secured from the Soudano-Sahelian Environmental Research Initiative and from the Danish Council for Development Research, for which I am grateful.

I would also like to thank those institutions and colleagues who have hosted me during the past years and who have provided excellent opportunities for me to present and discuss my work. I am especially grateful to Jean-Pierre Olivier de Sardan and Giorgio Blundo of the École des Hautes Études en Sciences Sociales, Marseille; Gareth Austin of the London School of Economics and Political Science; and Poul Engberg-Pedersen and Gorm Rye Olsen of the Centre for Development Research, Copenhagen. These academic sojourns provided intellectual oxygen for my work and the opportunity for regular feedback on my research and writing. I have also had the good fortune to be invited to present papers and chapters in progress at a number of institutions, in particular, African Studies Centre, Leiden; Copenhagen University; Food and Agriculture Organisation, Rome; Humboldt Universität, Berlin; Johannes Gutenberg Universität, Mainz; Johns Hopkins University, Baltimore; Laboratoire d'études et recherches sur les dynamiques socials et le développement local, Niamey; Max Planck Institute for Social Anthropology, Halle; Nordic Africa Institute, Uppsala; Université de Ouagadougou; University for Development Studies (Northern Ghana); University of Helsinki; University of Sussex, Brighton; University of Wageningen; University of the Western Cape, Cape Town; and the World Resources Institute, Washington, D.C.

Throughout my work, I have been fortunate to engage in ongoing discussions with students and colleagues at Roskilde University. The weekly seminars and the researcher training courses at the Graduate School of International Development Studies have been sites for stimulating critical analysis and the "eternal search for the argument," and I realize how much it has meant to my work. As many will know, it would have been impossible to juggle my academic duties while writing this book without the support of Inge Jensen, the conscientious and steadfast fixture of the Graduate School.

Along the way, many people have influenced the work more than they might realize. They have offered help, advice, and encouragement, and their questions and comments have often forced me to think again. It is not possible to acknowledge individually everyone who had a hand in this, who read and commented on greater and smaller parts of the manuscript, but special thanks are owed to Amanda Hammar, Andrew Wardell, Ann Whitehead, Ben Jones, Camilla Toulmin, Carola Lentz, Claude Mauret, David Pratten, Ebbe Prag, Eric Hahonou, Fiona Wilson, Gareth Austin, Giorgio Blundo, Helene Kyed, Henrik Secher Marcussen, Jean-Pierre Olivier de Sardan, Jeremy Gould, Jesse Ribot, Jimmy Weiner, Judy Longbottom, Karen Lauterbach, Keebet and Franz von Benda-Beckmann, Kojo Amanor, Lars Buur, Lisa Richey, Mahaman Tidjani Alou, Molly Bloom, Monique Nuijten, Neil Webster, Parker Shipton, Pauline Peters, Pierre-Yves le Meur, Ravinder Kaur, Richard Kuba, Rie Odgaard, Roger Leys, Sally Falk Moore, Sara Berry, Simon Batterbury, Sten Hagberg, Thomas Bierschenk, and Thomas Sikor.

In Ghana, I have also incurred many debts. Issues of politics, property, law, history, and power are obviously sensitive. To many of my interlocutors, acknowledgment by name could cause embarrassment. Nonetheless, numerous people have kept copies of letters, reports, newspaper clippings, petitions, and minutes of meetings, and I have encountered only trust and generosity as people let me make copies of their "private archives." They will have to accept my private thanks. Yet my listing must include Bakari Sadiq Nyari of the Regional Lands Commission for his boundless patience in mitigating my ignorance. Roy Ayariga of the Ministry of Agriculture; lawyer James Kaba; and Peter Ayaba, registrar at Bolgatanga High Court, also took pains to enlighten me on the intricacies of politics, property, law, and litigation in Bolgatanga. Christopher Asaare, who has recorded the history of many villages in the Bolgatanga area, kindly explained the sometimes fabulous stories of the area. Generally, the members of the public administration, chiefs, and politicians were extremely accommodating, and without their openness, I fear I would have given up halfway through this project. David and Lydia Millar stand out for their generosity, hospitality, and willingness to share their knowledge of the region, and I am grateful to Philip Ayamba, Joe Ayembilla, and Moses Aduko for their indefatigable assistance, guidance, and company, and to Andy Murphy and George Akoka for discussing and consistently challenging my work. The professional diligence of the staff in the Public Records and Archives in Tamale helped me to access a wealth of material, and I consider it a rare privilege to have "traveled back in time" under their guidance. Finally, my stays in Bolga were made especially pleasant by the helpfulness of the staff of the Sacred Heart Social Centre and the hospitality of the informal badminton club at the Black Star Hotel.

Some of the chapters have appeared in different forms, and I am grateful to the publishers for letting me use my work for the present book. Chapter 3 appeared in a different form in R. Kuba and C. Lentz (eds.), *Land and the Politics of Belonging in West Africa* (Leiden: Brill Publishers, 2006), 77–98; Chapter 6 was published in *Journal of Modern African Studies* 41, no. 4 (2003): 587–610; and a longer version of Chapter 7 was published in *World Development* 34, no. 11 (2006): 1887–1906 (Elsevier, Amsterdam). A French version, "En marge de la loi et au coeur de la politique locale. Colonisation agraire des forêts classées au Nord Ghana," appeared in *Revue Autrepart*, no. 30 (2004): 117–34 (IRD/Armand Colin, Paris). I am particularly grateful to Andrew Wardell, my coauthor of the last journal article and its translation, for letting me edit and use our common work for this book.

Finally thanks are due to my research assistant, Maj Forum, for helping me to put the manuscript in presentable order, and to Frank Smith, his editorial team at Cambridge University Press, and two anonymous referees for clear guidance in finalizing the book.

Christian Lund

Abbreviations

CCNT	chief commissioner of the Northern Territories
CO	Colonial Office, Public Record Office, London
CPP	Convention People's Party
DCE	district chief executive
GWS	Ghana Water and Sewerage
IDA	Irrigation Development Authority
IFAD	International Foundation for Agricultural Development
LACOSREP	Land Conservation and Small Holder Rehabilitation Project
LI	legislative instrument
MOFA	Ministry of Agriculture
NAG-A	Ghana National Archives, Accra
NDC	National Democratic Congress
NLCD	National Liberation Council Decree
NPP	New Patriotic Party
PNDC	Provisional National Defence Council
PNDCL	Provisional National Defence Council Law
SSNIT	Social Security and National Insurance Trust
URADEP	Upper Regions Agricultural Development Programme
WUA	Water Users' Association

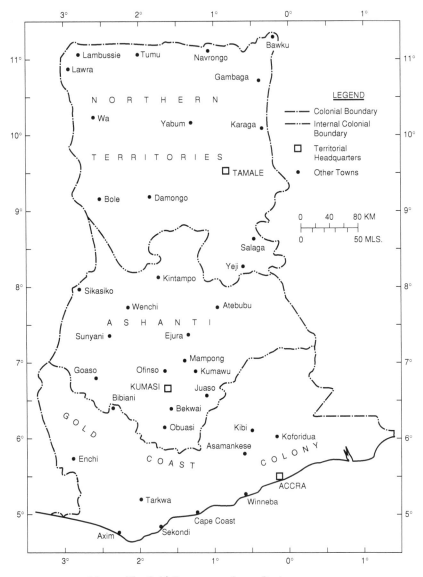

Map 1. The Gold Coast, 1907. *Source*: Bening, 1999: 25.

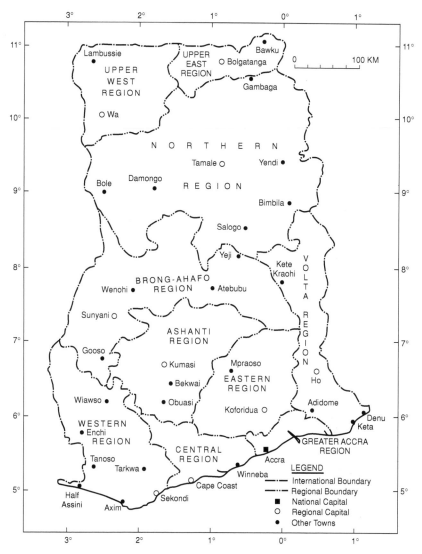

Map 2. Regions of Ghana since 1983. *Source*: Bening, 1999: 146.

I

Introduction

Any fool can turn the blind eye,
But who knows what the ostrich sees in the sand?
Samuel Beckett, *Murphy*

The Argument

An excerpt from the "Petition for the Payment of Compensation of Farm
Lands at Pobaga-Damweo Residential Area,"[1] dating to 28 June 1999,
provides a glimpse of some of the land issues people are facing in Bolgatanga
and the Upper East Region of Ghana:

> It would be recalled that on the 29th May, 1999, the inhabitants [of Damweo,
> Bolgatanga] entered to cultivate the land claimed by the Police Bureau of National
> Investigation (BNI) when they were met with threats of shooting them on sight if
> they were found entering the land. This unfortunate incident was reported to the
> Bolga Naba who invited both the incoming and outgoing Directors of BNI and
> the Regional TUC [Trade Union Congress] Chairman for amicable settlement. At
> the end of this dialogue, it was agreed that we go back and grow low crops such as
> groundnuts, beans, etc. It was based on this, that we went back to comply with the
> terms. We were again met with fierce resistance. This new development was again
> brought to the notice of the Bolga Naba who invited the BNI Director again for
> further discussion. . . . While dialogue was continuing, service personnel were seen
> cultivating the land to the provocation of the people, thus heightening tension in
> the area.

The land on which the police station stands was never legally acquired
by the government. Even when land was given back to its original owners
after passage of the Constitution of 1979, the police remained on the land
and were effectively squatting. No compensation has ever been offered to
the local population, so the people have now claimed it back by cultivating

---

[1] Material in private possession.

I

the grounds of the police station. Currently, an effective compromise seems to have been negotiated: on the grounds of the Police Bureau of National Investigation, the local population can grow only low crops, enabling the police to have a clear view from the buildings; on the adjacent, regional police station, the grounds have been divided between the local population and the service personnel, who themselves need to supplement a meager income by cultivating the grounds.

The openness and contingency of land issues in Africa make absolutely central the questions of how and to whose benefit settlements are reached, who has the capacity to endorse or enforce them, and how and by whom they are challenged. At this juncture, local politics and land tenure meet. Land struggles have intensified in the Upper East since 1979 because of rising land values, both in the towns and in parts of the countryside. However, land struggles have also played directly into local political struggles because of the confusion over whose land rights were "restored" by the constitutional changes of 1979. When the 1979 Constitution declared that land held in trust by the government was henceforth to be handed back to its "original owners," earthpriests, families, and individuals saw an opportunity to claim land rights from government and chiefs and to contest a political order that had developed throughout the twentieth century.

The book argues that, in the context of legal and institutional pluralism and the rising competition over land, the constitutional reversal of land tenure that took place in 1979 opened a hornet's nest of potential conflict over land claims *and* over competing claims as to who had the authority to settle those conflicts. Thus, struggles over land fanned the flames of political conflict over customary authority, which has reemerged as a burning issue in contemporary politics. Moreover, exclusivity of land rights is increasing at different levels. Whereas chiefs and earthpriests previously had somewhat overlapping authority over land, competing efforts are now being exerted by both parties to acquire more exclusive control. Chiefs and earthpriests alike have organized to obtain recognition from other institutions to this effect. For "ordinary" people, such organization produces a paradox. The restoration of property held the promise of greater command over the benefits of land for the "original owners." In competition, however, there is no guarantee that land users' claims translate into their own greater command. Their claims may be trumped by claims from customary authorities or from rival land users, leading to their exclusion. In consequence, land users tend either to gain more exclusive rights or to see their rights erode in political processes where skills in political organization of interests are tested.

The book studies what goes on in African politics at the local level when such conflicts occur. It explores how "local" issues do not confine themselves entirely within local arenas and demonstrates this through empirical analysis of the central concepts of property and law. Land, property, and

power obviously cannot be reduced to being only local matters. Broad structural power dynamics are at play, and national and international economies
and politics constrict peoples' opportunities and condition the working and
significance of local institutions. Nonetheless, a focus on local processes
emphasizes that, even in situations of historical and structural inequality,
law and property are dynamic fields. Political processes of competition and
exclusion are engaged in by people with different degrees of ambition and
appetite, of responsibility and resolve.

Property and law may be perceived as fundamental, legitimate fixtures
in society. In practice, however, they are quite ambiguous. Moore (1978:
1) reminds us that the "making of rules and social and symbolic order is
a human industry matched only by the manipulation, circumvention, remaking, replacing and unmaking of rules and symbols in which people
seem almost equally engaged." The political dynamics of property, that
is, the processes whereby rights over land and other resources are settled
and contested, are fundamental to how public authority is established and
challenged. Thus, the study of property dynamics is equally one of state
formation. The individual and institutional contestants' pursuit of control
over land involves them, willy-nilly, in the competition over public authority – its consolidation, reconfiguration, and erosion. This pursuit is done not
necessarily to achieve state formation at the local level but rather to check
and overcome competitors and to benefit from the advantages of power. The
result is, nonetheless, in part, institutional (Tilly, 1985).

The book is based on research in the Upper East Region in Ghana,
and although each corner of the world is the product of specific situations
and trajectories, many of the issues considered here are, I would claim,
emblematic for much of Africa. However, only by researching the historical configurations of particular situations, their dilemmas, conflicts, and
contradictions, are the institutional dynamics of property properly understood. History figures in two forms in this book. On the one hand, it is an
analytical category of how historical legacies of colonial rule, power struggles, legislative changes after independence, and the like impinge on local
dynamics of property and politics. On the other hand, history as an object
of study is a central part of the idioms and logics of local contestation where
people conjure up historical interpretations to back certain claims to power
and property. Without presuming further parallels, the historical studies of
the processes of European state formation by Norbert Elias (1994 [1939])
and of the development of private landed property in England by E. P.
Thompson (1975, 1991) demonstrate that large structural transformations
are fraught with conflict, ambiguity, and open junctures and are characterized by competing logics in the gradual production of a pattern. There is
little to suggest that processes of local politics and the dynamics of property
in Africa should exhibit any less ambivalence and contradiction.

Local Politics

A particularly fruitful field for the analysis of local politics is the reception, negotiation, and implementation of national policies, including land tenure reforms, decentralization policies, and public-sector reforms. The conventional view of policy processes as a rational sequence of specific decisions often requires modification when such policy is confronted with concrete "multirational" politics. No government policy is implemented in its entirety unscathed by the contingency of local circumstance and political negotiations. Rather, the reception of policies reflects an uneven playing field where some elements of policy can further existing projects and practice, and where others do not resonate with local political interests and conflicts. This is not to suggest that policies on land and other issues are irrelevant. On the contrary, state and government policies are important not only in their ambition to promote changes in resource allocation and organization but also in a more subtle sense. This tension is reflected in two, partly overlapping, literatures.

National laws and government policies constitute a structure of opportunities for the negotiation of rights and the distribution of resources, and the result is neither coherent policy implementation nor complete disregard of law and policy. While certain elements of the legislation will be absorbed into practices and systems with a much longer history and produce little change, other elements will provide justification for new ways. But instead of "replacing" old policies, new policies will often add a layer of legitimate references. Local actors may thereby use central government policies and directives to shore up their claims or underpin their own authority, and local government institutions often have some considerable margin for improvisation in carrying out the practical operations of policy implementation. As Mosse (2004: 655) suggests, policy may not generate events, but it helps stabilize the local interpretation of them. Policy is thus only a subset of local politics, and the latter can be quite deceptive. Not only are local issues not confined within local arenas, but politics is not the preserve of overtly political institutions. Everyday conflicts over land as well as more spectacular disputes often confront people within the same locality.

Local politics concerning property, therefore, is not a process isolated from wider influences. In fact, as Swartz (1968: 1) reflects, the very hallmark of local politics is that it is "incomplete in the sense that actors and groups outside the range of the local . . . relationships are vitally and directly involved in the political processes." Hence, national legislation and policy, political identification, alliances, and lobbying, as well as ideas about property and law, together constitute a web linking local politics to a broader context. Moreover, success in local politics does not hinge on astute individual and local management of social resources alone. Conflicts may be absorbed into broader political competition, where the actions and operations of the primary actors are couched in the mobilization of power on a different scale. The original dispute then becomes symbolic of the broader competition, other actors intervene, and the actions of the primary actors become far less decisive for the outcome. Furthermore, politics runs along informal as well as formal lines. While the formal institutional structure, inclusive of political parties, local and regional assemblies, governments, and administrations, to some degree meets the requirements of a mainstream polity in the "age of good governance," political issues are also dealt with through people's practices outside such institutions. This perspective on local politics owes a debt to the writings of the so-called Manchester school and to those who further developed their ideas (Gluckman, 1958, 1961, 1968 [1943], 1973; J. C. Mitchell, 1983, 1987; Moore, 1978, 1986; Olivier de Sardan, 1999a and b, 2005; Scott, 1985; van Velsen, 1967).

On the more subtle side, the state invades the field of local politics in the form of an idea (Abrams, 1988). The exercise of power and authority alludes to the state, and government policies symbolize the state and the idea of law. Hansen and Stepputat (2001: 8) suggest that states exist only when practical and symbolic languages of governance combine. The institutionalization of law and legal discourse and the materialization of the state in a series of permanent signs and rituals are integral parts of that language. This Gramscian idea of the state as the "successful effect" of a "will to class power" points to the active making of the state. When we deal with state formation in local politics, however, we might have to settle for less than the "successful effect." Mitigated, erratic, and even futile attempts to rule are also part of the picture, and while such attempts are "willed" competition over specific authority, they may not be undertaken with grand state-building ambition. Nonetheless, the idea of "a state" certainly informs the ways the attempt is made.

Work by Bierschenk and Olivier de Sardan (1997, 1998, 2003) demonstrates how the idea of a state – however seemingly distant – informs everyday politics. Thus, the language of the state is not the preserve of government institutions alone; other institutions strut in borrowed plumes. What transpires in local-level politics are certain forms of institutionalization and formalization of the exercise of authority alluding to state, law, and the bureaucracy, encoded in official language and often exercised with the paraphernalia of modern statehood. A variety of institutions may use the language of the state and its props in terms of contracts, deeds, and attestations and of stamps, stationary, and declarations. The irony of such "unstately stateliness" is that, while distinctions get increasingly blurred (in terms of who is exercising state authority), they become increasingly important (in terms of who can produce rights). Reality does not fall into neat dichotomies, yet people and institutions, at certain times, indeed maneuver as if the world could be divided into such compartments.

This situation produces another paradox. On the one hand, a compelling idea of a powerful state with intention and a higher rationality prevails. Likewise, law and property are referred to as stable, agreed-upon fundamentals of society. On the other hand, however, as public authority is exercised by competing and more or less transient institutions, the ideas of the solidity of the state are contrasted with the actual incoherence and incapacity of the multiple parallel structures and alternative sites of authority (a land commission, the courts, local assemblies, the ministries, chiefs, earthpriests, political factions, hometown associations, neighborhood groups, etc.). This contrast disrupts the notion of unity or rationality in the singular. Such plurality of institutions produces the ambiguous practical meanings of law and property. In a competitive institutional environment, the consequence of insisting on the unity of the state and clarity of property and law is that unity and clarity are undermined. This is a key to understand the dynamic of property and authority, which this book seeks to explain. This perspective on the state owes a debt to more poststructural views on the dynamics of the state, in particular in postcolonial societies (Abrams, 1988; Bourdieu, 1994; Comaroff, 2002; Das and Poole, 2004; Ferguson, 1990, 1999; Hansen and Stepputat, 2001; T. Mitchell, 1991; Steinmetz, 1999).

Although these two groups of authors – the Manchester school and the poststructuralists – differ on several accounts, some central elements are shared among them. First, the combined approach is nonteleological but nonetheless focused on history and the processes of reproduction and change. Second, the approach is nonnormative but is nonetheless concerned with people's norms, ideas, and agendas. Third, the approach does not privilege the state as a site of politics but nonetheless exhibits a keen interest in how the state, both as a set of institutions and as an idea, conditions local politics in a broader field. Finally, the idea of a field generated around a particular issue or concern is important. As a consequence, the analysis is not preordered according to specific theoretical concepts such as class, law, or discourse but rather is open to the dynamic relationships between different processes allowing for the contingency and complexity of the sociopolitical processes.

Moore (1978: 54–81) operates with the concept of a semiautonomous social field as an appropriate area for the study of law and social change. In her work, the semiautonomous social field is not defined by, nor are its boundaries identified with, its organization. Rather, the semiautonomous social field is defined by its capacity to generate rules and establish institutions to induce or coerce compliance with them. Many actors deal and compete with each other, and the field is thus partly constituted by the continuous interpretation – through conflicts and their settlement – of rules and practices.

A semiautonomous social field can be thought of as a broad social space, which is created substantially in relation to a problem, to something at stake – *in casu* land, property and authority. Thus, rather than government being viewed as an organizational structure, a semiautonomous social field denotes a process of governance. The field changes over time; specific actors, institutions, actions, and social relations are not equally important at all times but vary in significance with historical circumstance and opportunity.

In order to engage with local politics, it is useful to sketch out some of the elements of public authority. By authority, I mean an instance of power that seeks at least a minimum of voluntary compliance and thus is sought to be legitimated in some way. The "public" element should direct our attention toward two associated features. On the one hand, public authority connotes impersonal administrative operations in a general sense. On the other hand, it refers to public (as in "not secret") confrontations, discussions, and action in concert. Thus, we are dealing with institutions and groups that in the exercise of power take on the mantle of public authority (legitimated administrative operations) and in which their attempts to govern articulate notions of state. It is a specific form of power exercised publicly and legitimated with reference to the state. The institutions engaged in this enterprise, however, are characterized by movement in and out of a capacity to exercise public authority. They operate between public and private in the twilight between state and society (see Lund, 2006).

In Africa there is no shortage of institutions that attempt to exercise public authority. Not only are multiple layers and branches of government institutions (the judiciary, the administration, the customs service and police, the various extension agencies, etc.) present and active to varying degrees, but customary institutions bolstered by government recognition also vie for public authority. Much of the literature on African politics and its history details how government institutions and chieftaincy institutions, invented or otherwise, negotiate, forge alliances, and compete to constitute public authority and political control (Bayart, 1989; Berry, 1993; Boone, 1998, 2003; Gluckman, 1968 [1943]; Mamdani, 1996; Moore, 1986; Peel, 1983; Rathbone, 2000; van Rouveroy van Nieurwaal, 1999). In addition, associations and organizations that do not appear at first sight as political may also exercise political power and wield public authority. These may be hometown associations, professional guilds, cultural clubs, and the like. Similarly, occasions that would appear to be ostensibly nonpolitical, such as sporting events, inauguration ceremonies, and cultural festivals, may reveal themselves to be active sites of political negotiation and mediation over implementation of public goals or distribution of public authority in which local and regional identities and power relations are reshaped and recast (A. Apter, 1999 [Nigeria]; Bierschenk, Chauveau, and Olivier de Sardan, 2000 [(West Africa]; Cruise O'Brien, 2003 [Senegal]; Gilbert,

1994 [Ghana]; Hecht and Simone, 1994 [Africa]; Pratten and Gore, 2002 [Nigeria]; Worby, 1998 [Zimbabwe]).

In such cases, it is difficult to ascribe exercised authority to the "state" as a coherent institution; rather, public authority becomes the amalgamated result of a variety of local institutions' exercise of power and external institutions' imposition, conjugated with the *idea* of a state. Hence, the practice of governance varies from place to place, and even from field to field, whether it be "security," "citizenship," "property," "development," or some other domain (see Bayart, Geschiere, and Nyamnjoh, 2001; Lemarchand, 1992). Indeed, in some areas authority may be exercised by institutions with near hegemonic competence, while their authority in other domains at the very same time may be ferociously contested. It seems characteristic for much of Africa that enduring concentrated power over many domains within a single set of institutions is rare. Although hegemony always has the character of an unaccomplished project, the diversity of the local political scene in much of Africa often makes it hard to identify any project at all. This observation has given rise to rather frustrated academic and policy literature over the years, often termed "Afro-pessimism." Inspiring and influential examples include Bayart (1989), Chabal and Daloz (1999), Mbembe (2001), and Roe (1999). Although the authors will probably resist such crude classification and the lumping together of different and nuanced arguments, they do seem to measure the state in Africa by its distance from an idea of a "proper" state distinct from society. The acknowledgment of a blurred boundary between state and nonstate, however, makes it a dubious and often unrewarding enterprise to attempt to make an analytical distinction between state and civil society.

This observation is instead a privileged opportunity to explore the general theoretical fragility of clear separation between state and society and to investigate the social processes that simultaneously create and deny the distinction. Whether labeled state or not, it seems that a variety of institutions constitute themselves as de facto public authorities, albeit with greater or lesser success. This is the point. Public authority can wax and wane. Here, although the distinction between state and civil society is analytically unsatisfactory, it is useful when applied to the discursive and political organization of society, on a grand and small scale alike. If public authority – or "stateness" – can wax and wane, it follows that the state institutions are never definitively formed but are in a constant process of formation (Steinmetz, 1999: 9). This implies a certain fluidity in the character of groups defending shared interests. They may form or disintegrate in the course of struggle and can be seen undergoing both constant reproduction and transformation.

Institutions or groups of actors are, thus, simultaneously actors and arenas and manifestations of power relations. All three aspects are important for an understanding of the political processes involving institutions. First, as an actor, a politicolegal institution is personified by its governor, for example, the mayor, the district chief executive, the district commissioner, the magistrate, the chief, the party boss, the "strong man," defining and enforcing collectively binding decisions and rules – or, rather, *attempting* to define and enforce them, because this capacity is rarely fully accomplished and is often challenged. Consequently, while parties in dispute may go "forum shopping," taking their claim or dispute to the institution that they deem to be the most likely to produce a satisfactory outcome, institutions also use disputes for their own, mainly local, political ends. As Keebet von Benda-Beckmann (1981: 117) puts it, "besides forum-shopping disputants, there are also 'shopping forums' engaged in trying to acquire and manipulate disputes from which they expect to gain political advantage, or to fend off disputes which they fear will threaten their interests. They shop for disputes as disputants shop for forums."

Second, as Berry (1997: 1228) argues, social institutions such as household, family, and community should also be seen as "constellations of social interaction, in which people move, acquire and exchange ideas and resources, and negotiate or contest the terms of production, authority and obligation." An institution, therefore, is also an arena where competing social actors struggle to influence the way rulings are made.

Third, as arenas, institutions are also manifestations of power relations. Over time, they may be entrenched and thereby establish a structure of entitlements and prerogatives, while diluting other rights and rendering competing claims to authority and resources illegitimate. When an institution authorizes, sanctions, or validates certain rights, the respect or observance of these rights by people simultaneously constitutes recognition of the authority of that particular institution. In order to understand how political power is exercised, we therefore need to have an eye for the processual aspects of the formation of public authority and, in particular, how it is created through day-to-day social encounters. Yet legitimate authority is not necessarily legitimate authority indefinitely but must be vindicated and legitimated through a broad array of political practices. In essence, such practices constitute the negotiation of public authority in a particular context.

The Dynamics of Property in Africa

Negotiation in Inequality

Of all issues in African local politics, land remains perhaps the most prominent one. Questions of access to and control over landed property can quickly mobilize individuals and groups, and "the land question" is consistently an important item on the agenda of most African governments (Bruce and Migot Adholla, 1994; Peters, 2004; Toulmin and Quan, 2000; World Bank, 1996, 2003). There is, of course, no single "land question"; the burning issue varies from country to country and between various groups within different societies, but the mere fact that land questions are so contentious is a clear indication of the political and social transformative dynamics in the negotiation of property. Land tenure has in recent years secured a strong scholarly interest.[2] Increasing scarcity of land due to population growth, environmental degradation, and the slow rates of economic development has led to increased competition for land among rural producers (Berry, 2002b: 639). Urbanization combines these processes. It has meant that land values have gone up and that land has been taken out of agricultural production, resulting in land scarcity. In many growing urban areas, the result has been various forms of urban agriculture (Temple and Moustier, 2003). Land rights obviously vary tremendously throughout Africa, but *claims* to land all seem to be fashioned around social identity. Increasing land scarcity fuels politics of identity and belonging from the household to the societal level, defining boundaries between strangers and locals, insiders and outsiders, and people with entitlements and those without. Consequently, land becomes politically central, as it links important resources to authority in particular ways.

The institutional and normative plurality prevailing in most of Africa means not only that people struggle and compete over access to land but that the legitimate authority to settle conflicts is equally at stake. It is never merely a question of land but a question of property, and of social and political relationships in a very broad sense. Struggles over property are therefore as much about the scope and constitution of authority as about access to resources (Berry, 2002b: 640; Lund, 2002). The essential point is that property is distinguished from mere momentary possession or longer-term access by virtue of being recognized by others, through enforcement by society or the state, and by custom, convention, or law (MacPherson, 1978: 3).

The processes of recognition work in tandem. Recognition of property rights by an institution simultaneously constitutes a process of recognition of the legitimacy of this institution. From this perspective, property and

---

[2] Central works on land tenure in Africa include Basset and Crummey (1993); Berry (1985, 1993, 2001, 2002a and b); Bohannan (1963); Bruce (1986, 1993); Bruce and Migot-Adholla (1994); Chanock (1991a and b); Comaroff and Roberts (1981); Downs and Reyna (1988); Fitzpatrick (2005, 2006); Juul and Lund (2002); Le Roy, Karsenty, and Bertrand (1995); Moore (1978, 1986); Ostrom (1990); Peters (1994, 2002, 2004); Platteau (1996); Shipton (1989); Shipton and Goheen (1992); and Toulmin and Quan (2000).

the public authority of the institution are essentially precarious. Property is property only if socially legitimate institutions sanction it, and the institutions are effectively legitimate only if their interpretation of social norms (in this case, property rights) is heeded. Hence, public authority is continually constructed in the everyday practices of ordinary people and by the recognition by other institutions of their jurisdiction. The many rules relating to interests in land and other resources and the plurality of institutions of public authority turn the process of recognition into a political process of competition and negotiation. Thus, sometimes hitherto hegemonic institutions that have guaranteed property rights cease to be sufficiently powerful, and the status of the property they previously guaranteed becomes uncertain. Obviously, controlling land is not the only source of public authority. Security, citizenship, and development are but three alternative areas through which institutions can build up public authority. The centrality of land in most African societies, nevertheless, makes the field of property particularly propitious. The relationship between public authority and property is not a permanently established relationship, however. It is a social, politicolegal construction maintained and challenged through active and contested reproduction of property relations.

In a comprehensive article, Peters takes issue with recent increasing attention to the negotiability of rules and socioeconomic position in Africa.[3] Although the notion of negotiability was once a welcome challenge to simple economistic premises about the insecurity of all property that is not privately owned, Peters (2004: 305) argues that it has now gained so much currency that processes of inequality and social differentiation drift out of focus. We should pay as much attention to processes that limit negotiation and exclude certain groups. There is much to be said for this argument. Groups are marginalized economically and politically, and people are very unequally positioned in negotiating how land rights and property are to be defined. As Amanor (1999: 44) puts it, "[t]he majority of people are merely forced to abide by interpretations of what is determined to be customary by the powerful, or to operate outside legality." However, if efforts to contest prevailing patterns are ignored or classified as insignificant merely because they may have been unsuccessful, then actual outcomes become endowed with a quality of *inevitability*, which removes from the historical process its precariousness and multistranded nature.

While unsuccessful in radically overthrowing domination, actions of the dominated – however mundane or foolhardy – are hardly inconsequential for domination's configuration. At the very least, they reflect people's experience and grasp of opportunities at the time. In this book, "history" is allowed to unfold not as pure happenstance but with a due measure of openness toward

---

[3] For a debate between these positions, see Berry (2002b) and Peters (2002, 2004).

other possible outcomes of particular dilemmas, conflicts, and confrontations. In the words of Bendix (1984: 48), the task is to give "back to men of the past the unpredictability of the future and the dignity of acting in the face of uncertainty." Analyses that claim to have uncovered the singularly predominant or general logic in a particular case may easily fall into the trap of retrospective determinism – in particular, if counterexamples and questioning of the argument are kept to a minimum. Analyses that claim to uncover multiple entangled logics may conversely convey a sense of indetermination where fluidity is of the lowest possible viscosity. In most cases, however, several social logics are indeed entangled in complex ways.

Disentangling the variety of logics through careful analysis may, in the best of cases, enable us to understand what happened in a particular situation and suggest how to draw more general parallels with other similar cases. The intention is therefore not to argue that anything could have happened in a particular case but to keep in mind that things did not turn out as they did because they could not have turned out otherwise. The meticulous recording of relevant events and of the contextual, historical situation of the argument is a valid way to undergird plausibility. The challenge is to link small-scale, open-ended transactions and larger processes of increasing exclusivity of rights and intensified competition over jurisdictions controlled by no individual. Watershed events are interesting in this respect, as they reshape the general structure of opportunities. Events like land reforms may entitle some while disenfranchising others. However, the 1979 reform in northern Ghana, reverting land to "original owners," provided an opportunity primarily for chiefs and politicians, landowners, and tenants to reassert positions and interests. The reform privileged a certain register of traditional authority and ownership to be "filled out" by these groups.

In this perspective, the agency of decisive transformative capacity is in principle attributed to all actors whose concrete, discrete, individual acts form patterns when aggregated. The weight of small players may be significant, sometimes because of their numbers and sometimes because of serendipity or special skills. This does not mean that power does not enter into the process or that events are completely arbitrary. Although poor and disadvantaged people may sometimes negotiate improvements to their lives, these may just as swiftly be winnowed out again.

The Significance of Land: Settled Facts or Facts to Settle

Property in land had been central for political control in the colonial and postcolonial eras in Ghana. As a consequence, efforts to register, fix, consolidate, and institutionalize particular meanings of land and particular rights and responsibilities between groups and authorities vis-à-vis land have been exercised by actors of different shapes and sizes. However, the significance of property in land changes over time with shifts in economic and sociopolitical contexts.

The institutionalization of legal pluralism owes much to the process of colonization in Africa. The development of customary law and, particularly for the British colonies, the implementation of indirect rule were deliberate attempts to formalize what was seen as the equivalent, albeit it in less sophisticated forms, of law and polity in the imperial centers. If the political structure of society and access to land were linked before colonization, the policies and practices it introduced seemed to integrate polity and land tenure in a complex of indirect rule and customary law. In the first phase of colonization, British and French authorities claimed extensive authority over land. "Specific legislative instruments varied from one colony to another, but they conveyed a common message. From Senegal to Malawi, French and British authorities claimed that 'by right of conquest,' all 'vacant and ownerless' land belonged to the colonial state. Vast tracts of land were often judged 'vacant and ownerless' on the basis of cursory inspection or none at all" (Berry, 2002b: 641–42). Some land was sold or granted to settlers or companies in different colonies, but, in practice, most land remained under African control. The history of Ghana is interesting for its diversity. In the South of the country, in the Colony and Ashanti areas, the elite, powerful chiefs and the intellectuals, mainly lawyers, managed to prevent the colonial government from seizing the land as crown land. In the Northern Territories Protectorate, however, land was vested in the crown and became the source of future disputes over the extent of control by government and traditional authorities and actual land users (Bening, 1995; Edsman, 1979; Ladouceur, 1979; Meek, 1946; Nyari 1995).[4]

The British colonial administration generally relied on Africans in the exercise of its tasks. Over time, they made a virtue out of necessity, and with Lord Frederick Lugard, the governor of the Protectorate of Northern Nigeria, the concept of indirect rule took shape. Indirect rule was based on three fundamental principles: recognition of chiefs as native authorities and mediators between government and the population, the creation of native courts, and the creation of native treasuries and a tax system (Mann and Roberts, 1991: 19–21). Indirect rule was viewed as an affordable form of government, allowing some room for "civilising development."

[4] The Gold Coast was divided into three areas, namely the Colony, Ashanti, and the Protectorate of the Northern Territories. The British also controlled a part of the former German Togoland after World War I. This area was later to be integrated into Ghana. The Northern Territories were proclaimed a British protectorate under the governor of the Gold Coast Colony with the promulgation of the Northern Territories Order in Council on 26 September 1901 (Gold Coast Colony, 1902). The reorganization of the administrative boundaries of the former Protectorate of the Northern Territories included the establishment of the Northern Region in 1957. It was subdivided in 1961 to create the Upper Region. In 1980 the Upper Region was further subdivided into the Upper West and Upper East Regions.

However, it was soon realized that much more had to be known about African societies, their political structures and customary practices. This led to the commissioning of a large number of anthropological studies and surveys to identify and describe customary polity and law. The surveys in the British colonies ultimately resulted in *An African Survey* edited by Lord William Hailey (1938) and *Land Law and Custom in the Colonies* by Meek (1946).[5] For the Northern Territories in Ghana, R. S. Rattray, special commissioner for anthropology, undertook a major study resulting in *The Tribes of the Ashanti Hinterland* (1932). As Berry (2002b: 643–45) points out, however, the information about customs and institutions was not merely gained through ethnographic surveys.

Officials acquired and processed information about "native laws and customs" through their daily interactions with chiefs and commoners, litigants and judges, witnesses and petitioners, laborers and vagrants, taxpayers and defaulters.... In the process, they found themselves engaged in an on-going quest for knowledge which proved frustratingly elusive – partly because Africans societies were themselves undergoing change. Far from the timeless web of accepted practice that colonial officials imagined (or hoped for), "custom" proved in practice to be a shifting kaleidoscope of stories and interests that eluded codification. Officials' efforts to get customs right – by inventing them if necessary – were often as destabilizing as oppressive.

The ambition of the colonial administration was to rationalize indigenous rules into customary law so as to fit the format of the metropolitan state and the colonial administration and to entrench the dichotomy between modern and customary law. The process entailed a long-drawn-out debate that remains inconclusive to this day.

In his article on the limits of invention in British colonial Africa, Spear (2003) argues that the recent infatuation with the notion of invented traditions has often overstated colonial power and its ability to manipulate African institutions. Rather, Spear argues, we should see traditional institutions and customary law as the result of historical processes whereby African institutions and agendas as well as colonial ambitions shaped the outcome. "Less invented than transformed, codified, expanded and criminalized under specific historical conditions, customary law was neither traditional nor modern, African nor European, but quintessentially colonial" (Spear, 2003: 14).[6] The colonial administration was not the only party with

---

[5] See also Hailey (1951). For a description of the political, academic, and logistical challenge of this enterprise, see Cell (1989).

[6] A similar ambition characterizes the work of Lentz and Nugent (2000: 6): "If the ethnicities of the twentieth century were not simply hangovers from a pre-colonial past, nor were they simply plucked from the air."

ambitions in the enterprise of codification, yet even within the administration, views differed. This assessment does not render customary institutions and law less socially constructed, but it broadens the number of "constructors" and stretches the construction time from a circumscribed period to an endless process. As a result, ambitions of codification and simplification were often frustrated by competing interests. Far from putting an end to debates over authority and property, colonial codification laid out institutional and semantic structures, which we encounter even now in contemporary conflicts.

The simplification process was not reserved for indigenous institutions but also concerned concepts and their meaning. For several reasons, concepts such as ownership do not travel between different societies without complication. First, when certain forms of property in an African society are translated into ownership, there is a tendency to forget that the meaning of ownership not only varies between different societies but everywhere serves as an approximation for the primary right holders' property rights (see Lund, 2002). The idea of ownership as "total exclusion of the right of any other individual in the Universe" (Blackstone, here from Rose, 1998: 601) is exactly an *idea*. In concrete societies, African as well as "Western," ownership is always circumscribed by others' rights limiting the exercise of the abstract total right to property. Thus, when Kasanga (1988: 31) states that customary land rights are "indefeasible, indeterminable and inheritable," it may be so from a narrow legal positivist point of view. From a political, anthropological, or historical point of view, however, it is an empirical challenge to ascertain the extent and limits of ownership and account for them (see Rose, 1994, 1998; F. von Benda-Beckmann, von Benda-Beckmann, and Wiber, 2006).

Second, many forms of property encountered in Africa are significantly less exclusive than what we would normally associate with the term "ownership" (see Berry, 1988). This is not to argue that African land tenure is essentially communal, but several layers of interest in property are typically recognized as legitimate. Mindless translation of certain indigenous property concepts into the language of ownership tends to strengthen exclusivity, benefiting the primary right holder at the expense of others. This leads to the third aspect; the difficulty of translation, which is not merely an academic challenge, proves an opportunity or a liability for those with vested interests in the land. Although customary law presupposed segregation between European and African concepts, Africans soon began to use European terms as open to interpretation as local ones, at least in their communication with the colonial administration. Translating certain indigenous terms for forms of property into Western concepts also entailed an opportunity for changing the actual significance in terms of the extent, duration, and beneficiaries of the property rights. Obviously, less fortunate right holders would see their land rights dwindle as a consequence. The phenomenon prevails today (Toulmin and Quan, 2000) and is hardly reserved to Africa (Scott, 1998). Claims to traditional jurisdiction or traditional land rights are often based on reference to the past while argued in simplified terms of ownership and authority, despite the fact that the historical references hardly had the meaning then as is adduced to them now.

Property and land tenure regimes in Africa, however, owe their ambiguity to more than what is lost or added in translating concepts between cultures. Most indigenous land tenure systems in Africa are characterized by a coexistence of multiple rights that are often held by different persons as a function of their status or position in society. Moreover, there are often multiple ways of getting access to land and justifying claims to it. Shipton's (1994: 348) list extends to "birth rights, first settlement, conquest, residence, cultivation, habitual grazing, visitation, manuring, tree planting, spiritual sanction, bureaucratic allocation, loan, rental and cash purchase." These different sorts of claims do not necessarily contradict each other but can be seen as dynamic "nested hierarchies of estates." The normative repertoire does not constitute a differentiated systematic hierarchy, and the norms are of varying specificity. Some deal with substantial entitlements and obligations, some with specific behavioral requirements and restrictions, some with more abstract codes of conduct. As Kintz (1990) demonstrates in her essay on Burkina Faso, there are not only rules but also rules for how to circumvent them in a proper way. The norms are therefore neither inherently contradictory nor compellingly complementary, but they are invoked so as to impose rival constructions on agreed facts and thus are brought into conflict by virtue of the strategic and pragmatic contingencies that arise out of conflicts of interest (Comaroff and Roberts, 1981: 70–106; Fortmann, 1995; Lentz, 1998b; Rose, 1994). In addition, people's property rights are often linked to their social identity. Social identity does not guarantee rights but seems to entitle a person to claim them. However, the boundaries of the property-holding group are rarely a settled fact but rather are a "fact" to settle. Consequently, social identities become a contested terrain, and seemingly simple and clear categories such as "firstcomers" and "latecomers" become the objects of intense, sometimes refined, sometimes coarser, negotiation. In situations of increased scarcity, belonging tends to become an instrument of exclusion, as Peters (2004: 305) points out:

The proliferating tensions and struggles between generations and genders, or between groups labelled by region, ethnicity or religion, are intimately tied up with the dynamics of division and exclusion, alliance and inclusion that constitute class formation. . . . as land becomes a property or a commodity, so we see developing a very different sense of "belonging" – from someone belonging to a place to a property belonging to someone; in short, a shift from inclusion to exclusion.

Another source of the sometimes nebulous character of land tenure lies with the very notion of space. The bounded nature of a particular space, which has become almost second nature to the thinking about land, is not necessarily the only valid perception. Again, Ghana provides a good illustration: borders between earth shrine areas of earthpriests and chiefs' territories can be difficult to define. While individual fields and plots generally have been marked off by various forms of linear borders, delineation has not always characterized the areas of control of earthpriests or chiefs. Lentz (2006c: 9) suggests that they "were probably perceived not as flat homogeneous territories, but as fields of ritual or political power, with a well-defined center . . . in the inhabited and regularly cultivated space surrounded by concentric circles of influence, thinning out towards the uncultivated bush or forest beyond which the neighboring settlements lay." The areas controlled by firstcomers also were not necessarily continuous but consisted of various stretches of land, interspersed with areas controlled by neighboring communities. Areas of influence are not necessarily contiguous and may often overlap with ensuing friction and negotiation.

This possibility becomes increasingly complicated when the source to the claim of influence over an area is factored in. For example, while the influence of the earthpriest is derived from a claim to privileged contact with the spirits of the land, the influence of chiefs is, by contrast, derived from a claim to control over the people who inhabit it. This leads to two contrasting perceptions of space. One sees space as property where the rights to the land are central, and any authority over people within that space seems a derived secondary effect. It differs from a perception of space as territory, politically controlled through the allegiance of people in the area to a chief. Control over land within the territory seems to be a derived secondary effect to the control over people. The two perspectives need not conflict, but when the land acquires monetary value, competition intensifies. The colonial idea about the natural propinquity of chiefly authority over the people and control over their land consolidated chiefs' territorial claims. However, such interpretations are not "natural," irreversible conclusions. If the right opportunity comes along, effective challenges can be organized.

The past plays a central role in local political conflicts over land and power in the Upper East Region of Ghana. What seems just as characteristic is the inconclusive nature of the settlements reached. People will draw on the rich ambiguity of the past when the recurrent opportunities of the present allow and suggest it, in order to press claims for the future (and this time, they hope, make them stick). Strong forces can labor for a particular interpretation of the past. Through the colonial period and a good thirty years on, an alliance between government and chieftaincy secured the latter's position. Now, one could imagine that with time such an institution would become established, stable, and predictable, and if challenged at all, then the new claim might come from government ambition for land reform. However, the fact that some rights and social relations appear to endure and remain stable is not a sign that nothing is happening. On the contrary. Various actors, both individuals and organizations, actively reproduce these social relations and confirm property rights. Social institutions such as property regimes are not "things" that are present or not; they are what people do. Moreover, institutions are only as robust, solid, and enduring as the ongoing reproduction or reenactment that enables them to persist. One might lose sight of this when talking about "old" institutions, as if they were perpetuated from the past by some mysterious force. They are no more solid than people make them; however, as they generally reflect prevailing power relations, they are not haphazard constructs.

The challenge of a particular constellation of property rights and public authorities is most likely to be successful when organization and opportunity coincide. Organization has two meanings: a formalized structure of social relationships and resources with some form of purpose, and the process of organizing. Organization in the first sense of the word is inherently interesting. Wolf (1990: 590) points this out clearly:

> Organization is key, because it sets up relationships among people through allocation and control of resources and rewards. It draws on tactical power to monopolize or share out liens and claims, to channel action into certain pathways while interdicting the flow of action to others. Some things become possible and likely; others are rendered unlikely. At the same time, organization is always at risk. Since power balances always shift and change, its work is never done. . . . Even the most successful organization never goes unchallenged. The enactment of power always creates friction, disgruntlement, foot-dragging, escapism, sabotage, protest or outright resistance.

In addition to organization as an outcome – what I call an institution – Wolf's point about the processual aspect of organization deserves our attention. Here, I would like to emphasize the importance of improvisation in the face of opportunity and risk; the linking up with other groups; the creation of temporary or enduring alliances with resourceful actors; the choosing of a forum for vindication of claims; and the orchestration of expressions of interest in durbars, petitions, meetings, demonstrations, newspapers, and radio and at the odd press conference. Obviously, not everybody is equally capable of organizing at the moment of opportunity.

Many controversies over property are played out over the question of whether certain resources are public, private, or something else, as if these distinctions are fixed through time. However, as a result of people and institutions trying to determine such questions, the defining lines tend to move. As Geisler (2000) and Rose (1994) argue, landownership is muddy, and the apparently clear distinction between public and private does not hold up well to empirical scrutiny. What is considered public is often perforated by private interests in terms of permits, leases, and simple possessor interests in use. What is considered private, on the other hand, is often bound by an array of restrictions separating, at least partly, ownership from control. However, although the categories of public and private cannot be found in unadulterated form empirically, they do exist as political and discursive concepts around which interests are argued. A similar figure can be drawn up over the legal-illegal distinction. What is legal at one point may be rendered illegal at another. Changes in what is legal and illegal, public or private, occur not merely as a result of government legislation but equally as an outcome of many local, everyday negotiations of property and propriety. Although laws and regulation reflect a political will of government, farmers, chiefs, traders, and bureaucrats in local settings often have other ideas. Their interest and power may rearrange distinctions in practice.

Outline of the Book

The story of Upper East Region in Ghana in the present book puts land at the center of local politics. The history of land tenure in colonial and postcolonial northeastern Ghana is marked by a number of very significant watershed events. In 1901 the British government declared its jurisdiction over the Northern Territories, which entailed formal government control of all land in the area. The adoption the Land and Native Rights Ordinance and indirect rule (c. 1932) centralized government control over land in villages and towns. By appointing, gazetting, and in many places "inventing" chiefs in the Northern Territories, chiefs became an extension of government, and land control was officially delegated to them. Transactions in land, however, had never been the business of political chiefs in the northernmost parts of Ghana. This responsibility had been the domain of another group of customary authorities, namely the earthpriests. The "discovery" of earthpriests did not sit well with colonial ideas of an intimate linkage between chiefs and land tenure. In the British perception, chiefs were publicly appointed authorities *and* custodians of the land. The colonial administrators thus preferred to stick with this simplified idea and to ignore the earthpriests. In practice, however, private, individual transactions in land and the work of earthpriests in land matters continued but were invisible to the law. When Ghana gained independence, government as well as the chiefs had an interest in retaining formal control over land. By masking the fact that private land transfers and earthpriests' authority continued in practice, the apparent postcolonial continuity of the legal basis for land tenure consolidated the political alliance between government and chieftaincy. This was disrupted with the Constitution of 1979.

This book is not a comprehensive history of property and public authority in the Upper East Region of Ghana. Its contribution to the intelligibility of the pattern of property and authority is rather a series of histories of debates and conflicts that illuminates some central issues. Microhistories have a number of advantages (see Berry, 2001; McCaskie, 2000; Moore, 1986, 1994). First, if combined with processes of a larger order, they provide a lens with which to look at the generation of opportunities and constraints. Microhistories offer a way of situating agency, choice, and negotiation in historical circumstances where cards may be dealt in advance but not played mechanically. As McCaskie (2000: 20) argues, this form of analysis tends to remain provisional and resist closure, and "its focus on individual agents within localised fields of action can – and does – supply a nuance and texture otherwise inaccessible to analysis." I have therefore aimed to situate each of the stories in contexts allowing the significance of the conflict to stand out. Multiple microhistories also allow for polyphony. By juxtaposing cases of conflict over property and public authority from different settings, the uneven processes of negotiation and differentiation become evident.

The book privileges conflicts because they make structural interests and change more visible to the observer. The cases selected, therefore, focus primarily on areas where land values are rising, namely urban and suburban localities, forests, and irrigable areas. I cannot pretend to have planned this in detail from the outset. But land controversies in a place like Bolgatanga are not exactly secret, and people proved to be very generous with information. To access and understand these microhistories in Ghana, I benefited from public and private archival sources and interviews and discussions with farmers, politicians, chiefs and earthpriests, public servants, clergymen, lawyers, and journalists, as well as members of associations, unions, and societies. In addition, my stays in Bolga allowed me to observe courtroom hearings, durbars, and political meetings, all contributing to a dense web of local politics. As field research was carried out in periods of one and a half months over several years, I was able to share my writing widely with informants and friends in Ghana. This created a vital dialogue for me. My knowledge was often extended and complemented, new leads and contacts were identified, and my analysis was frequently challenged by very knowledgeable people. As will be evident by now, the approach is not restricted to any single academic discipline but moves between legal anthropology, political economy, sociology, and history in the hope of cross-pollination.

During the colonial period, paramount chiefs in the South of the Gold Coast managed to invent traditions relating to land in collaboration with the colonial administration, thus consolidating and centralizing the power of chiefs, while making land administration simple from the colonial administration's point of view. The alliance confirmed the relationship we see today between property and authority of the chiefs. Chapter 2 analyzes how, in the Northern Territories, similar dilemmas of centralized government control over land versus delegation of control to customary authorities and the "true nature" of the indigenous rules about land were debated. A number of interests had to be balanced out. With indirect rule as the official ideology from 1932, the policy of the British was to transfer important aspects of administration to the chiefs and native authorities, while retaining the right to appropriate all the lands that the colonial administration decided it needed through the Native Rights Ordinance. Chiefs were central to indirect rule (Bening, 1975a; Hawkins, 2002: 116–22; Lentz, 1998a; Saaka, 1978). Leaving land matters to chiefs was somewhat frustrated, however, as it gradually dawned upon the colonial administration, in particular the lower echelons dealing directly with the population in present Upper East and Upper West regions, that land was not controlled by a well-organized centralized chieftaincy. The "discovery" of the earthpriest, who, in contrast, wielded little political power, made land matters too complicated for comfort. Colonial administrators preferred to stick with the simplified idea of chiefs as custodians of the land and to ignore the earthpriests, who contradicted the colonial idea of the linkage between native political structure and native land rights.

The chiefs' position has historically been supported by the administration.[7] Chiefs are gazetted; they have recognized institutions, the Regional and National Houses of Chiefs; they recover taxes for the district administration; they appear at every durbar; and they have endorsed land leases. They thus exercise public authority and are endowed with much of the accoutrements of state. Nonetheless, the prerogatives of chiefs have become severely challenged recently – not by government but by the earthpriests, once described as an outworn secret cult.

The emerging challenge from the earthpriests depends not only on individuals' talents for positioning and fortune in the exercise, although without it few challenges would succeed. The advancement of interests takes place in many ways in local politics in northern Ghana. Chiefs, organized in the regional House of Chiefs, constitute a powerful group, but political parties (more or less ethnically based), youth, and hometown associations also try to influence local politics at different levels with greater or lesser effect. The earthpriests' creation of the Association of Tindambas of Bolgatanga

---

[7] The government's periodic animosity and even hostility toward chiefs may well have curbed the latter's power at times (Rathbone, 2000), but there was little doubt as to the prominence of chiefs as traditional authorities in all customary matters, even in land and even in the Upper Regions.

in 1997 was a formalization and organization of interests, which developed an increasingly vocal position during the 1980s and 1990s. The strength of the organization lay not merely in numbers but rather in solid contacts with men of letters – lawyers. They were able to lodge claims, not directly with the state for recognition but indirectly via the courts for compensation for the government's improper, or nonlegal, acquisition of land.

Chapter 3 explains in detail how the opportunity to pursue this avenue was created when the new Constitution of 1979 declared that land in the North of the country should no longer be vested in government but in the original owners. The relative success of the earthpriests soon led to conflicts between them and the land users over their respective command over land. The competition over land is also a competition over the past. Chapter 4 shows how rival perceptions of the past are marshaled by chiefs and earthpriests in order to best justify their respective claims. Earthpriests look to the past as an unbroken timeless tradition, whereas chiefs prefer to look for significant historical events as precedents to validate their current claims. However, space also figures in such contests in more than one way as either legal property or political territory. The dual logics of past and space play into one another in questions of decentralization, local tax collection, and the creation of a district.

Claims are not necessarily relinquished just because rights are extinct. The 1979 Constitution, the relative success of earthpriests, and the resulting institutional uncertainty made the organization of interests on a smaller scale and the renegotiation of their land rights a promising prospect for many. Chapter 5 presents a series of microhistories that reveal how individuals and groups of people were able to renegotiate their terms of tenure, exploiting the legal and institutional uncertainties of the day. Obviously, not all attempts at change are crowned with success. For every success, there are probably countless attempts that are neutralized, defused, obstructed, and prevented by those who thrive in current circumstances, and the chapter deals with success and failure alike.

Although the instances described in Chapter 5 were crucial to their participants, some conflicts in local politics may gain quite different significance. When chieftaincy conflicts, ethnic cleavages, and party politics coincide, an important political fault line is created and reconfirmed. The conflict between Kusasis and Mamprusis over the chieftaincy in Bawku is central to Chapter 6. It demonstrates how different governments tried to curry favor with the different sides. The "Bawku skin affair," as it is known, is multifaceted and has resulted in violent conflict on several occasions. Politicians have politicized cultural events and lobbied government in Accra. Ethnically based youth associations have looted the Traditional Council in Bawku, petitioned government, and participated in riots. People have been forced off their land in villages and out of their shops in town. And chiefs have been put in and out of office with government changes to such an extent that most villages around Bawku have a current as well as a former (and possibly future) chief. This last aspect points to the inconclusive nature of conflicts over land in general. For every settlement of a controversy, there seems to be an occasion ahead for its renegotiation. Such occasions are often provoked by government policies and the introduction of national laws, as mentioned earlier, but may also be brought about quite locally. For this reason, many people collect small private archives of documents (leases, copies of laws, transcripts of speeches, newspaper clippings, letters, etc.), which they anticipate will be useful in overturning or confirming the present situation at an opportune moment.

The case of the Red and White Volta Forest Reserves, discussed in Chapter 7, demonstrates how legal use of the forest has gradually become interpreted as illegal use. This transition has occurred not to prevent a particular kind of use but to be able to elicit bribes for not enforcing what is seen as the law. Successive attempts to decentralize authority were undertaken already during the development of forest policy in the Northern Territories of the Gold Coast Colony between the 1930s and 1950s. From 1960, however, this trend was reversed. Forest policy was thenceforth characterized by centralization, exclusion, and restrictive legislation that ignored the property and use rights of the local population enshrined in official documents. The accompanying rhetoric was equally one of conservation of resources and restriction of local people's access. However, the actual governance of access and use of forest resources differed from the declared policies of exclusion. In reality, a much more subtle, negotiated, and politically sensitive form of arrangement tolerating people's access prevailed under the colonial administration and continues today. Furthermore, the generally assumed illegality of people's use of the resources, and the nonenforcement of the law by formal means, provided a context for informal monetary and political rent seeking by political agents offering protection and indulging people's use of the forest resources.

The public-private conundrum is analyzed in Chapter 8. The construction of irrigation infrastructure increases the value of property, and the very operation involving public investment occasions a renegotiation of land rights in ways over which government has only partial control. Landowners, tenants, beneficiaries of government allocation, and stranger-farmers alike engage in a host of small-scale negotiations, thus adjusting and transforming property relations and the significance of legislation. While the Ministry of Agriculture managed to render private land public for the purpose of irrigation in the 1950s and 1960s, the farmers managed to effectively render the public infrastructure private in the 1990s. This paradox of

government control over private land and private control over public infrastructure can be understood only if the transactions are seen in the broader
context of government control over land before 1979 and private control
thereafter, following the divestiture enshrined in the 1979 Constitution.
The generalized notions of property may influence people's behavior much
more than the formal details of law.

2

"This Situation Is Incongruous in the Extreme"

The History of Land Policies in the Upper Regions of Ghana

We are the makers of manners.

Shakespeare, *King Henry* V

What useful discovery did Socrates learn from Xanthippe? Dialectic, Stephen answered.

James Joyce, *Ulysses*

Introduction: Philosophies and Dilemmas

Even when a state has only limited ambitions of direct interference in land matters, land issues can be greatly affected by its ambition to organize and reorganize the local political structure. Thus, there is often an intimate linkage between a certain polity and the land tenure regime. Martin Chanock (1991b: 64) argues that there is a profound connection between the use of the chieftaincy as an institution of the colonial government in the British colonies and the development of the customary law of land tenure. In northern Ghana, certain dilemmas animated debates and legislation about land rights during the colonial period, and it could be argued that a relatively innocuous compromise was reached over time: on the one hand, the government retained the right to appropriate all the lands it decided it needed by the Native Rights Ordinance; on the other, indirect rule seemed to allow the natural evolution of land tenure to unfold unfettered by impatient stereotypical legislation. However, recasting local political institutions and practical and managerial concerns by the colonial administrators had, in fact, a fundamental impact on land administration. This chapter looks at the period of colonial rule in northern Ghana and investigates how, at various stages, local administrators in their pragmatic efforts to deal with a number of dilemmas in effect made dramatic decisions on the land tenure system.

Northern Ghana was occupied by British troops in 1898, and in 1901 an Order-in-Council formally established the British government's jurisdiction in the Protectorate of the Northern Territories (Agbosu, 1980: 114; Bening, 1995: 228). This marked the beginning of a rather ambiguous land policy in northern Ghana. Two philosophies of landownership have, since then, collided. One philosophy, embodied especially in Governor Gordon Guggisberg's policies, was that the government should seize total control over all lands in the North to keep costs of development down and eliminate speculation in its wake.[1] Guggisberg's chief (but eventually failed) ambition to link the North to the South with a railway line would have supported this approach (Bening, 1995: 237; Nyari, 2002: 9–10). The opposing philosophy was coined by Lord Lugard (1965 [1929]: 301–2), whose influence on British policy in its West African colonies was renowned:

> It seems preferable that the natural evolution of land tenure should not be arbitrarily interfered with, either on the one hand by introducing foreign principles and theories not understood by the people, or, on the other hand, by stereotyping by legislation, primitive systems which are in a transitional state. Each advance should be duly sanctioned by native law and custom, and prompted by necessities of changing circumstances. Such a policy of patient progress is best adapted to the country.

The two philosophies reflect different concerns: directing change or letting custom evolve.[2] Guggisberg promoted visions of particular projects that could integrate the Northern Territories into the colonial economy, whereas the concerns expressed by Lugard were primarily aimed at ensuring the success of the colonial administrative structure. Although the two philosophies to some extent reflect two phases of colonial government, namely direct rule from 1902 to 1932 and indirect rule from 1932 to 1945, the ambiguity was built into the legislation from the very beginning and has continued to inform the administration of and legislation about land in the North. Colonial administrators were navigating between these concerns and had to negotiate certain dilemmas. It was assumed by the colonial government, in particular early on, that it was imperative to promote the evolution of some form of private property rights in land. At the same time, however, individual tenure was seen as inherently un-African.

---

[1] Frederick Gordon Guggisberg first came to Ghana in 1901 and worked until 1908 as a surveyor. He returned to serve as governor from 1919 until 1927.

[2] In his work on British and French colonialism, Cooper (1997) shows how different concerns were negotiated in most of Africa. Development ideology was originally supposed to sustain empire, not facilitate transfer of power. But administrative expediency and fiscal neutrality created arguments and opportunities that could be seized by political groups, nascent political parties, chieftaincy organizations, trade unions, and the like, who thus developed political space for the negotiation of political power. See also Moore (1992) and Mortimore (1999).

Chanock (1991b: 63) remarks for the British African colonies in general that while the colonial period opened with the dominance of ideas about the evolutionary superiority of Western concepts of individual property rights, it closed with a general atmosphere of suspicion of individual rights. In his *Land Law and Custom in the Colonies*, Meek (1946) thus describes how the British crown early on failed to secure its control over land in the South of the Gold Coast, the Colony, and Ashanti, owing to the opposition of some chiefs and other persons involved in the land issue.[3] The failure to secure control over land was later lamented by the British and seen as the major cause of dispossession of natives as well as the intense and widespread litigation over land, known as the "curse of the country" (Meek, 1946: 172). Consequently, there were serious fears among the colonial administrators that local chiefs and landholders in the Protectorate of the Northern Territories would be subject to land speculation and ultimately be victims of alienation from nonnatives, in particular the educated, thrifty, and dexterous southerners, if countermeasures were not taken.

This fear was linked to the concern for the administration of the protectorate. Thus, if we view land tenure systems in the light of the broader political system and in the conception of the British policy, the right to use and access land was dependent on allegiance to a chief whose authority in turn rested with his control over land. Nonetheless, absolute ownership seemed not to be the appropriate institution to underpin chiefs' authority in the Northern Territories. As Meek (1946:10) states, "the grant . . . to individuals of absolute rights of ownership would tend to disrupt the native polity, and so, too, would the indiscriminate sale of land by chiefs." To match this problem, the colonial administration decided to hold the land in trust for the natives to prevent alienation, and it established a system of leasing through Rights of Occupancy in the Land and Native Rights Ordinance as the "vessel in which government policy is conveyed to the natives."[4] The colonial government saw itself as the only institution with administrative capacity to manage the land, and sufficient political power to protect the interests of the natives. Because this policy should not be a burden on the state coffers, however, discussions were going back and forth between different parts of the colonial administration about the need to establish, on the one hand, comprehensive procedures for the granting of rights and for recovering property tax and, on the other, a pragmatic

---

[3] Among such "other persons" were John Casely Hayford, born in Cape Coast in 1866, educated first locally, then in Freetown, and finally in London where he was called to the bar in 1896. On his return, he became very active in the Aborigines' Rights Protection Society and published extensively on land issues (Hayford, 1913). For the history of education in northern Ghana, see Bening (1974b, 1990).

[4] "Land Tenure in the Protectorate and Its Development under the Land and Native Rights Ordinance" (1948). NRG 8/1/57.

approach that could be practically undertaken by the administration. With indirect rule as the official policy from 1932, the ambition of the British administration was to transfer important issues of the administration to the native authorities, whose creation began that year.

Concerning land, however, this policy was somewhat frustrated, as it gradually dawned upon the colonial administration that the traditional polity and the land tenure system, in particular in the extreme north of the Northern Territories, was not one of a well-organized, centralized chieftaincy owning the land. Thus, the discovery of the *tindana*[5] – the earthpriest – in what is now the Upper East and Upper West regions made indirect rule of land matters too complicated for comfort. Colonial administrators preferred to stick with the idea of chiefs as custodians of the land and to ignore the earthpriest, because involving the latter was incongruous to the colonial idea of the linkage between native political structure and native land rights. The result was that land continued to be vested in the government even after independence. Private, individual transactions in land as well as the customary authority in land matters – the earthpriest – continued to be invisible to the law, whereas chiefs were considered rightful native authorities in land questions.

Early Land Policies in the Northern Territories: "Taken for the Government"

In the first decade of the twentieth century, the British began to recognize the existence and possible significance and utility of the indigenous African government in the Northern Territories. The colonial administration's initial engagement with the local polity, however, was characterized as a failure by one of the first chief commissioners, A. E. G. Watherston, who attributed this to:

- The lack of really big chiefs;
- The breaking up of what were, in a certain sense, kingdoms by Samory and Babatu [warrior and slave trader respectively];
- The absolute imbecility of 60% of the present elected chiefs;
- The want of any common law, even among tribes speaking one language with regard to land, matrimony and so forth;
- The constant stream of traders passing through the country who prefer to bring their matters to the white man rather than to the local chief.[6]

---

[5] Tindana (sing); tindambas (plur.). The spelling varies somewhat between sources. In direct quotations I have maintained the respective authors' orthography verbatim.

[6] A. E. G. Watherston, "The N.T.s of the Gold Coast," *Journal of African Societies* 7 (1908–9): 344, quoted here from Saaka (1978: 27).

The toils and travails of the British to establish governable entities in the Northern Territories reflect their concerns with land and property as well. Before the establishment of British rule in northern Ghana, the area consisted of rather dispersed political entities and ethnic communities. Of larger kingdoms, the Northern Territories could boast of only the Gonjas, the Dagombas, the Mamprusis, the Nanumbas, and the Walas (Allman and Parker, 2005; Bening, 1975b, 1996; Hawkins, 2002; Ladouceur, 1979: 19–35; Lentz, 2000a). Some of these kingdoms were, moreover, somewhat amorphous, as smaller entities around their borders defied and repudiated their authority. In addition, so-called acephalous or stateless societies without distinct political leaders were encountered by the British administrators in the northernmost parts of the Northern Territories as they familiarized themselves with the area under their protection. The efforts of the British were soon directed at reconstituting the existing stronger and weaker kingdoms, wielding together hitherto independent settlements to form cohesive communities that could be governed, and creating chiefs for the stateless societies in the North (Bening, 1975b, 1996; Ferguson and Wilks, 1970; Ladouceur, 1979: 32). Initially, the Colonial Office in London supported the policy suggested by the first commissioner and commandant of the Northern Territories, Lieutenant Colonel H. P. Northcott, to use the chiefs as the primary agency of the administration. Hence, the British administration first attempted to restore the larger kingdoms, as they were seen as protostates or native states. Governor Guggisberg thus saw a possible form of indirect rule as he made his annual report in 1921:

What we aim at is that some day the Dagombas, Gonjas, and Mamprusis should become strong native states. Each will have its own little Public Works Department, and carry on its own business with the Political Officer as a resident and advisor. . . . The question is what steps are to be taken as a foundation on which to build this edifice of the future. I would like the Chief Commissioner to draw up and submit to me in due course a policy for the Northern Territories, showing a definite scheme for fostering the formation of these big states.[7]

At this stage the ambition was to model states on the modern ideas of government and public administration, whereas the Lugardian idea of allowing the native polity to unfold at its own evolutionary pace was less prominent. The idea meant that the British administration appointed or recognized a significant number of chiefs during the first few decades of the century. Efforts to form larger entities led to the amalgamation of independent settlements and their placement under the authority of paramount chiefs, establishing a hierarchy of seniority with only a few paramount

---

[7] Report by Governor Guggisberg, 1921, NRG 1/8, here from Ferguson and Wilks (1970: 334). See also Stopford (1903).

chiefs. The political instrument of promotion and demotion of chiefs has been a frequently used strategy of the government, colonial and independent alike. By rewarding chiefs with paramountcy, government simultaneously can diminish the power of already established paramount chiefs, and by demoting paramount chiefs it "elevates" those who keep their title.

The acephalous sociopolitical structure did not meet the administrative expectations of the colonial officers, and a stereotypical notion that many of the northernmost peoples in the Northern Territories lacked any political organization took root in the early decades of the century (Hawkins, 2002: 107). As it was noted in a report, "large tracts of the Northern Territories appear to be uninhabited or sparsely populated by rude savages without recognized headchiefs or central forms of government, and the Gold Coast system would be quite inapplicable to such tracts."[8] In the process of consolidation of the native states, the acephalous societies were simply put under the authority of a chief, either freshly created or with noble pedigree as the case may have been.

The official policy was intended to revolve around the local political institutions, but as was evident from the first ordinance for the protectorate – the Northern Territories Administration Ordinance (Cap. 111) of 1902 – the administration reserved the right to control land unfettered by any custom. Although it provided that "native tribunals shall exercise the jurisdiction heretofore exercised by them in the same manner as such jurisdiction has been heretofore exercised,"[9] the ordinance gave the chief commissioner sweeping powers to acquire lands:

It shall be lawful for the Chief Commissioner or any persons appointed by him with all necessary workmen and other servants to enter upon any land required for public service, he shall cause such land to be marked out, and a notice to be posted

---

[8] Enc. 3 in No. 90, African (West) no. 652, pp. 45 and 83, CO 879/67, here from Bening, 1995: 229. The same quote in Agbosu's (1980: 114) article reads "nude" rather than "rude." One wonders which is worse. In fact, nudity remained a public concern well into the 1950s. In March 1959 a meeting was held among the Department of Social Welfare and Community Development, the Ministry of Health, the chairmen of the local councils, the All African Women's League, and representatives of the religious missions to this effect. "Nudity, particularly of females, in public places of the Northern Region" was discussed, and "appropriate propaganda" as well as distribution of free clothing through the All African Women's League and the missions was suggested. NRG 8/1/6.

[9] Section 16 of the Administration (Northern Territories) Ordinance Cap. 111, here from Bening, 1975b: 125–26. As Bening (1975b: 125–26) notes, "[u]ntil the introduction of Indirect Rule in 1932, the chiefs and their councils exercised very little real authority over their people." In fact, the vague formulation of the ordinance was allowed, in Bening's words, to "fall into abeyance and authority of the chiefs atrophied. The jurisdiction of the native tribunals was trivial and they acted mainly as courts of arbitration for only the indigenous people. . . . The chiefs . . . took no real part in the administration of the country but merely implemented the instructions and ideas of the District Commissioners. They were thus more the agents of the central government than chosen representatives and rulers of their people." See also Bening (1975a).

in some conspicuous part thereof, which notice shall be in these words, viz.: "Taken for the Government."[10]

Later, in the 1920s, the colonial administration discussed plans for the construction of a railway line linking the remote and neglected Northern Territories to the Ashanti and Gold Coast Colony. According to Bening, this occasioned an interesting disagreement within the administration reflecting the two colonial philosophies on land tenure. In 1922 the secretary of native affairs[11] observed that the Northern Territories were not a colony as such but a *protectorate*. Moreover, the Treaties of Friendship and Freedom of Trade and Treaties of Protection did not mean the surrender of ownership of the land to the British crown (Bening, 1995: 235). As Agbosu observes, the sovereign rights of the traditional authorities had not been ceded to the queen. Similarly, the terms of the treaties did not cover land matters (Agbosu, 1980: 108). Hence, granting of leases by the chief commissioner was *ultra vires* – beyond his proper jurisdiction. Consequently, the secretary of native affairs argued that an ordinance similar to what prevailed in the Colony and Ashanti was promulgated explicitly vesting the lands in the tribes and communities of the North (Bening, 1995; Daanaa, 1996). The governor and the secretary of state were opposed to this idea. The latter noted in a letter that no special formalities had been observed and that the government simply had acquired land whenever it was necessary.[12] The governor supported this practice and found the chief commissioner ill-advised in instructing his officers to obtain Deeds of Gift from the chiefs (Bening, 1995: 236).

Such a deed would constitute a de facto recognition of chiefs' land rights, and, as the secretary of state noted, the chiefs in the Northern Territories have no clear conception of the nature of private property in land, and it is undesirable to encourage them in the idea that they have power to make such grants.[13] However, while land technically speaking was not the property of the colonial government or the governor, the people of the Northern

---

[10] Administration (Northern Territories) Ordinance Cap. 111. This minimal formal requirement for government acquisition was taken seriously by the administrators, though, as the letter from Acting District Commissioner Syme to the chief commissioner of the Northern Territories in 1931 shows, some confusion existed as to the number of notices required: "Nangodi Veterinary Immunisation Camp. No government land which has been acquired recently up here has got notices posted on *four* conspicuous places. Section 27 s.s. (2) NT Cap. I would seem to require 'a notice to be posted in some conspicuous part,' and this is all that has been done. I am now arranging to have four notices posted forthwith" (NRG 8/1/4, acquisition of land).

[11] Arthur J. Philbrick, who later became chief commissioner of the protectorate.

[12] Duke of Devonshire to Governor, November 1922, NAG-A, ADM 12/3/32, here from Bening (1995: 236).

[13] Duke of Devonshire to Governor, November 1922, NAG-A, ADM 12/3/32, and GC Conf. of 28 September 1922 and Encs., NAG-A ADM 12/3/38, here from Bening (1995: 236).

Territories regarded the treaties of trade and friendship signed with the queen as having taken away their sovereign rights (Agbosu, 1980: 109). This perception was indeed largely shared by the colonial administration and later by the administration of independent Ghana. Agbosu notes that government assumed complete administrative control over the lands, treating them as if they were crown lands, although there was no legal basis for doing so (Agbosu, 1980: 113; see also Nyari, 2002). Until 1927, the Administration (Northern Territories) Ordinance of 1902 was the central piece of legislation affecting land tenure in the North. It provided sweeping powers to the governor to acquire land and promoted an understanding that land had already been "taken for the Government."

The Land and Native Rights Ordinance: A Question of Trust and Administrative Expediency

By the end of the 1920s, political debates over the future political administration of the Northern Territories eventually favored indirect rule and the transformation of native states into native authorities with more regularized administrative responsibility (Ladouceur, 1979; Saaka, 1978; Staniland, 1975).[14] Strongly inspired by the indirect rule system developed in Northern Nigeria, it was hoped that chiefs would learn to exercise authority within a simplified framework of modern government. Under the Native Administration Ordinance (Northern Territories), a native authority was a chief, or other native, or group of natives, appointed to be a native authority. Assisted by a Traditional Council, the native authority would, it was envisaged, be responsible for local public works and for certain judicial tasks with the Native Authority Courts, and it was empowered to levy taxes. The ordinance marks the high-water mark of the policy of indirect rule (see Allot, 1960: 128).

In order to put indirect rule into operation, however, it was realized that much more had to be known about the nature of the native institutions that were "to be recast into a modern form," as Ladouceur (1979: 54) coins it. For these reasons, a great research project was launched by the government to record the histories, customs, and institutions of the peoples of the North. District officers were instructed to investigate these matters in their respective areas, and the government's special commissioner for anthropology, R. S. Rattray, undertook a major study on the whole of the Northern Territories, resulting in his *The Tribes of the Ashanti Hinterland*.[15] Moreover,

---

[14] See Staniland (1975: chap. 5) for an account of the battle over indirect rule in northern Ghana.

[15] Other studies of significance were A. Duncan Johnstone and H. Blair, *Enquiry into the Constitution and Social Organisation of the Dagbon Kingdom* (1932); St.-J. Eyre-Smith, *A Brief Review of the History and Social Organisation of the Peoples of the Northern Territories of the Gold Coast* (1933); and E .F. Tamakloe, *Brief History of the Dagbamba People* (1932); all published by the government in Accra. Of other

conferences were organized to record the laws, customs, and political organization of the various peoples.[16] These conferences laid out rules of succession, systems of rank, and allegiance. The conferences were followed by intensive campaigns to consolidate and amalgamate political entities, an approach that was seen as the most suitable in the face of the administrative challenges of the future. The process of formalizing the native states into larger units underpinned by systematic recording and representation of "native customs and constitutions" entailed a fundamental strengthening of the role of the chiefs as the central pivot in local administration.

It was in the context of these overall efforts that the Land and Native Rights Ordinance attempted to deal with the land issues. Land speculation and maladministration of stool (i.e., chieftancy) lands by chiefs in the South increasingly became a concern for the colonial government during the 1920s. Fears that this situation would spill over into the Northern Territories prompted the colonial government to formalize the rules and procedures already followed in the North, and in 1927 the Land and Native Rights Ordinance (Cap. 143) declared all lands, whether occupied or unoccupied, to be native lands and placed these under the control of the governor and subject to his disposition. It provided that land was to be held and administered for the use and common benefit, direct and indirect, of the natives. These laws provided that no compensation was to be paid for any land acquired (Land and Native Rights Ordinance No. 1 [1927]).[17] The ordinance was opposed by intellectuals in the Gold Coast Colony, who saw it as state confiscation of lands. The governor, on the other hand, argued that vesting the lands of the Northern Territories in the government was a measure to prevent speculation, alienation, and the subsequent landlessness of the natives.[18] The revised ordinance saw the light of day in 1931. In

reports, one can mention "The Kusasis: A Short History," by District Commissioner Syme from 1932. See Lentz (1999) and Ladouceur (1979). These studies were part of an even greater African survey (Hailey, 1938). See also Cell (1989). One of the earliest reports was made by George Ekem Ferguson (see Arhin, 1974).

[16] The most important conferences were those of Gonja (May 1930), Dagomba (November 1930), Kusasi (March 1931), Mamprusi (December 1932), and Wa (July 1933) (Ladouceur, 1979: 54).

[17] At the same time the forest resources were legislated for, for the first time in Forests Ordinance No. 13, Cap. 157, amended by Ordinances No. 16 of 1928, No. 31 of 1928, No. 38 of 1929, and No. 10 of 1932. The Forests Ordinance No. 4 of 1929, applied to the Northern Territories. NAG-A ADM 56/1/280.

[18] Governor Slater thus stated that the new ordinance sought to preclude the natives from the temptation to dispose of their lands outright without due regard for the requirements of their descendants, and for totally inadequate payments; to ensure that such profits as are derived from the land are used for the benefit of the community as a whole and not for any particular section or individual member of it; and to minimize the possibility of ruinous litigation. Sir R. Slater's speech to the Legislative Council, 1 March 1932, here from Metcalfe (1994: 634). The ordinance was revised in 1931. While the revised Native Land Rights Ordinance of 1931 recognized that the land remained the property of the people, it vested the land in trust with the governor.

the amendment it was made clear that indigenes who occupied land under customary law needed no other title.[19] Moreover, the governor stated that the crown acquired no title to the lands. The land remained the property of the people, but the governor became the trustee for and representative of the people (Bening, 1995: 242–44). As Der points out, however, while the intent of the ordinance may have been to protect the local people's rights over their lands, it had the indirect effect of dispossessing them (Der, 1975: 138).

The practical challenges of enforcing the ordinance and making full use of its developmental potential reiterated the two opposite positions in terms of calls for a controlled, comprehensive planning approach (including certificates of occupancy) versus a more pragmatic, incremental, and adaptive one. The acting commissioner of lands, G. W. Stackpole, thus wrote to the acting colonial secretary in 1932 concerning, among other things, the issuing of certificates of occupancy.

The time has come to address you from the point of view of this Department upon the subject of the necessity for providing in the Northern Territories some facilities for the provision of more accurate plans and descriptions of pieces of land which are to be dealt with in legal documents. . . . Certificates of Occupancy issued under the Land and Native Rights Ordinance 1931 require plans of the land comprised in the certificate. . . . During the five years ending 20th November 1936 all non-natives are by section 3a of the Land and Native Rights Ordinance 1931 required to prove their titles in the prescribed manner. It will be necessary then to record the fact that the title has been proved and to evidence the consent of the Governor a right and a Certificate of Occupancy will normally be granted. . . . [H]owever, . . . as the Surveyor-General has no surveyors available for regular work in the Northern Territories there is very seldom any one available who can make a plan which is even approximately correct. . . . This situation is incongruous in the extreme.[20]

Because certificates of occupancy were required only by nonnatives, the administrative and operational burden of the task was greatly reduced. Still, the task seemed daunting to Acting Commissioner of Lands Stackpole. A possible reason for concern was that some groups of the African population, namely the Lobi, were not considered as natives but rather as French because they were believed to originate from the French territories. The Hausa and Yoruba communities, originating from Nigeria, posed a similar challenge.[21] A few years later, in 1937, a "Memorandum Relating to the Application of

[19] Land and Native Rights Amendment Ordinance 1931, Section 2. See also Bening (1995: 244). In the amendment, "Native lands" were substituted for "Public lands."

[20] NRG 8/1/6, case no. 450/2169/C.S. 149. Letter from G. W. Stackpole to the Acting Colonial Secretary, 5 July 1932.

[21] "Surely it is not contemplated issuing Certificates of Occupancy and preparing plans for the thousands of illiterate non-natives in the Protectorate with their semi nomadic habits and systems of shifting cultivation; if so we shall require the services of several Surveyors for some years." Letter from Chief Commissioner NT to Commissioner of Lands 1326/55/1928, 27 July 1932. NRG 8/1/6.

the Land and Native Rights Ordinance of 1931" saw the light of day. The author is not identifiable, but it is likely to be the chief commissioner of the Northern Territories.[22] It neatly defined the Hausa, the Lobi, and other similar groups either as native with no need for certificates of occupancy or as foreigners with no right to it. The parallel policy of legislating the Northern Territories into modern land management, while in practice following a less cumbersome route of letting indigenous tenure evolve by itself, could proceed. The memorandum echoes Lugard as it continues by stressing the limited direct impact of the ordinance on the majority of people in the Northern Territories.

In cases where no estate right or interest in the land is acquired, no action is desirable nor is [it] required under the Ordinance. The nature of the occupation is in accordance with native custom and no written licence or agreement between the parties is necessary. It would not be advisable in these instances to attempt by means of a written document to ensure that the occupation is one only at the will of the native owner, as any such document would confuse the uneducated native mind which otherwise has a perfectly clear idea of the nature of the occupation.[23]

One wonders whether confusion would beset merely the uneducated native mind. The reasons for the systematic efforts to reduce the impact of the ordinance were the administrative difficulties of enforcing it. Stackpole, now promoted to commissioner of lands, seemed to think that the procedure of delivering a certificate of occupancy, if undertaken at all, should be adhered to properly. If people did not have sufficient means to have surveys conducted, transactions could be postponed until a more propitious moment.[24] This policy would fit in with a notion that people would be either natives conducting their land transaction within the confines of tradition in a nonmonetary fashion or detribalized urban people with ambitions to secure legal protection of their property; a distinction between rural custom and urban law. However, people seem to have fallen between the categories, as reports of land sales were not infrequent. Thus, chief commissioner of the Northern Territories, Mr. Jones, reported in 1939:

I would mention that a report received this morning from the D.C., Krachi [part of former German Togoland included in Northern Territories], shows that illegal

---

[22] Letter from Commissioner of Lands, Mr. Stackpole refers to this memo as authored by the C.C.N.Ts. NRG 8/1/6.

[23] "Memorandum Relating to the Application of the Land and Native Rights Ordinance of 1931." NRG 8/1/6.

[24] "I am not in favour of any relaxation of survey requirements antecedent to the issue of a C. of O.... There is however no necessity for a C. of O. to issue at any particular time.... I have always succeeded in obtaining surveys although sometimes after some delay. With the additional help of licensed surveyors matters should improve." Minute by the Commissioner of Lands (Mr. G. W. Stackpole), 9 July, 1938. NRG 8/1/6.

sales are continuing, and that they will continue so long as the chiefs and elders concerned are free from punishment. In its present form the Land and Native Rights Ordinance is nothing more than a piece of empty legislation; it does not enable us to fulfil the requirements of paragraph 2 of Article V of the Mandate.[25]

Later the same year, the district commissioner residing in Gambaga thought it necessary to seek advice from the chief commissioner concerning the development in the two major towns in his area, Bolgatanga and Bawku. As a part of the efforts to facilitate sanitation and the commercial development of Bolgatanga, a survey was made and a town layout was designed and demarcated in 1938. The Bolga native authority allocated a large number of plots to both natives and nonnatives. However, as A. F. Kerr, the district commissioner, points out, guidelines concerning the recovery of rent were difficult to ascertain.

The Bolga Native Authority is very vague as to the conditions on which plots were allocated for occupation by these strangers.... I understand ... that the Mamprusi Native Authority had, on the suggestion of Colonel Gibbs, decided to impose a rent of £1 a house per year on all "strangers" – by which was intended, I believe, all non-natives of the Northern Territories – who lived in the towns of Walewale, Bolga and Bawku. I can find no reference to this than its inclusion in the Native Administration revenue estimates, and no rules have been made – nor could, I think. As yet no one has paid in Bolga: in Walewale the eight Yorubas have paid, Moshi etc. being regarded as natives, having lived there for a generation or so: and I am enquiring about the situation in Bawku. [While typing the letter, Mr. Kerr received the information about Bawku and appended it as a P.S.] In Bawku £1 a year rent is payable by all Yoruba and "Coast" house-owners, an arrangement which has the virtue of simplicity, but appears to lack any legal, economic or ethical justification.... In view of the apparent urgency in getting this matter settled as all plots have been allocated and some already built on, I would be grateful if Your Honour could give me some preliminary indication as to the terms on which anyone who wants may start building on a plot which has been allocated to him, as I imagine that it may be some time before the matter is finally decided.[26]

Considering the amount of correspondence on the issue of certificates of occupancy after the passage of the first ordinance in 1927 and the related discussions about who should constitute the customary authority in land matters, it is striking that the actual number of certificates of occupancy turned out to be relatively modest. Assistant Commissioner of Lands Pogucki thus

---

[25] Letter by C.C.N.Ts Mr. Jones 17.1.39. NRG 8/1/6.
[26] Letter no. 549/17/1932 of 14 August 1939 from District Commissioner (Gambaga/Mamprusi) to Chief Commissioner, Tamale. NRG 8/1/28.

recorded that from the adoption of the ordinance until he did his report in 1951, a mere eighty-two certificates had been issued, twenty-eight of which were issued to missions (Pogucki, 1951). There is no reason to believe that this number in any way reflects the number of land transactions of a private and monetary character. It is more likely that the majority of such transactions merely remained out of the legal and administrative horizon of government and the state.[27]

The correspondence between the different elements of the colonial administration reflects that several concerns were voiced at the same time. First of all, the overarching ambition to legislate on land issues was predominant. It was untenable for the British colonial administration to leave the management of this resource outside the scope of the law. Second, the administrators' concerns with administrative feasibility, especially the ordinance's implementation, led them to take measures to define most of the population out of the ordinance's immediate areas of concern. What remained within the scope of the ordinance – namely, rent for plots in urban areas – was likewise dealt with in a highly pragmatic fashion. Indeed, the somewhat concerned letters indicate that negotiated settlements between individuals and local authorities greatly outnumbered regularized access as prescribed by the ordinance. While land was ultimately held in trust by the governor, the everyday transactions seemed to flow along channels that were never mastered by the trustee.

Although Guggisberg's concerns with government control over land seemed to prevail in a formal sense, everyday concerns with feasible administrative procedure nonetheless led administrators to interpret the legal framework in ways that had the least cumbersome consequence and the least apparent impact on local practices. While this "pragmatic compromise" may seem innocuous, the concerns for feasible management had a significant impact on the land tenure system and, in particular, on the ways in which indigenous institutions and authorities were integrated into the system of indirect rule. Consequently, the "discovery" of the earthpriest did not sit well with administrative priorities.

The "Discovery" and Disregard of the Earthpriest

In *The Tribes of the Ashanti Hinterland*, government anthropologist Captain Rattray (1932, xi) argued for a reassessment of the colonial administration's

---

[27] The difficulties of conducting a policy of segregation between the developed educated part of the urban population, on the one hand, and a more conservative indigenous population, on the other, was gradually recognized by the local administrators. See District Commissioner Irving Cass's essay on "The Traditional Native Authority in Urban Administration in West Africa" from 1948. NRG 8/2/22.

conventional ideas about native polity and native land tenure, at least for the northernmost parts of the Northern Territories:

Over the whole area . . . we had, it was found, a people who possessed a practically uniform religion, a uniform tribal and totemic organization, and an identical political constitution or system of tribal government. The outstanding feature of the last names was the *Ten'dana* . . . or priest king. "In the past, in the Northern Territories, there were no Chiefs, only *Ten'dama*" is a statement which I have frequently heard made. Such a statement is the result of confused thinking and shows complete lack of knowledge of the local social organizations under which these tribes formerly lived, and in many cases still live. The case should rather be stated thus: "In the past the *Ten'dama* were the only Chiefs known." Had a series of events . . . not greatly affected the local constitutional system, these *Ten'dama* or Priest-Kings would undoubtedly have evolved into the type of Native ruler with whom we are familiar among the Akan; that is a ruler who was not only high-priest and custodian of the land of his tribe and of the ancestral spirits, but one who was a Chief or King on a territorial basis whose sanctions were secular and physical rather than spiritual. . . . Here in the North this natural process of evolution, from the Priest-King to the Territorial ruler was interrupted by external influences which produces a really remarkable state of affairs. These it is well we should understand before embarking on schemes for Indirect Rule or a new native Administration.

Rattray was insisting on an evolutionary paradigm modeled on the Akan social structure that he knew from the South. The earthpriests would have evolved into territorial chiefs, he believed, had it not been for the invasion of warrior tribes who settled in the North and, in particular, for the British colonization. The secular territorial rulers who invaded the North were too superstitious to interfere with the work of the earthpriest according to Rattray (1932: xvii):

The result was that among many of these tribes, before our advent, there had been evolved a kind of dual mandate. There was the secular ruler descended from the leader of the earlier warrior bands. He was recognized by every one as a kind of titular head, he had a red fez and wore clothes, but really interfered hardly at all with the life or private affairs of the masses. All religious or magico-religious concerns continued to be managed and conducted by the former priestly rulers, who now, however, functioned nominally under the territorial chief. The former continued to assert his original title to be custodian and trustee of the land of his people, a claim which few, even of the most arrogant secular chiefs, ever dared to dispute, even to the present day. "The people belong to me, the land belongs to the Ten'dana" is a statement I have repeatedly heard made.

The colonial encounter, however, was more harmful to the earthpriest, according to Rattray. In many places, the earthpriests, "having seen what had happened to their fraternity, who had appeared before the officials of the other Continental powers," preferred to thrust forward some "wholly unimportant and often useless individual" (Rattray, 1932: xvi) to be an emissary to meet the white man.

In the course of time, however, many of these individuals came to dig themselves in and became more assured and confident of their positions. . . . Some of them are fine men, and all are most careful to function satisfactorily before the European Official. From a Commissioner's point of view they are often most efficient and hard working Chiefs. They realize very fully that they would not hold their position for a day without Government backing, so take good care to please the local Government representative. I myself have seen this type of Chief stand up and declare that the land of the tribe was his and that no *Tin'dana* existed or ever had existed in his division. This extreme type is happily somewhat rare, but he exists and is a real menace. . . . These upstarts would not survive long were we to leave the country. . . . A remedy is simple and need cause no great upheaval. All that is necessary is to insist that every rightful *Tin'dana* who is not actually a Chief and the *Tin'dana*'s hereditary elders should act with the Chief as his councillors. (Rattray, 1932: xvii)

The writings of Captain Rattray have been discussed and critiqued by Carola Lentz (1999), among others, for the way in which he insisted on viewing the native polity as an embryonic but interrupted form of the Akan structure. There can be little doubt that this was indeed the case. Nonetheless, his work was important for the knowledge it provided about the earthpriest. While Rattray was not the first of the British colonial administration to discover the earthpriest, he was the first to conduct a more systematic anthropological study of northern Ghana and, together with District Commissioner Eyre-Smith of Lawra District, the first to reflect on the possible role for the earthpriest in the modern administration of the protectorate.[28] Rattray (1932) did not see the earthpriest as a relic from a chaotic past but rather as a contemporary political figure holding natural legitimacy and thus disinclined to despotism.

Immediately after Rattray, another British anthropologist, Meyer Fortes (1940, 1945), began his studies among the Tallensi just south of Bolgatanga. While Fortes was not in the colonial government's employ, his research was presented to and discussed with the colonial administration. Fortes believed that the existing image of customary authority as exclusively chieftaincy was seriously misinformed. But whereas Rattray had an idea of an arrested evolution of the social system, Fortes was keen to see the Tallensi society representing some form of equilibrium[29] (Allman and Parker, 2005:

---

[28] For an analysis of colonial ethnographies, see Lentz (1999). See also Hawkins (2002: 104–37).

[29] This is actually somewhat of a paradox in Fortes's writing. In an early article on "culture contact," he demonstrates an eye for change and diversity. He thus argues that the "unit of observation must be a

199–206; Fortes, 1945: 231–58; Manoukian, 1952: 65–69). The discovery
of the earthpriest produced a challenge to the colonial administration. In
the British conception of indigenous land tenure and customary law, the
linkage between them was ensured by the chief. He was considered the
custodian of land as well as the natural political authority. The existence
of a "land authority" without matching political power, capable of carving
out "land" from the chiefs' domain, introduced an unsettling thought of
fragmenting customary authority. Hawkins (2002: 119) argues that these
"new" findings were largely ignored by administrators, and the long-term
effect was the elimination of the earthpriest from the administrative perspective.[30] However, this was not a foregone conclusion, as debates and
correspondence among and between colonial administrators testify.

Rattray's and Fortes's work kindled an interest in the earthpriest among
certain administrators and, in particular, inspired the commissioner of lands,
who made a visit to the Northern Territories in 1948. Afterward, he made a
number of observations and recommendations for possible amendments to
the law in view of the realities he encountered on the ground. His report,
"Land Tenure in the Protectorate and Its Development under the Land and
Native Rights Ordinance" (1948), merits some attention. In the report, he
made some observations along the lines noted by Rattray and Fortes:

Throughout the Protectorate the control of land is in the hands of one or other of the
land priests known as Tindana. . . . These priests are in absolute control of the land
under their jurisdiction both as regards tenure and the practical rules of agriculture,

---

unit of life and not of custom" and "the population falls into a large number of discrete communities,
the social boundaries between which do not become apparent to an ethnographer bent on tracing
this uniformity of custom" (Fortes, 1936: 26). He even concludes that the "extraordinary thing is not
that native society changes, but that any of its traditional forms of social life survive the process of
civilization" (Fortes, 1936: 55). Nonetheless, his writing on earthpriests (1940 and 1945) carefully
avoids "change," even though Fortes must have been aware of newer land transactions, such as sales.

[30] The rejection of the earthpriest by the colonial administration was in a symbolic sense reinforced
by Guggisberg's passion for chiefly medallions! Medals issued varied in size in accordance with the
relative importance of the chief. To my knowledge, no medals were awarded to the earthpriests.
Arguably, it was also compounded by the (early) opinions of the Agriculture and Forestry Departments of Africans' "wasteful" and "unsound" land use practices. For example, Forestry Departments
throughout West Africa were instrumental in constructing the conceptual dichotomy between the
realms of the "modern" and "scientific" approach to fire control and/or management and the "traditional" and "haphazard" use of fire as a land management tool by, for example, farmers, herders,
hunters, and honey gatherers. This approach veiled complex historical, ecological, and sociocultural
realities and has resulted in the persistence of the bush fire "problem" despite repeated attempts
by West African states to legislate against bush fires. One of the functions of the earthpriests as
custodians of the earth was (and remains) the ritual use of fire in customary land use practice. In the
eyes of a modernizing development administration, earthpriests and their role are the antithesis of
progress. I owe thanks to Andrew Wardell for drawing my attention to this point. See also Tilley
(2003).

and can eject an occupier who is unsuitable or who farms in an unhusbandlike manner. I would here mention that the Tindanas are usually unwilling to enter into any negotiations with Government. They appear to keep in the background but have a strong influence and are strong minded obstinate men who are so convinced of the immutability of the state of affairs of which they are the living custodians that, to them, it seems infinitely wise to admit, say and agree to, nothing, remaining wise and inscrutable in the assurance of their sacred trust. Up to a point they may be acting wisely.[31]

The commissioner of lands seemed, however, less confident than Rattray and Fortes in the immutability of the situation:

Such incidental matters as for instance the embrace of Christianity are also sapping the old powers of the Tindanas for we find a Christian refusing to obey the customary rules regulating farming days. He says the day he must not farm is Sunday, not Friday. This is tolerated by the Tindanas. Nor does it seem a long way from the time at which a recalcitrant occupier will refuse to leave the farm merely because an incensed priest plants a twig before his door. These times are passing.[32]

In practice, however, chiefs and earthpriests were recognized by the colonial administration to have (at least for practical purposes, some) legitimate interests in land. The commissioner of lands pointed to a clause in the Land and Native Rights Ordinance that excluded all titles to land lawfully acquired before the issuing of the ordinance from government control.[33] By deduction, the commissioner of lands considered such lands – in fact, most lands – outside immediate government control. The cross purposes between the ideal command by the colonial authorities and the necessity to rule via some local legitimate authority were glaring. The land tenure system was not practically operational for the administration without the involvement of either chiefs or earthpriests; still, involving them could be seen as relinquishing government control. In fact, these considerations led the commissioner of lands to suggest a series of amendments to the ordinance to allow a formalization of the customary land tenure system. The particular copy of the report at my disposal is a photocopy from the Lands Commission in Bolgatanga. Two people have made comments in the margin; one of whom appears to have read it at the time of its issue and in a

---

[31] "Land Tenure in the Protectorate and Its Development under the Land and Native Rights Ordinance" (1948), para. 4–5. NRG 8/1/57.

[32] Ibid., para 15.

[33] "In a number of cases in town the Chiefs have from time to time granted leases to non-natives of land falling within the exception in section 3(a) [of Land and Native Rights Ordinance (cap. 143)]. Such leases have in the past been regarded as invalid, and the lessee has been required to take up a right of occupancy and then a certificate of occupancy has been issued to him. . . . I do not consider that Government had any right to take this action." Ibid., para. 22.

Table 2.1. *Land Tenure in the Protectorate and Its Development under the Land and Native Rights Ordinance, 1948 (NRG 8/1/57), with Marginal Anonymous Comments*

"Land Tenure in the Protectorate," paragraphs 47–50	Anonymous Commentator
My view is that it would be politic and expedient to amend the Ordinance in the following respects:	It is true for their *use* only.
To recognise that, as on the Colony, all the land in the Protectorate belongs to the native communities.	
To recognise the Tindanas as Land Authorities.	NO.
To permit Tindanas to make grants of lands to natives in accordance with native custom.	They already do so for farming purposes.
Clearly to recognise the right of the Tindana to dispose of land in or on behalf of the community [subject to obtaining prior written consent of the Governor].	Not to non-natives at all & not to anybody in urban areas.
It is suggested that each Tindana's position be recognised, and that each should be given statutorily a seal by which he would execute all documents	NO.
disposing of land and that such seal should be affixed by the Tindana in the presence of the District Commissioner and the Chief who would sign or mark an attestation clause to that effect.	NO.

professional capacity. The identity of the commentator is unknown. It could have been the governor, or it could have been someone with a lesser charge. Be that as it may, the double reading of the report with the commissioner of lands echoing Lord Lugard's philosophy of "natural" evolution of land tenure, on the one hand, and the anonymous commentator's objections in curt barks, on the other, illustrates the debate and disagreement within the colonial administration (see Table 2.1).

The handwritten comments were obviously not the only reaction to the suggestions made by the commissioner of lands.[34] The district commissioners were saddled with the unenviable task of reconciling the natural evolution of land tenure with the sanctity of custom. While they saw the marginalization of the earthpriest as a natural process whereby an outworn fetish cult was made redundant, they deplored the commercialization and alienation of land as a departure from custom whereby the chief protects the general interests of his community. Other reactions to the commissioner of lands' report, such as a letter from the district commissioner in Gonja/Salaga, also cautioned against reversing the tide of evolution. Again, the concerns for administrative expediency shine through:

[34] Letter from District Commissioner Cass (Dagomba) to Chief Commissioner in Tamale, 18 August 1948. NRG 8/1/55.

I feel that the position has moved from the strictly theoretical one to a point where the Tindana and the chief both have rights. The position may be . . . the result of an administrative arrangement, but I do not think we should be justified in making a legal retreat from it. . . . I therefore believe that we have already arrived, or are very rapidly approaching, a new system of land tenure in the North and that the position described . . . by the Commissioner of Lands has in effect been reached. While I agree that this system probably varies from place to place and is without definition, I do not see that this means that it is based on a fallacy. I suggest on the contrary that it is based on a workable compromise which has grown up, no doubt, through Administrative pressure, but which nevertheless has been worked out by the people themselves to their own satisfaction without our direct intervention and indeed without our noticing what has been going on.[35]

Likewise, the assistant chief commissioner sent a condensed survey of the administrative officers on the commissioner of lands' report to the governor:

Mr Amherst's views:

- Land does not belong to the native communities
- We must not go the way of the South. . . .
- Not even the Governor should be allowed to grant complete ownership. . . .

Mr Dobbs' views:

- The Chief and the Tindana should become the joint land Authority . . .

Mr Crabb's views: . . .

- Usually there is a "working agreement" between Chiefs and the Tindanas.
- But the tendency is, and will be, for Chiefs to assume control of land [added in pencil: "But not ownership or right to alienate"]. . . .
- Not desirable to give Tindanas seals.
- It *might* be desirable to make it compulsory for Native Authorities *and* Tindanas to sign land documents. . . .

Mr Gass' views: . . .

- The Native Authority [i.e., chiefs] should be recognized as Land Agency. The Tindana lost that long ago.[36]

The reports from the various parts of the Northern Territories confirmed Rattray's "discovery." The earthpriest had played an important part in land allocation in the past. However, the dominance of kingdoms in some parts

---

[35] Letter from District Commissioner (Gonja/Salaga) to Chief Commissioner in Tamale, 16 August 1948. NRG 8/1/51.

[36] Survey of the views of Administrative Officers on the Commissioner of Land's Memorandum, 6 January 1949, signed by Assistant Chief Commissioner. NRG 8/1/51.

of the Northern Territories (Gonja, Dagomba, Mamprusi, Nanumba, and Wala) – basically what is now the Northern Region – matched well with an evolutionary perspective on land tenure and native polity. The inevitable evolution toward a full-blown Akan-like society had reached the southern and central parts of the Northern Territories, whereas this development had not yet unfolded in the northernmost parts of the protectorate, basically what is now the Upper East and Upper West regions. The earthpriest, it was recognized, had not disappeared totally from land transactions in the northernmost parts. The consensus among the administrators was, nonetheless, that the "natural evolution" should not be interrupted; if anything, it should be helped along by "administrative pressure" as the district commissioner of Gonja put it. However, it should not go beyond the convenient point of chiefly control. Individualized private tenure with possibilities of alienation was not administratively attractive.

Assistant Commissioner of Lands Pogucki (1955) describes this historical process as "tribalisation." He argues that allodial ownership to land in northern Ghana historically was held by kinship groups or clans.[37] Hence, land was under the control of the earthpriest. However, in many cases, and in particular in what is now the Northern Region, a process of conquest and tribalization of land occurred – a process aided by the British ideas of indirect rule.

It is however, interesting to note that in all these areas the tribal basis, if one may speak of it as such, is being stressed by members of the ruling groups, whereas representatives of the subject groups usually (except in the presence of chiefs and their relatives) express the opinion, that land from the point of view of allodial ownership is still vested in the kinship groups. In all such instances where this process of tribalisation proceeds, the usually expressed opinion is, that allodial rights to land are vested in the paramount chief as a representative of all his people and, that the divisional and sub-divisional chiefs, or headmen of villages, are only representing the paramount chief in connection with the land, and do not hold any rights of their own. These alleged tribal rights are, however, superimposed, and do not grow organically out of the organisation of the respective areas, although attempts are being made to justify the claim to such rights. . . . [T]hese purported

---

[37] The allodial title is the highest customary title capable of being held in Ghana and, in principle, subject only to such limitations, restrictions, or obligations as may be imposed by the general laws of the country (Rocha and Lodoh, 1995: 3). The term "allodial title" denotes a customary law interest in land not traditionally held by a tenant from a lord. Allodial title is therefore also known as "absolute" or "ultimate" title (Woodman, 1996: 56). In Osborn's *Concise Law Dictionary*, allodium is described as "Lands not held of any superior, in which, therefore, the owner had an absolute title and not a mere estate" (Osborn, 1964: 23). Allodial title is, or rather was, established through discovery and first settlement and is essentially communal. Historically, as Woodman (1996) and Rocha and Lodoh (1995) argue, allodial title could also be acquired by conquest and subsequent settlement. For doubts about the "absolute" nature of allodial title, see Tait (1952). See also Chapter 3.

tribal rights, claimed by members of the ruling tribe, exist in a large number of places simultaneously with the rights claimed by kinship groups of the first settlers of the subject tribe. They do not operate, however, concurrently, but rather side by side. Usually the form of operation of these rights consists of a stranger approaching the chief for permission to use land for farming. But simultaneously the same stranger, perhaps in order to be on the safe side, would approach the Tindana in order to obtain his approval as a representative of the originally land owning kinship. The extent of the exercise of allodial rights depends upon the strength of the community of the subject tribe in a particular locality. (Pogucki, 1955: 19–21)

While Pogucki seems to be in doubt about the validity or justice of the chieftaincy claim to land, carefully referring to *alleged* and *purported* rights, he nonetheless recognizes the "facts" of history: land rights are in some places successfully vindicated by paramount chiefs. In the second part of his report,[38] aimed at providing material for discussion of further development of land law in the Northern Territories, Pogucki (1951: 6) strikes a more pragmatic tone as he tries to summarize the Lands Department's position:

Many of the concepts of customary land law in the Northern Territories have reached a more developed state, although some notions remain still in a formative stage. It may therefore be desirable to maintain measures of control to guarantee further normal evolution of customary law, which on the one hand would prevent a sudden disruption of social security through uncontrolled desires for economic betterment by individuals and through growth of speculation in land, and on the other hand enhance security of tenure which may be required for further economic development at that stage, both by groups and individuals owning, or acquiring rights in land. These objects can best be achieved through organised measures of control, a codified system of law and registration of land all having in view that [here Pogucki moves on to quote a dispatch from the governor][39] "the parallel existence of individual and communal rights in land are not necessarily inconsistent with African conceptions of land rights. Individual security of title can be combined with a measure of community control; and the object in planning . . . is in large measure to ensure that advantage is taken of this valuable African conception of land tenure, before it has been irreparably weakened by the spasmodic growth of ill-defined, and possibly inconsistent, individual rights."

This statement again echoes a number of considerations and attempts to balance them. It emphasizes that to let the control over land go from the state to the chiefs, or, worse, from chiefs to land users, was not an option.

---

[38] Pogucki's reports were first published in 1951. The first part of the report was later, in 1955, republished. Because the 1955 edition is more readily available, I prefer to refer to this version of the first part. The second part was not, to my knowledge, republished.

[39] H.E.'s Conf. Despatch No. E.L.13/189, 30 June 1949. Here from Pogucki (1951: 6).

Nevertheless, it praises some of the perceived virtues of African land tenure. Its recommendation is a pragmatic combination of the two approaches.

Conclusion

It can be argued that a compromise between two philosophies of government control and the natural evolution of land tenure was gradually reached in the administration's pragmatic negotiation of its challenges. Whereas Guggisberg's ambition to seize total control over land was accomplished by the Native Rights Ordinance, the Lugardian ambition to allow the natural evolution of land tenure to unfold unfettered by impatient stereotypical legislation would seem to be accommodated by indirect rule. The government retained the right to appropriate all the lands, which it decided that it needed, and there was a "natural fit" between the ambitions of indirect rule and this particular idea of native custom collapsing political authority and indigenous tenure into one figure, the chief. While this compromise would seem quite innocuous, it had a significant effect in the areas where "tribalization" had not already deleted the importance of the earthpriest.

The close linkage between polity and land in the British colonial administration of Ghana meant that changes in the political structures had consequences for land management, even if the colonial ambitions in this area were effectively modest. Hence, the favored position of the chiefs in the system of indirect rule led to the disregard of other indigenous land authorities. It was preferred to keep them in the dead angle as a cult soon to vanish. Thus, even though the British had no ambition to "rewrite" custom, their efforts to solidify it meant change. By empowering a certain segment of the customary authorities and disregarding another, land control and political office were seen as conjoined. This image endured even after independence, and chiefs were regarded by the state as the legitimate representatives of the population as well as its customs. That, however, need not be a permanent position. What is at one point considered insignificant and tolerated transactions, orchestrated by symbolic leaders of waning secret cults with no authority, may in different historical circumstances turn land administration upside down, a point I develop in the next chapter. To most rural producers, the practical terms of access to land did not change much with colonial imposition. Whether this can be attributed to the fact that the government was holding the land in trust, and thereby preventing speculation, is difficult to say. In towns, exclusion was more of an issue, as government seized land for development purposes. On balance, however, this imposition was still quite modest in scale. The most important impact was rather that the colonial "protection" of the Northern Territories through selected indigenous political institutions – the chiefs – laid the foundation for future claims and conflicts over jurisdiction and resources.

3

Who Owns Bolgatanga?

The Revival of the Earthpriest and Emerging Tensions over Property

What made the "emergency" was the repeated public humiliation of the authorities; the simultaneous attacks upon royal and private property; the sense of a confederated movement which was enlarging its social demands.

E. P. Thompson, *Whigs and Hunters*

Introduction

Property rights in Bolgatanga and northern Ghana[1] have been the object of much debate and struggle during the past three decades. A legal situation that was established in 1927 essentially remained in effect after independence. The Land and Native Rights Ordinance (Cap. 143) declared all lands in the Northern Territories, whether occupied or unoccupied, to be native lands and placed them under the control of the governor. When the 1979 Constitution divested the state of its trusteeship over most lands in the Northern and Upper regions, the need to address the question to whom these lands were to be given became acute. The new legal situation provided an opportunity for reassessing the past, resettling old accounts, reasserting belonging in terms of prerogatives and jurisdictions, and renegotiating ownership to land. Chiefs and earthpriests intensified their competition over the control of the land.

This chapter deals with the history of landownership in Bolgatanga as a story of competing claims to customary authority and clashes between public and private interests in land. The chapter starts with a brief glimpse into a report of the lands commissioner, from 1948, which illustrates the evolutionary perspective on customary land tenure promoted by both anthropologists and administrators during the colonial period. It also shows the

[1] Northern Ghana (or the Northern Region) was essentially the former Protectorate of the Northern Territories of the Gold Coast. In 1960 the Upper Region was carved out of the Northern Region, with Bolgatanga as its capital; in 1983 the Upper Region was subdivided into the Upper West and Upper East Regions, with the regional capitals of Wa and Bolgatanga, respectively. See Bening (1999).

difficulties that the commissioner (and other observers) encountered in assigning traditional landownership, whether to the earthpriests or to the chiefs. I then discuss some of the relevant legal stipulations and administrative practices concerning land that have prevailed since independence. The legal controversies that have developed since the 1980s, which I subsequently analyze, demonstrate that the evolutionary sequence of customary tenure – shifting the control over land from earthpriests to chiefs – is not as inevitable as suggested. Rather, contemporary conflicts show that we are dealing with negotiations whose outcome depends on the political context and the organization of interests of the contestants. Moreover, the cases suggest that we are witnessing competition not only between different customary authorities but also between the customary authorities and land users with customary freehold. The controversies illustrate how claims of belonging are being used to justify property rights and, more generally, how stakeholders attempt to exploit the fluidity of property rights as well as to fix them to their own advantage.

Land Tenure in the Upper Regions and Bolgatanga

In most of Ghana, the customary offices are occupied by the chieftaincy institution – the *stool* in the South and the *skin* in the North. In the Upper East and Upper West regions, however, they also comprise the earthpriest, the custodian of the earth. The roles of chiefs and earthpriests appear to be complementary: the chief constitutes the political authority, while the earthpriest fulfills more religious or spiritual functions. Indeed, prior to each season of cultivation, the earthpriest must propitiate the land and sacrifice to the gods, and it is also he who must appease the gods in the event of sacrileges committed against the Earth (Kasanga, 1996: 8). Generally, the earthpriest is a descendant of the first settler in an area and belongs to the senior segment of the firstcomer lineage (Fortes, 1940, 1945; Pogucki, 1951, 1955). However, the homology and complementarity between the offices of the chief and the earthpriest that Fortes (1940: 255) emphasized do not necessarily prevail in spatial terms (Lentz, 2006a). In Bolgatanga, for instance, four different earthpriests are responsible for the ritual initiation of the land before cultivation, while only one chief, the Bolganaba, constitutes the political customary authority. The former are known as the earthpriests, or tindambas, of Tindanmolgo, Tindansobliogo, Dapooretindongo, and Soe, respectively.

   In Bolgatanga, as in other parts of northern Ghana, chiefs and earthpriests disagree on the question of who holds the allodial rights to the land. The allodial title is regarded as the strongest customary title to land, subject only to limitations and obligations imposed by the general laws of the country (Rocha and Lodoh, 1995: 3) and therefore also known as "absolute" or "ultimate" title (Woodman, 1996: 56).[2] Individuals and families from the landholding group, on the other hand, hold the "customary freehold" denoting the near maximal interest in land. They are generally referred to as "owners." Ownership is never absolute nor is it constant over time, however. It is a historically contingent set of property rights that always leave a greater or smaller set of residual property rights with other agencies than the "owner." As mentioned earlier, it is an empirical challenge to ascertain the extent and limits of ownership and to account for them (see Chapter 1). Hence, when in the following discussion reference is made to "the owner," it is an approximation. It refers to the person who has hereditary rights to a piece of land, who can bequeath it to kin, and who can let others have temporary use rights, through either a formal lease or an unwritten agreement. Transactions of transfer are generally to be endorsed by the allodial right holder. This principle is valid for all parts of Ghana where the allodial title is vested in the wider community represented by chiefs and earthpriests (Kasanga, 1988: 31). This relationship is not carved in stone but is subject to friction and negotiation. Therefore, in addition to the question of who among the customary authorities has allodial title, the actual extent of control of allodial titleholders and landowners is also at issue. Somewhat schematically, a "horizontal" competition over the allodial title thus intertwines with a "vertical" competition between allodial titleholders and ordinary landowners.

Allodial title is essentially communal and was established through discovery or first settlement as well as conquest and subsequent settlement, as Woodman (1996) and Rocha and Lodoh (1995) argue. Colonial administrators and government anthropologists saw the earthpriests as a waning institution, leaving room for a "tribalization" of land tenure with chiefs as the conquering and dependable landholders (see Chapter 2). While the ambiguity of the allodial rights was observed by the commissioner of lands as he toured the Northern Territories in 1948, he was convinced that the native authorities, that is, the chiefs, would one day control the land.[3] Hence, recommendations to favor the chiefs were not seen as taking sides but merely as an acceleration of the inevitable.

Government and economic and social pressure are both tending to raise the Native Authority [i.e., chiefs] to a point of influence in land matters, which at least for practical purposes, will in the normal course cause the Native Authority to be

---

[2] In Osborn's *Concise Law Dictionary* (1964: 23), allodium is described as lands "not held of any superior, in which, therefore, the owner had an absolute title and not a mere estate."

[3] "Land Tenure in the Protectorate and Its Development under the Land and Native Rights Ordinance" (1948), para. 4–5. NRG 8/1/57.

regarded as the land owners, or at least as being in control of the land, and much of the mysticism attached to the existing tenure to be forgotten. . . . [I]n some areas African applicants for land make their applications to the Chief who himself makes the necessary arrangements with the Tindana, while whenever Government acquires compulsorily a piece of land for public purposes arrangements are made with a Chief and his Council who themselves consult the Tindana. . . . [I]t will be accepted, I think, that continual pressure will tend to create the general impression and later acceptance of the fact that all land will be under the control of the Native Authority.[4]

These observations bear witness to long-standing frictions between earth-priests and chiefs and to their overlapping jurisdictions. They also show that in the daily administrative practice, the colonial personnel in fact recognized customary land rights and, though with some trepidation, actively involved customary authorities in land matters, although this policy was clearly at variance with the Land and Native Rights Ordinance that boldly declared all lands, whether occupied or unoccupied, to be native or public lands under the control of the governor.

The commissioner's findings, particularly the hypothesis of the irreversible erosion of the earthpriests' power vis-à-vis that of the chiefs, are typical of much of the older literature on land tenure in northern Ghana. It may well also reflect the opinion of many stakeholders, because such "authoritative texts" often fed back into the society. As recent research on colonial ethnography has shown, however, the image of an original "egalitarian, spiritually legitimated, democratic, decentralized society," under the authority of the earthpriests, that inevitably evolves into a hierarchical centralized polity based on chiefs was challenged already during the colonial period, when some of the British administrators forwarded alternative images of the precolonial past (Lentz, 1999: 166). The earthpriests themselves, as we shall see, were (and are) not always willing to let themselves be marginalized, nor do they necessarily represent egalitarian and inclusive principles of land rights.

Legislation and Politics

The commissioner of lands' tour report did not lead to any amendments of the ordinance, and when the Northern Territories were united with Ashanti and the Gold Coast Colony in 1951, land continued to be vested in the governor of the Gold Coast. As independence approached, however, politicians in the Northern Territories requested that the government transfer its trusteeship to local political authorities – notably the Northern Territories

---

[4] Ibid., para. 15–17.

Council – to avoid the possibility that control over land of the North would fall into the hands of an independent government dominated by people from the South (see Ladouceur, 1979: 136–43).[5]

A bill was drafted to this effect but was met with opposition from the chiefs, who by then were relatively well organized. They agreed that the trusteeship of land should revert to local authorities of the North, though not in the guise of the Northern Territories Council but rather in the form of the chiefs themselves as traditional authorities. It is worth noting that no mention was made of the earthpriest, the clan, the elders, or family heads (Bening, 1995: 248). The bill was never adopted, and on independence in 1957 the governor-general continued to hold the lands in trust in accordance with the 1927 ordinance. When the country moved from independence to become a republic three years later, the State Property and Contract Act of 1960 (Act 6) confirmed that the land was vested in the government, or rather in the president.

Two significant acts were passed in 1962, the Administration of Lands Act (Act 123) and the State Lands Act (Act 125). The first confirmed and extended the state's power to acquire stool and skin lands, and it is on the basis of this act that the control and management of all lands in the Northern and Upper regions were vested in the state in 1963.[6] The second made a subtle distinction between land *vested* in the state and land *owned* by it, and stipulated that land could be vested in the state "free from any encumbrance whatsoever" (i.e., owned by the state) only through the publication of a specific law or executive instrument. By contrast, land merely vested in the state, under Act 123, still belonged to the original allodial titleholder.[7] While vested lands in the North were virtually administered and controlled in the same manner as lands properly and legally acquired by the state under compulsory acquisition statutes, there was a subtle – hairsplitting – difference between the two forms of land tenure, which was to become a source of contemporary clashes over public and private property.

---

[5] See "Memorandum for Consideration by the Northern Territories Council in Connection with the Proposed Amendment of the Lands and Native Rights Ordinance, CAP 121, and the Northern Territories Council Ordinance, 1952" (7 January 1954) and "Resolution of the Northern Territories Council on the Transfer of Trusteeship of Northern Territories Lands to the Northern Territories Council" (27 August 1954). Both, NRG 8/1/129.

[6] Stool Lands (Upper Region) Instrument 1963 (EI 87) and Stool Lands (Northern Region) Instrument (EI 109). The executive instruments provided that, in the event of any acquisition of land by the state, the state did not have to pay compensation for the land itself but only for "unexhausted improvements [basically houses] and economic trees and other works on the land."

[7] Thus, when Woodman (1996: 58) argues that the 1963 compulsory acquisition of land in the Upper and Northern Regions by the state extinguished all allodial titles, it needs to be qualified: although the rights that such titles bestowed were certainly dramatically curtailed, they were completely extinguished only when land was acquired as state land – that is, state *property* – through Act 125.

When in the 1960s the capital of the new Upper Region was set up in Bolgatanga, government facilities were needed urgently. Because most such projects were executed under crash programs, the proper formalities of a legal acquisition of the construction sites by the state were rarely completed. Public interest was vaguely defined and in practice quite elastic. As Mettle (1972: 131) argues,

In its present form the terminology of the State Lands Act, 1962 [125], makes it possible for the President, under the guise of land required "in the public interest," to take land belonging to the Leader of the Opposition and give it to his girl friend to build thereupon. It should surprise no one, therefore, that there was a rampage for land in the urban areas both in the heyday of the Nkrumah administration and during the short-lived Busia government. The circumstances were tainted with suspicion and corruption.

In short, the government had the means to acquire land even quite arbitrarily but, in most cases, failed to *legally* acquire the land it seized. As land was already managed by the state, in accordance with Act 123, government institutions assumed that there would be no problems with their occupancy, because it was considered to be in the public interest, even when no appropriate executive instruments were published. Although subsequent developments were to prove the opposite, until the adoption of the new constitution in 1979 the problems were contained. For all land vested in the state but not physically occupied by it, the ordinary owners with customary freehold were in practice unaffected by the legislation.[8]

During the 1970s pressures mounted against state control over the land in the North. It seems that a confluence of three different forms of interest were decisive for the move to divest the state of the land. First, the northern elite, enlightened chiefs and intellectuals whose marginal political position had previously rendered their efforts fruitless, actively campaigned for the divestiture in order to put the North on par with the rest of the country (Alhassan, 1996; Bening, 1996; Kunbour, 1996; Ladouceur, 1979; Lentz, 1998a: 576–81). In addition, major agricultural investments had been made with World Bank assistance. Two large-scale irrigation schemes and a general investment in the modernization of agriculture through the URADEP (Upper Regions Agricultural Development Programme) attempted to promote modernized, private capitalist agriculture, which in itself was incongruent with state ownership on the land (see Konings, 1986: 154–57, 229–314; Shepherd, 1981: 187–90). Finally, the national political situation may also explain why interests in divestiture finally persevered. The Acheampong administration was governing from crisis to crisis and had to

---

[8] It could thus be argued that the overall effect of the state control over all lands provided certainty of title and a virtual absence of title litigation (Kasanga, 1992: 10).

The peace + her small place: let politics + nat useful in post-colonial MM

maneuver in the face of stiff opposition. Konings (1986) and Hansen and Collins (1980) suggest that the government tried to appease the influential groups in the North and create a political alliance with them in order to resist the opposition. The "political price," it would appear, was to set up a committee to investigate the possibilities of divesting the land and turning control over it to the traditional landowners. As a consequence, the Alhassan committee was set up in 1978.[9]

According to Agbosu (1980: 127) and Bening (1996: 23), although no detailed studies were undertaken, the committee's report did attempt to specify the roles of earthpriests and chiefs to some degree (Government of Ghana, 1978). In this regard, it reflected reality, yet it failed to provide clear-cut instructions for the apportionment of land rent. For the Frafra area around Bolgatanga, the report offered the following recommendations:

[L]and within the Bolgatanga . . . Area was vested in the various clan Tindanas in trust for the people of his clan community. However, with the advent of the whiteman and the establishment of chieftaincy . . . the chief with time got actively involved in the administration of community land with particular reference to a stranger settler/farmer. The chief had therefore to consult the Tindana in all land cases where a stranger came in to the area, with the Tindana however having the upper hand. In these divisional areas, it is therefore recommended that the lands be vested in the various and individual Tindanas in trust for the people. The chiefs should however concur in all documented land transactions whether by a stranger or an indigen.[10]

The opacity of this statement notwithstanding, when a new national constitution was drafted in 1979, the committee's overall recommendations were taken into consideration, and the lands of the Northern and Upper regions were indeed divested from the state. No further specifications were made, however, except that lands were to return to their previous owners and were now vested "in any such person or in the appropriate skin without further assurance than this clause" (Article 18 [3]). It is clear that the lawmaker assumed that the chiefs were the "natural" customary authorities. The Constitution thus guaranteed the institution of chieftaincy (Article 177[1]) and gave chiefs representation in the Lands Commission (Article 189[1]). Authors like Ninsin (1989: 176) see the changes in landownership embedded in the 1979 Constitution as a "restoration of communal lands in the North to those authorities through whom the leading classes could more easily appropriate communal lands for private commercial purpose."

---

[9] The committee was headed by lawyer Roland Issifu Alhassan.

[10] "Report on Northern Lands of 1978 relating to the Frafra Traditional Council," p. 3 (Regional Lands Commission, correspondence ref.: 11803f, 2001). See also Government of Ghana (1978).

However significant a milestone the constitutional clauses were, they were also significant in what they omitted – namely, any specific clarification of who the owners of the land were or who was authorized to engage in legal transactions concerning land. The 1992 Constitution (Article 257) confirmed only the general thrust of the 1979 Constitution, again without further specifications of the ownership of northern lands, but it did add that the traditional authorities and the district assemblies were to receive some sort of income from land leases.[11] Although the divestiture did not affect land that had been legally acquired by the state, it did embrace all plots that had been developed by the government without any formal legal acquisition. Such cases were indeed numerous, comprising ministerial buildings, police stations, schools, government-owned companies, government staff bungalows, power transmission lines, and other properties.[12] Two interrelated issues were therefore now at stake. First, who holds the allodial title and to whom accrues the land rent destined to the stool or skin? Second, to what extent and how do people try to recover land or get compensation for the land that should have been handed back to them but upon which various government structures now stand?

The Renegotiation of Land Rights

The two issues of allodial title and the tension between private and public interests in land have not been resolved by the recent legislation. Legal changes, rather, have been introduced to provide opportunities for various groups to renegotiate status and entitlements. This renegotiation takes place in a range of different fora and by different means, ranging from court cases, political networking and lobbying, and more conspicuous manifestations like large meetings to subtler practices such as the actual occupation and sales of land. The range is broad and outcomes are often contradictory and temporary. Nonetheless, a few significant events appear to have set the stage for how people attempt to institutionalize, or reinstitutionalize,

[11] According to Article 267 (6) of the 1992 Constitution, "[t]en per cent of the revenue accruing from stool lands shall be paid to the office of the Administrator of Stool Lands to cover administrative expenses; and the remaining revenue shall be disbursed in the following proportions: (a) twenty-five percent to the stool through the traditional authority for the maintenance of the stool in keeping with its status; (b) twenty percent to the traditional authority; and (c) fifty-five percent to the District Assembly within the area of authority of which the stool lands are situated."

[12] The Upper East Region Lands Commission has listed some forty plots of varying size, mainly located in Bolga, which are proposed acquisitions by the state in the Upper East Region, and an unknown number of plots have not even been proposed for acquisition. These lands are not legally acquired but merely occupied by public institutions. The list was established around 2000, long after the occupation of the land by the government was a fact. Interview with the Regional Director of the Lands Commission, Upper East Region, Mr. Nyari, 14 November 2001.

positions and have them recognized, as well as for how these attempts at institutionalization are undermined, challenged, and rendered ambiguous by yet other actions. The following cases may appear disparate, but taken together, they demonstrate that customary landownership does not develop according to any predetermined evolutionary pattern, nor are we witnessing a mere pendular movement between chiefs and earthpriests. Evidence also shows that recent conflicts accentuated by the increasing monetary value of land not only form a pattern of tension between competing customary authorities but also pit such institutions against the actual land users.

Defamation of Character

During the first years after the adoption of the 1979 Constitution, the earthpriests did not figure anywhere in the official administration of land. Hitherto, land leases had read that land was held in trust by the government *for* the Bolganaba, the paramount chief and skin of the Frafra area. The latter was also entitled to all land revenue destined for the "traditional authority."[13] However, the number of leases endorsed and hence the income accruing from this function were limited. After 1979, when land was no longer held in trust by the state, it was not clear who could lease out land or endorse such leases – a situation that offered opportunities for the earthpriests to reactivate old claims. Already in the early 1970s, two literate members of one of the earthpriest clans – Asam Suo, a teacher, and Michael Atongo, a retired policeman working as commissioner of oaths and active in the District Council – began to agitate for the earthpriests' cause. In a series of letters and petitions to various authorities, they confronted the Bolganaba. For example, they complained to the regional commissioner that the Bolganaba had usurped their authority not only in land but also in religious matters,

The Bolganaba should refund back the land revenue collected and . . . refrain from making sacrifice to the gods of the land and proven . . . protectors of the lives of the people. We are the tindambas and landowners of the Bolgatanga canton and responsible for all land questions in Bolga town area. From . . . time immemorial all land questions and acquisition was directed to us, the tindambas, which fact cannot be denied by the Bolganaba as he or his ancestors own no land and knows [*sic*] nothing about our land questions. Grandfathers of the Bolganaba never interfered with our matters and customs, but the Bolganaba Martin A. Abilba III has been interfering with our land matters by collecting the land revenue and making

[13] The name Frafra is derived from the greeting of the Gruni people and has remained a common generic sobriquet for all people of the Bolgatanga area (R. Thomas, 1983: 69). The Frafra Traditional Council covers Bolgatanga district.

sacrifices and pouring libation whenever the need arises which is against custom. Bolganaba should refund all monies collected as land revenue from 1954 up to date.[14]

During the first years after Jerry Rawlings's second coup d'état in 1982, the political rhetoric favored the "downtrodden and exploited," and the political apparatus was dominated by radicals (Nugent, 1995). Emboldened by this atmosphere of revolution and reversals, Asam Suo began to sign and endorse leases to land – or, rather, to assist the earthpriests to do so. The unpredictability of the regime made the Bolganaba, and the chiefs in general, lie low. Thus, for some years both the earthpriests and the Bolganaba signed and endorsed leases as if the land was their allodial property. However, although the revolutionary period allowed the earthpriests to voice their interests, the administration was hardly operating. Therefore, it never recognized the earthpriests' claims or effectively dismissed those of the chiefs. During the first years, 1982 to 1983, the land administration was virtually suspended; until 1997 the National Lands Commission did not operate on a regional level, and the local communities were not granted any representation.[15] In this open-ended situation, both sides, the chiefs and the earthpriests, attempted to institutionalize their claims of ownership. Both sides endorsed land leases.

In December 1987 the Bolganaba sent a petition on the Bolgatanga Tindanaship to various political authorities such as the Provisional National Defence Council (PNDC) district secretary, the police, the regional lands officer, the regional town and country planning officer, the Traditional Council, and the Tindana of Dapooretindongo (one of the four earthpriestly sections of Bolgatanga); in it, he accused the latter of being a fake. A few weeks later, a second petition, Bolgatanga Tindanaship Affairs; "Petition for Recognition and Redress," was sent to the same addressees by a Mr. Agyre Abanga.[16] Both petitions challenged the legitimacy of the Tindana of Dapooretindongo, arguing that that latter became earthpriest only by looting the "Gods," that is, the fetishes and "jujus" connected with the earthpriestly office, from Agyre Abanga's house. Moreover, they claimed that the Tindana of Dapooretindongo had forged a petition of the earthpriests. Finally, as the Bolganaba pointed out, whenever the earthpriest

---

[14] Bolgatanga Tindambas to Regional Commissioner, Upper Region, 11 August, 1978, file FCD/8/ SF.1; quoted in Konings (1986: 244).

[15] Interview with Regional Director of Lands Commission Upper East Region, Mr. Bakari Nyari (13 March 2002).

[16] I was unable to locate copies of these two petitions in the court archives or with the persons to whom they were addressed in Bolgatanga. However, extensive references are made to them in two cases of defamation of character in the archives of the High Court of Bolgatanga: *Tindana Adingo Ayure vs. Bolganaba Martin Adongo Abilba* (1988), and *Tindana of Dapooretindongo vs. Mr. Agyere Abanga* (1989).

performed certain rites and poured libation before official functions – for example, the Centenary Celebration of the Public Works Department – the "Gods of the Bolgatanga skin" rejected "his sacrifices and libations." Indeed, these rejections had become a "cause of concern and embarrassment to the Bolganaba, the elders, and the people of the Frafra traditional area."[17] In short, the petitions described the earthpriest as an impostor who had usurped the office, an accusation allegedly corroborated by the supernatural disdain for his offerings.

These petitions prompted the earthpriest to file suit against the Bolganaba and Agyre Abanga, claiming compensation for defamation of character. The earthpriest argued that ever since he took office, he had been recognized and held in high esteem by the Regional Council, the Frafra Traditional Council Office, the police, the other earthpriests, and not least the Department of Lands. He also emphasized his "important role in the processing and grant of leases of lands by the Lands Commission in the Bolga area." Moreover, he mocked the Bolganaba for his ignorance of earthpriestly matters, asserting that the earthpriest "sacrifices to the 'Gods' of Bolgatanga lands, 'Gods' unknown to the defendant [the Bolganaba], and does not sacrifice and pour libation to the 'Gods' of Bolgatanga skin which the plaintiff [the earthpriest] has nothing to do with." In addition, he asserted that the making and unmaking of earthpriests in the Frafra Traditional Area was not the chief's business.[18]

The earthpriest's lawsuit against the Bolganaba and Agyre Abanga was met, in turn, with counterclaims in which, for instance, Abanga insisted that *he*, and not the earthpriest, "played and plays an important role in the processing and grant of leases of lands by the Lands Commission in the Bolga area," and that he was the one "held in high esteem by the Lands Department."[19] Abanga also alluded to the involvement of the Bolganaba in the selection of the Tindana of Dapooretindongo. Normally, when an earthpriest dies, the successor is selected by a diviner who is not from the area. On the occasion of the election of a new earthpriest in Dapooretindongo in 1976, the Bolganaba had supported, albeit unsuccessfully, Abanga, whom he expected to be less hostile to the chief than either Michael Atongo or Asam Suo. According to the earthpriest's followers, the Bolganaba and Abanga had attempted to sabotage the divination procedure in the hope of making the earthpriest's accession to office invalid.[20]

---

[17] High Court of Bolgatanga, Tindana Adingo Ayure vs. Bolganaba Martin Adongo Abilba (1988).

[18] Statement of claim, 12 April 1988.

[19] Statement of defense, 10 June 1988.

[20] Interview with family members of the Tindana of Dapooretindongo, 14 March 2002. Among the people present were the teacher Francis Amiyinne; Robert Abiro, the assemblyman of Dapooretindongo; Asofo Akumamme, a brother of Adingo Ayure; and Agyre Abanga, a son of Agyre Abanga.

Neither case, whether it dealt with the earthpriest's claims or the Bolganaba's counterclaims, was concluded. Both were adjourned indefinitely. The earthpriest continued to be the tindana of the area, and when the first district assemblies were inaugurated in 1989, Asam Suo was elected assemblyman. Whether this outcome played a role is not clear, but from that time onward, the Lands Commission in Accra no longer processed leases in the name of the Bolganaba but in the name of the landholder leasing out his land. However, the royalties accruing to allodial titleholders, according to the 1992 Constitution, went to the Bolganaba as the representative of the skin and in conformity with what was the practice in the South of the country.

Petitions, letters, and lawsuits are public commemorations of political claims, which are never easily relinquished. The Bolganaba thus bolstered his claim to allodial title by referring to the chiefs' conquest of the Frafra area, and it cannot to be ruled out that his claim may one day prevail.[21] Similarly, the earthpriest's case for damages for defamation of character and his indirect claim to allodial title may, under the appropriate circumstances, be one day successful. As Moore (1992: 32) observes, "It is a question whether what happens in the court is to be defined in terms of the ebb and flow of local micro-politics or in terms of a central government standard, a rule oriented, delegating judicial/bureaucratic model." In our case, the 1979 Constitution created not a standard procedure but rather an open juncture in which competing claims to allodial title could be asserted. The ebb and flow of micropolitics were ambiguous, and neither the Bolganaba nor the earthpriests were able to impose their interests definitely. The latter's position as allodial titleholder, however, was to be consolidated by a number of quite different cases.

SSNIT Affordables, Ghana Water and Sewerage, and the Organization of Interests

The Social Security and National Insurance Trust (SSNIT) makes a variety of investments to ensure its solvency, some of which are in real estate. In pursuing such an investment in 1989, the Bolgatanga branch of SSNIT applied to the then Bolgatanga District Council for land along the Tamale Road. A site plan was drawn up, which effectively earmarked the land that was to be acquired by SSNIT to the exclusion of any other person.[22] However, SSNIT never acquired the land legally and never paid compensation; it simply began to erect affordable houses on the premises.

---

[21] Bolganaba, "Petition against the Role of the Tindana in the Bolgatanga Land Tenure System," 3 November 2000. Material in private possession.

[22] High Court of Bolgatanga, Tindana of Tindansobliogo and Anafo Azane vs. SSNIT, 1 February 1999.

During the first few years, there was minimal official response. The military regime was reluctant to encourage people to take on the established institutions such as the SSNIT, in part because the appropriation of the land had followed the long-established pattern of legally incomplete acquisitions by government. By 1995, however, three years into the latest democratic phase and sixteen years after the constitutional divestiture of the land, the Tindana of Tindansobliogo and Anaho Azane, the head of the family whose land was primarily concerned, engaged a lawyer and filed a case for compensation against SSNIT. Though protracted, the case was eventually closed in 1999 and decided in favor of the plaintiffs, who received 228 million cedis in compensation. This amount was divided proportionally between landholders in Tindansobliogo and neighboring Kalbeo, who had both been affected by the establishment of the SSNIT Affordables housing project.

Around the same time, a similar case was conducted against Ghana Water and Sewerage (GWS) by the Tindana of Tindanmoligo. As structural adjustment policies promoted the privatization of public-sector enterprises, GWS was sold off in the late 1990s. One of the immediate consequences was that GWS discharged a good part of its employees. As occurs in other privatizing state enterprises, discharged staff was to receive severance pay (Appiah-Kubi, 2001), which, in the case of Bolgatanga, was given in the form of land, by simply parceling out plots of the GWS grounds that were not taken up by GWS installations. It was only when construction of residential houses began that the local population reacted. The families of Tindanmoligo and Kalbeo, whose lands GWS was using, were for the most part still living on the land, but had, of course, abandoned farming where GWS structures had been erected.[23] These sixty families and the Tindana of Tindanmoglo now engaged a lawyer[24] and filed suit against GWS. Basically they claimed they were due an annual rent for the land beginning in 1980 (the year after the adoption of the 1979 Constitution) and compensation for the land occupied by GWS structures. They filed for compensation because GWS had never legally acquired the land, and because both the 1979 and the 1992 constitutions stipulated that the allodial titleholders' control over the land was to be restored. It took the court only a year to decide in favor of the plaintiffs who were awarded compensation in the amount of 227 million cedis for the entire area.

These two cases were followed with keen interest by many because they were the first to deal with the issue of compensation and because the court, in

[23] It is worth noting that when the government acquired land for various developments, it generally took much more than was immediately required. See Kasanga and Kotey (2001: 24). This precautionary measure was obviously wise, but it also led to huge areas not being developed. In many instances, government institutions tolerated that local inhabitants continued to occupy and cultivate land that was not immediately needed. This created grounds for expectations to continue using the land.

[24] The very same who had been the earthpriest's lawyer in the two cases of defamation of character.

accepting the claims, recognized the earthpriest as the allodial titleholder.[25] This was a watershed decision. Moreover, as a result, the Lands Commission decided that the income from the ground tax destined to the allodial title-holders should henceforth go to the local earthpriests who signed the lease and no longer to the Bolganaba, as had been the case until that point.[26] Not inclined to acquiesce, the latter mounted a campaign with petitions, deploring the management of land royalties and pointing out that older documents stated that the land was held by the state in trust for the skin and not the earthpriest. Because the 1992 Constitution explicitly recognized the chiefs with their traditional councils and not the earthpriests, the latter enjoyed no official status.

The Constitution recognises the institution of Chieftaincy as opposed to Tindanaship, and guarantees the said institution together with its Traditional Councils. . . . This is the more reason why the Chiefs are gazetted and the Tindanas are not. Legislatively, therefore, while the skin has that constitutional backing the Tindana lacks it. There is even no statute whatsoever establishing the office of the Tindana let alone accord him allodial title landholder of the Traditional Area. . . . There are no uniformity in the traditional land administration, when many Tindanas rival over land ruled by one chief. Many of these Tindanas are very confused as to which areas they have their jurisdictions to exercise their functions and eager to make money insofar as endorsement of leases is concerned, chaos and anarchy is likely to set in, in the long run.[27]

Obviously, the Bolganaba would not let the allodial title slip away that easily after having enjoyed it for so long. For their part, the earthpriests were not about to accept the status quo either; in 1997 they formed the Association of Tindambas of Bolgatanga and held a large gathering in town at which representatives of earthpriests from many places of the Upper Region

---

[25] Interestingly, the local population was obviously not fully aware of the consequences of its victory in court. Receiving the compensation for the entire area meant that it now belonged to GWS and that they had to vacate it. They went from *tolerated locals* and *landowners* to *squatters* in one swift move. When they realized this, the affected families and the earthpriest refused to accept the compensation, which to this date is sitting in the safe of the High Court of Bolgatanga. GWS and the people still both occupy and use the GWS grounds.

[26] The Bolganaba would continue to receive income from the ground tax for the leases issued in his name up to that date. A letter from the Lands Commission Secretariat in 1996 to one of the earthpriests in Bolgatanga demonstrates the uneasy position held before the court's decision on the GWS case: "The department has no legal or customary right to determine ownership right over land under dispute, you are therefore advised to re-direct your petition to the Upper East Regional House of Chiefs to ascertain the rightful allodial title holder of the subject land" (Regional Lands Commission, correspondence no. 9507, 3 June, 1996).

[27] "Petition against the Role of the Tindana in the Bolgatanga Land Tenure System," sent by the Bolganaba, 3 November 2000. Material in private possession.

were present.[28] The Bolganaba, as was to be expected, did not attend. The association asked the director of the Regional Lands Commission to attend the inaugural meeting and thereby to imbue the event with official recognition, but the invitation was declined. Nonetheless, at the inauguration of the Regional Lands Commission in 2000, the chairman of the tindambas' association was allowed to present a speech, addressed to the minister of lands and forestry and to the members of the Lands Commission and their "distinguished entourage," which neatly summarized the aspirations of the association:

We . . . wish to place on record that other traditional rulers and state agencies have exploited us for a long time and strongly warn that such exploiters no longer have a chance left. . . . Some traditional rulers with their positions and links with certain government agencies sideline, ignore, undermine and exploit us. . . . People cannot just pretend that we do not exist. . . . To arrest the above-mentioned problems, we humbly wish to appeal to the Minister to initiate appropriate legislation to include the Tindaamas in the Regional Lands Commission. . . . We further re-iterate that appropriate legislation be enacted quickly enough to allow Tindaamas to be part of the Traditional Council. Also it is our wish and desire that planning committees for festivals and commemorative days such as NAFAC, Independence days etc. always exclude us [*sic*! this should, no doubt, read *include* us].[29]

The desire for recognition is obvious from this speech and was confirmed in my interviews with the members of the association. In fact, the official recognition of the earthpriests was a central priority of the association's activities. In addition to official addresses and formal claims of recognition, the association also let it be known that the earthpriests, as a response to the Bolganaba's recent petition, which was directed against their aspirations, would not perform the customary funeral rites for the chiefly house. This was considered a serious humiliation. Finally, the association began to be more vigilant with respect to leases of land issued by subordinate chiefs and other persons, notifying the District Assembly of cases in which the chiefs still attempted to control land (and probably got away with it from time to time).[30]

---

[28] It is considered taboo for the earthpriests of Bolgatanga to meet in person. Therefore, all meetings in the association were conducted by representatives.

[29] Speech by the Chairman of the Tindaama's Association of the Occasion of the Inauguration of the Regional Lands Commission, 12 April 2000. Material in private possession.

[30] The vigilance of the earthpriests was recorded in the *Ghanaian Times*, 25 March 2004. "Mob disrupts chiefs' meeting. A meeting of local chiefs and elders that was scheduled to take place at the Bolgatanga Traditional Council to find a solution to a dispute over the payment of royalties in respect of land within the Bolga Municipality had to be abandoned following the intrusion of a mob. The intruders, who numbered about 500, were mostly supporters of the landowners, the Tindanase."

The cases of the *Tindana of Tindansobliogo vs. SSNIT* and the *Tindana of Tindanmoligo vs. GWS* changed the balance of power in favor of the earth-priests. For the earthpriests and their supporters, securing the allodial title meant that the office of the Bolganaba no longer covered land issues as before. He was considered a "stranger," created and implanted by the British, and not a genuine authority in land matters. However, while the Lands Commission's disbursement of land revenue to the earthpriests consolidated their position, it would be premature to write off the chieftaincy and naive to consider the current situation in any way as finally settled.

Earthpriests versus Landholders

Paradoxically, taking the Bolganaba out of the property equation did not make the question of ownership in Bolgatanga much clearer. The hopes of those who thought that land rights were now finally settled were dashed when new disputes developed, this time between the earthpriest and his clan and the local landowners over the limits between allodial title and customary freehold. In 2001 the Bolgatanga District Assembly came up with plans to relocate the charcoal sellers from the center of town to an area laid out as "light industrial zone," along the Tamale Road, and these plans set in motion a series of negotiations.

The area in question is known as Kalbeo – bordering on, or part of, Tindansobliogo. In fact, that was one of the contentious issues. It is commonly held that the ancestors of the people of Kalbeo were settled there more than 100 years ago by the Tindana of Tindansobliogo, whose successors have since then been responsible for all land-related sacrifices and the shrines in Kalbeo. When the District Assembly identified the area of Kalbeo as one that it wanted to develop, it asked the assemblyman from Kalbeo to contact the local chief, the landowners, and the Tindana of Tindansobliogo. The district chief executive (DCE) called a meeting, in January 2002, to ascertain the ownership of the land of the future industrial zone. The Kalbeo assemblyman and the Tindana of Tindansobliogo assured the DCE that the inhabitants of the area had been settled there by people from Kalbeo – a distinct proof of the fact that they controlled the land. Even families from Tindansobliogo who had wanted land in Kalbeo had been obliged to ask for it in Kalbeo.

The people of Kalbeo had indeed requested the Town and Country Planning Department to draw up a site plan, and over the years individual landowners in Kalbeo had leased out plots to a number of small entrepreneurs. As one of my informants explained, "land along the Tamale Road is selling like hot cake." The Tindana of Tindansobliogo had endorsed these leases and received 100,000 cedis from both the lessor and lessee for his services. The transaction itself, however, was not between the Tindana of Tindansobliogo and the lessee, but between the landowner from Kalbeo and the lessee. The fact that the earthpriest had endorsed the leases implied that he had recognized the plot holder's right to lease out his land rights in exchange for money. In other words, the Tindana of Tindansobliogo had recognized the plot holder as a landowner with customary freehold. To underscore their harmonious relationship with the Tindana of Tindansobliogo, the representatives of Kalbeo also pointed out that the earlier SSNIT compensation had been shared between the two communities in proportion to the land affected by the SSNIT project, giving the people of Kalbeo 31 percent of the total of 228 million cedis. The DCE was satisfied, and scheduled a further meeting to actually mark out the plots for the charcoal sellers.

During this meeting it transpired that the District Assembly wanted forty plots of 100 square yards each. Normally, in this area plots of this size would fetch 3 million cedis, but this price was far beyond the means of the municipality. The DCE offered a sum of 500,000 cedis per plot, arguing that this was a fair price if one considered all the side benefits, in terms of jobs and other economic activities that the local population was going to enjoy. Because the offer was not immediately accepted, another meeting at the Assembly Hall was scheduled. Meanwhile, the people of Kalbeo decided to accept the offer, provided that the owners received a written promise from the DCE stating the price of the plots. During the subsequent meeting, however, the DCE withdrew his former offer and argued that people should give up their plots for free, in light of the general development of the town.

Subsequently, another community meeting was organized in Kalbeo, this time with the participation of the Tindana of Tindansobliogo and members of Tindansobliogo Youth, the community association of Tindansobliogo. Whereas the landowners of Kalbeo were adamant that they would not relinquish their land without compensation, the earthpriest now changed position and began to argue that people should give it up. The District Assembly, he argued, would compensate in kind, namely through the construction of a community center. However, this center would be located not in Kalbeo, but in neighboring Tindansobliogo. The people of Kalbeo then accused the earthpriest and the Tindansobliogo Youth of conducting parallel negotiations with the District Assembly and selling out Kalbeo interests for their own benefit. The arguments soon became very heated. The earthpriest and the Tindansobliogo Youth denied having negotiated with the DCE and argued instead that it was the earthpriest, not the people from Kalbeo, who was the legitimate owner of the disputed plots. The present earthpriest, who only recently took office, had been properly selected by divination, they explained, while his predecessor, who had allowed the people from Kalbeo to lease out land, had been acting as deputy only in place of his recently deceased father, until a substantial earthpriest could be divined.

Against all custom, this "interim tindana" had sold out Tindansobliogo interests in Kalbeo, by allowing the people of Kalbeo to lease out the land. From this moment, the earthpriest now declared, all previous transactions made by the people in Kalbeo themselves without the involvement of the Tindana of Tindansobliogo were considered null and void.

During the following days, a series of smaller violent confrontations between Tindansobliogo Youth and young people from Kalbeo occurred. The latter claimed that members of the Tindansobliogo Youth were erecting roadblocks and preventing them from reaching Bolgatanga; the Tindansobliogo Youth, on the other hand, claimed that they took the people of Kalbeo to task only because of the latter's lack of respect for tradition and "for only wanting to chop."[31] A week later, a delegation of elders from Kalbeo paid a visit to the Tindana of Tindansobliogo in order to resolve the differences and have the earthpriest recall his threat to confiscate the land. However, this was to no avail. The delegation was met by a crowd from the four founding communities of Bolgatanga, namely Tindansobliogo, Tindanmolgo, Dapooretindongo, and Soe, who insisted that they owned the land and could retract it, if the people of Kalbeo attempted to transfer it to others in order to make undue profit out of what had initially been given to them only as a usufructuary right. In fact, rather than having customary freehold, the earthpriests insisted that the people of Kalbeo were, essentially, strangers. The following day, the Tindana of Tindansobliogo announced on local radio that all leases to land in Kalbeo were illegal and invalid and that any current leaseholder should report to him in order to have the lease rectified, stating that the land was leased by him, the Tindana of Tindansobliogo, and not "some settler."

The question was now whether the Tindana of Tindansobliogo, supported by the Tindansobliogo Youth and the tindambas' association, would be able to assert his status as landowner in Kalbeo, with the liberty to expel truculent tenants, and to grant land to the District Assembly? Or would the interests of the inhabitants of Kalbeo prevail, as their rights to settle other people on the land and to lease it to small entrepreneurs had been confirmed by a former Tindana of Tindansobliogo and by virtue of the SSNIT compensation paid to them? There was consensus that the Tindana of Tindansobliogo did in fact perform all land-related rituals in Kalbeo, but there was disagreement on the tenurial implications. Similarly, there was agreement that the people of Kalbeo could use the land as long as they wished and that this could even be bequeathed within the family. However, no consensus was reached whether they also had the right to lease out the land. In October 2002 the DCE set up a three-member

---

[31] Interviews with Youth of Kalbeo, 14 November 2002, and interviews with Tindansobliogo Youth leadership, 15 November 2002.

committee to unravel the affair,[32] but the committee's work has not yet been concluded.

The conflict over land in Kalbeo shows that the reconfiguration of property relations in the wake of the 1979 Constitution is not limited to competing customary authorities. It also involves the relationship between customary authorities and "ordinary people" over the effective, concrete, and practical implications of ownership or split ownership between them. It is not surprising that this is not settled. Landowners in Kalbeo may manage to wrest more control over the land from the Tindana of Tindansobliogo and his clan, or the earthpriest may roll back the Kalbeo landowners' control. In either case, it signifies increasing exclusivity of property. If the Kalbeo landowners prevail in their demands, it means that it is unclear who then actually guarantees these new extended rights. We may thus in Kalbeo have had a glimpse of more exclusive, yet less certain land rights.

Conclusion

Customary tenure is not immutable. The history of property claims in the Upper East of Ghana shows how questions of property and the authority to determine it have been negotiated in words, law, and action. Chiefs and earthpriests have, on the one hand, schemed, acted, and debated to vindicate their claims to allodial title and the ensuing benefits. The government, on the other hand, has reduced or denied these rights at various points in time, at least on paper. In practice, however, different governments were often forced to let customary institutions exercise some authority. In addition, government policies have been far from consistent, and different agencies have pursued very different philosophies. When the state divested itself of the northern lands in 1979 and – out of ignorance, negligence, or design – failed to identify the allodial titleholders, a long-standing dispute was reanimated. The potential compensations at stake were – and continue to be – considerable, as government institutions became squatters at the stroke of a pen, and planning was complicated as people aspired to reclaim past entitlements.

The conflicts over land between the colonial government and the population, between the chiefs and earthpriests, and between customary authorities and land users illustrate the ambiguity of land rights and the concurrent

---

[32] The committee was asked to "1) determine whether land in the disputed area had been designed (earmarked?) for any purpose, 2) find out if leases had been granted by the Lands Commission; 3) to identify who granted and signed such leases; 4) to determine the actual owner of the land [sic!]." Inaugural address delivered by the District Chief Executive in the Land Dispute between the People of Kalbeo and Tindansobliogo in the Conference Hall of the Assembly, 8 October 2002. Material in private possession.

difficulties of terminology. On the one hand, land rights are manifold, nested within each other, and often enjoyed by different actors. The rights, for example, to cultivate, transfer, tax, and let strangers settle are not necessarily vested in the same person or agency. On the other hand, however, as opportunities arise, the various actors, be they government, chiefs, earthpriests, or landowners, tend to claim rights wholesale – a strategic simplification of the tenure system. The divestiture of land to the original owners spurred on a "horizontal" contest between chiefs and earthpriests over the allodial title, not least because this "ownership" now included rights to accrue land rent and to receive compensations, and it therefore became economically interesting. Furthermore, as the example from Kalbeo shows, a "vertical" competition became apparent. Earthpriests (and their respective communities) and landowners vie over the extent of the latter's right to sell land and reap the profits from development. This resulted partly from the rise in the economic value of urban land and was propelled by the earthpriests' success in court, and the compensation paid to the landowners in the SSNIT Affordables and Ghana Water and Sewerage cases. The emerging conflict over the respective rights of earthpriests and landowners represents a process of exclusion whose outcome is still in the balance. The significance of the dividing lines of property rights grew with the economic value of the land. Moreover, the preceding struggles between chiefs and earthpriests over the allodial title in Bolga rekindled the ambitions of the earthpriests and their families and stirred them up for conflicts over property.

In all the cases discussed here, belonging plays a central role. In the competition between chiefs and earthpriests, the respective prerogatives were called into question by challenging the legitimacy of the opponent's investiture into office.[33] The loss of the allodial title may eventually further undermine the legitimacy of the chief's claim to office. In the case of the population of *Kalbeo vs. the Tindana of Tindansobliogo*, the qualification of ownership obviously also goes through first arrival, belonging, and the capacity to settle strangers. However, politics and legal circumstance make the criteria seem malleable.

Viewed in isolation, the competition between chiefs and earthpriests may appear to be a movement, back and forth, between alternative claimants of customary authority. Over time, entitlements have been lost and gained with the political winds. However, things are more complicated than that. The stakes and the circumstances have changed, and keep changing. As land values go up, controversies between different customary authorities and

---

[33] The setback of the Bolganaba even provoked the reopening of an older case against his enskinment, by the family of the candidate to chiefly office with whom he had competed in 1972. Proceedings in the Matter of Appeal, *Asingbe Agana, Adongo Awogeya and twenty others vs. Martin Adongo Abilba.* 1/AJ/80; National House of Chiefs, Kumasi. The case has been pending since 1980.

actual land users intensify, and increased exclusivity seems to be the ambition as well as the consequence. Moreover, the various instances described here show that claims are not extinct just because rights are. The divestiture of lands may have presented itself as an innocuous reform back in 1979. However, the inherently ambiguous nature of customary law and customary authority is not diminished when they are brought to prominence in new legislation. When political opportunity arises, rights will be asserted anew.

It would seem that as long as political circumstances, administrative procedures, or economic opportunities are likely to change, new hands will be dealt, and few will be able to say who owns Bolgatanga with any degree of certainty. What seems to be of a more enduring character is *how* Bolga is owned. No single domain is in itself decisive, but those who master successful ownership have juggled legal, economic, and political strategies and have timed them to take advantage of opportunities presented by national legislation and political circumstance. And they have been known to persevere, at least for a while. Moreover, as these maneuvers unfold and benefits and rents from property become consequential, the historical split ownership between allodial title and customary freehold will be challenged. The "horizontal" competition between authorities gave an impulse to the "vertical" competition between authorities and ordinary landholders. This, in turn, has raised the question of what *ownership* means in practical terms. Practice seems the place to look, as the following chapters demonstrate.

4

Seizing Opportunities

Chieftaincy, Land, and Local Administration

Have you never heard, Mr. Visconti said, that beer is much more
intoxicating drunk through a straw?
Surely that is a legend.
There speaks a Protestant, Mr. Visconti said. Any Catholic knows that a
legend which is believed has the same value and effect as the truth.

Graham Greene, *Travels with My Aunt*

Introduction

The presence of the past in the present is notable in Bolgatanga.[1] Conflicts
over land and chieftaincy are characterized by an intense reference to the past
as the source of unadulterated legitimacy of claims to the future. The past
and lines of heritage are frequently rehearsed in Ghana. It is a pastime in
which everyone who depends on pedigree for position or privilege engages
with passion. However, two different forms of *past* are often at play at the
same time (Berry, 2004). On the one hand, reference is made to *tradition*
as a timeless past, a reservoir of "how things have always been done" in
the constant flow of time. On the other hand, there is a past made up of
significant *historical events*, of actions and transactions that are invoked with
various vindications. The two pasts are rather different from one another.
One justifies claims to the future as a seamless continuation of the past; the
other justifies them as the result of salient fortunate events.[2] Those who
belong to different social positions in the Upper Regions of Ghana, such as
earthpriests and chiefs, are thus more readily justified by reference either to
time immemorial or to historical events of their creation, respectively.

The past, however, is not the only ambiguous shibboleth in conflicts over
land and chieftaincy in northern Ghana. *Space*, just as the past, is malleable

---

[1] I owe this neat turn of phrase to Maurice Bloch (1977: 287).

[2] The two forms of the past do thus not represent a ritual versus a more mundane conceptualization,
as described by Bloch (1977), but are, rather, parallel, both reflecting ritual and mundane elements.

within a concrete cultural setting.[3] Similar to the way the past is invoked in two forms, space figures in two, occasionally compatible, occasionally competing forms. As *territory*, space has certain political connotations, whereas *property in land* moves space into a legal domain.[4] As territory, space is governed but not owned by its governing agency. As property, space is owned but not governed by its owners. By owner is meant anyone with a recognized property claim to a particular resource in a given space. Thus no one has exclusive ownership but only property rights circumscribed by others' property rights. Often property claims overlap and compete, making the issue of property inherently complex and contentious. By juxtaposing property and territory, I do not want merely to throw in more complexity but to provide a lens through which it can be read. Obviously, the ambiguity between territory and property becomes poignant when actors slide between categories – when governors claim to own, or owners pretend to govern.

The preceding chapters show that while government's property rights to land were legally quite limited, the common interpretation, right up to 1979, differed. The way the state managed its trusteeship of land developed an interpretation, shared by lay and learned alike, that tended to conflate governance of territory with extensive property rights. This interpretation was generalized thanks to government's unconstrained seizure of land and the fact that the state actually did possess some plots of land on terms equivalent to those of private individuals or institutions. This ambiguity of space is not reserved for national government and legislation; it goes right down to the smallest political entity of society, as the present chapter demonstrates.

The semantic openness of the past and of space affords certain patterns of argument and organizational procedure as opportunities arise. In his essay on the past as a scarce resource, Appadurai (1981) argues that the past does not have infinite semantic plasticity. Its rhetorical and strategic applicability depends on some sort of consensus and convention about how the past can be meaningfully debated in a particular society. As a general hypothesis, similar limitations must be expected to prevail for space. The question is what type of argument and what form of political rhetoric is available for whom and with what effect. The two ideas of the past and the two ideas of space favor certain forms of vindication. However, while each

---

[3] See, e.g., Bening (1973); Comaroff and Roberts (1981); Lentz (2000b, 2006b); Peters (1994); Thompson (1991); and Walker and Peters (2001).

[4] Sack (1986: 19) conceptualizes territorialization as "the attempt by an individual or group to affect, influence or control people, phenomena and relationships by delimiting and asserting control over a geographic area." This comprehensive definition would include territory (the political dimension) as well as property (the legal dimension). In order to identify the tensions between the two strategies, the versatile construction of arguments and their subtle movement between political and legal institutions, I find it useful to distinguish between these two modern forms of controlling space.

claim avails itself more easily to either one or the other social position, there is sufficient adjacency between territory and property for certain actors – whether established by tradition or history – to be able to operate both lines of argument.

Political opportunities for competition, opposition, and debate over space and the past emerge from many corners, but the fecundity of national events, reforms, and politics is often impressive in this respect. Analysis of government reforms easily lends itself to an administrative perspective, where the process is assessed on its deviance from "the plan."[5] Indeed, national policies and politics matter a great deal as they create intended and unintended dependencies and opportunities. In their work on political change in Ahafo, Dunn and Robertson (1973; see also Lentz, 2002) nonetheless caution against seeing either end of the causal relationship, local or national, as simply an inert or wholly predictable force. Aside from their intended objectives, administrative reforms and procedures constitute moments of opportunity for local political players to assert (or reassert), to negotiate (or renegotiate), entrenched or more volatile positions in the fabric of local politics. Thus, the changes and readjustments in local government structures and procedures also provide for significant sociopolitical rearrangement beyond a reform's intended scope. Such movements bring together an amalgamation of legal and political conflict, passionate invocation of history, and tradition, as well as images of space as either territory or property in an intense courtship and lobbying for support from without as well as from within the locality.

This chapter presents two instances of local political competition arising at moments of opportunity where strategic reference to *the past* is brought to bear. Various aspects of decentralization, local tax collection, chiefly rivalry, and the creation of (yet) a new district had direct impact on the ways *space* equally became a domain of competition, and how conflicts were conducted and perceived. Thus, various domains of local politics interlock and agendas cast in different discourses of space and the past collide to undermine or underpin each other.

Chiefs and Taxes in Zaare

The case of Zaare shows how two families struggle over power in a village at the outskirts of Bolga. Competing interpretations of the past are employed

[5] The political relationship between central government and the population in Ghana has been mediated through local political institutions such as chiefs and native authorities during the time of indirect rule and, since 1951, a variety of local government structures at district and subdistrict levels (Ayee, 2000; Staniland, 1975). The political arguments accompanying readjustments of local government structures and processes often focus on service provision, accountability, and the degree of discretionary powers accorded to the decentralized bodies (Ayee, 1994, 2000; Crook, 1987, 1994; Crook and Manor, 1998; Dunn and Robertson, 1973; Ladouceur, 1979; Ribot, Agrawal, and Larson, 2006).

under circumstances that neither party controls. Because one party's argument about the past was not vindicated, a more spatial strategy is engaged with particular readings of space in an attempt to guard its interests.

In May 2002 violent fights broke out in Zaare. People were at each other's throats, attacking each other with cutlasses and catapults, and homes were burned to the ground. Several people were killed in the confrontation. The army was brought in, and a dusk-to-dawn curfew was issued for Zaare for some weeks. While the degree of violence had understandably shocked the inhabitants of Bolga and surrounding villages, there was no shortage of explanations of the conflict. This was an "old affair" that had been rekindled and brought to a head by circumstance. What had finally triggered the violence was the fact that one leading clan or family, the A-urugubiisi, had denied members of the chief's clan, the Ayorebiisi, access to its lands. The A-urugubiisi claimed that whatever lands had been granted through time were now withdrawn by them – the descendants of the original earthpriest of Zaare.[6] The history of political leadership and land control in Zaare is a result of competing, time-honored claims and fortuitous accidents occurring during the colonial and postcolonial eras, making the context more or less propitious for rival narratives. The case is neither more nor less intricate than what prevails in most villages in the area, but it demonstrates how political claims to the future depend on mastery of the past.

The common rendition of the history of Zaare tells about an original settlement of two brothers, the founders of the A-urugibiisi clan.[7] By virtue of seniority, the oldest was entrusted with the religious affairs of the community and earned the title of earthpriest, with responsibility for the fertility of the land and overseeing its allocation. The younger was entrusted with the functions of the administration and earned the title of chief, with political responsibility of the population within the village territory. Henceforth, the earthpriests would be sought and identified by soothsayers, whereas contestants for the Zaare skin among the A-urugibiisi clan would let the Mamprusi king, the Nayiri, perform the enskinment of the chief. The two brothers also had a sister, who married and left Zaare. However, she was widowed at an early age and returned with her children. Her firstborn sired

---

[6] Zaare is the home of some ten families or clans. Two of them are particularly relevant here in order to understand this particular controversy. The other clans seem more or less equally divided in their allegiance to the two camps. The necessary "simplification" of the complexity of the intertwined family and political relations is not meant to belittle or neglect any Zaare citizen.

[7] There was a striking convergence in the "Zaare histories" and genealogies from among various litigants. The difference lies with the different relative weight attributed to tradition and history by the respective litigants. The following is based on interviews with the leading protagonists of the two competing clans, Paul Atalanga (Ayorebiisi) and James Azure (A-urugibiisi) and other opinion leaders. The convergence may to some extent be the result of the work of Christopher Asaare, amateur historian: "Zaare: Clan and Skin History" (unpublished, but quite widely circulated, material in private possession).

the Ayorebiisi clan. Over the years, this family grew numerous and relatively powerful; however, the family members were always reminded of
their descendance from a "female" line, although this proved not to be an
impediment to promotion with the intervention of the colonial administration.

In 1910 the British wanted to punish the Nayiri and transfer the enskinment authority of Zaare to the Bolganaba. The latter seized the opportunity
and enskinned a chief of the Ayorebiisi clan. At this point, there were effectively two chiefs in Zaare. The chief enskinned by the Nayiri, Anea (and in
particular his son, Agana), refused to accept this arrangement and, together
with the earthpriest, refused to let people inter their dead if they did not
recognize his authority. In September 1911 Anea thus refused the burial
of a deceased man and ordered the corpse to hang from a tree. The family
did, nonetheless, bury the corpse. Then it called the district commissioner
from Zuarungu, who, upon arrival in Zaare, had Anea and his son arrested
and charged for refusing the burial of a dead man and with the intent to
cause pollution.[8] In the presence of the villagers, the district commissioner
requested Anea's red cap, which the latter had received upon enskinment
as a symbol of authority, and destroyed it.

Unfortunately, ["our" chief] is not a strong man and Agana still troubled him, but
he refrained from reporting him. This trouble arose the other day over a funeral
custom for a Zaare man and Agana interfered and stopped it. His excuses for doing
so were because the man's people refused to follow him altogether as the deceased
did. I brought in Anea who is a small hunch-back man, very short sighted and a
permanent wriggle of the nose and head and he is to sit down in Zuarungu till I
hand him over to Capt. S. D. Nash. I destroyed his red fez and told him that he
was not recognised by the Government as a chief. I am sending Agana to Gambaga
for 6 months as a political prisoner.[9]

This marked the change of family, or *gate*, for the Zaare skin: The A-
urugibiisi gate, enskinned by the Nayiri, was out, while the Ayorebiisi clan
had come to power, thanks to the colonial intervention. There were a few
scuffles, but it soon ceased as the British colonial administrators swiftly
sent any "troublemaker" to the prison in Navrongo. Nonetheless, relations
between the competing clans remained sour. For the following enskinments
of chiefs in Zaare (in 1952 and 1955), no one from the A-urugubiisi family
presented himself as a candidate, owing to fear of the colonial administration. Moreover, the tindanaship also moved to the Ayorebiisi clan. Sometime

---

[8] A concoction of cow dung and the residue from the dawa-dawa nuts was prepared. Apparently, this
produces an especially vile odor, and it was smeared all over the walls of the hut of the deceased; the
whole area was bathed in an offensive stench at the arrival of the district commissioner.

[9] Notice from District Commissioner of Zuarungu, 1911. NAG-A, ADM 68/5/1.

in the early 1950s, the A-urugubiisi earthpriest died, and until a soothsayer would divine the new earthpriest, the tasks were entrusted to the Ayorebiisi clan. Apparently, the clan managed to put off the soothsaying indefinitely. Thus, the political office of the chief as well as the religious office of the earthpriest had been transferred from the original family to the "female" line of Ayorebiisi.

When the chief of Zaare, the Zaare-naba, died in 1992, however, the British were long gone, and it was an opportunity to confirm or reverse the situation. It would be a while, however, before the formal funeral was organized and the various candidates could "knock on the skin" and announce their ambitions to become chief of Zaare. The funeral was postponed by the Bolganaba and the regent, Paul Atalanga, nephew to the late chief; the former wished to extend the period during which potential candidates could ingratiate themselves with gifts to him to the maximum, whereas the latter needed time to be able to make the necessary savings to perform the funeral and "conduct a campaign" for the skin. The competing A-urugubiisi family, on the other hand, was increasingly impatient, and eventually let the Bolganaba know that if the procedure was drawn out any further, the family would go to the Nayiri, who had enskinned chiefs in Zaare before the Bolganaba's emancipation from the Mamprusi king.

During the same period, the tindanaship was also contested. One of the descendants of the original earthpriest vindicated his claim to the tindanaship. He thus wrote several letters to the Survey Department arguing his case and pointing out the injustice of the situation that the Ayorebiisi family was in control of the skin, had an assemblyman, *and* controlled the land because proper soothsaying procedures to identify a proper earthpriest had been put off since the 1950s.[10] The Survey Department and Land Commission did not respond to the petitions, however, and Paul Atalanga, the regent of Zaare and "his" earthpriest continued to endorse leases.

The two families both reached for the past in justifying their claims to chieftaincy and the tindanaship, linking the original office to significant events. Members of the A-urugibiisi clan claimed their right to the skin and the tindanaship through their first settlement and the recognized tradition that authority flows from this feat. The disruption of their reign was instigated by the colonial administrators, strangers to the area as well as to tradition, and was to be attributed to the temporary transient exception of

---

[10] I did not manage to retrieve the first letters in this correspondence, but only Letter from Regent of Zaare, Paul Atalanga to Survey Department, "Demarcating Plots in Zaare," 1 May 2001; Letter from Issakar Amooda to Survey Department, 10 February 2002; Letter from Chief of Zaare to Regional Lands Commission, Bolgatanga, "Installation of Zaare-Naba, Naba Akumasi a Babalgesake," 11 February 2002; and Letter from Naba Akumasi to Survey Department, 14 April 2002. Material in private possession.

colonial rule. The fact that the district commissioner passed the skin to a "female line" was ample proof of the colonial administration's disregard for tradition. The Ayorebiisi family, on the other hand, argued differently. The destoolment of the infamous Anea was merely an administrative confirmation by the colonial officers of the popular will in Zaare. Chieftaincy was not reserved for a single family, and the colonial intervention only precipitated the historical change under way. Moreover, the peaceful government of successive Zaare chiefs proved its capacity and right to sit on the skin.

Finally, in 1999, the funeral was performed, Paul Atalanga of the Ayorebiisi family was formally appointed regent, and the contest for the Zaare chieftaincy could begin in earnest. The Bolganaba invited the contestants to formally announce themselves.[11] The duel was to be between Paul Atalanga and James Azure (A-urugubiisi). The two contestants regularly visited the Bolganaba and donated cattle and money; during the last eleven days before the enskinment, such visits occurred on a daily basis. In the span of almost two years until the enskinment took place on 21 July 2001, each candidate had spent around 12–15 million cedis and offered between 7 and 10 cows.[12] Neither of the two could mobilize such funds on his own and sponsors were drawn in from all over Ghana and abroad, from places such as Germany and the U.S. state of New Jersey. At the day of the enskinment, the candidates arrived at the Bolganaba's palace. The two candidates and their respective retinues were invited into the Bolganaba's hall. In private, shielded from the public eye, the paramount chief let them know that because both had fathers still alive, neither could get the skin.[13] Both candidates were taken aback because the Bolganaba had known about the existence of each candidate's father throughout the campaign without letting either know about the futility of his ambition, and they protested loudly. There was, therefore, some confusion as the Bolganaba sprinkled a fistful of flour on Paul's father, Akumasi Asana, and announced him the new chief of Zaare. In the commotion, James was also powdered with flour and as he left the chief's hall he was equally cheered by his awaiting followers, just as Akumasi had been received by his and Paul's people. Thus, at the end of the day, two

---

[11] Seven people announced their candidacy. If representatives of an eligible clan – a gate – fail to present themselves at such an occasion, the gate will be closed and henceforth will have forfeited its claim to the skin. Thus, five out of the seven candidates were nominal only.

[12] Interviews with Paul Atalanga and James Azure, 7 and 21 November 2002; 5 and 6 March 2004; 13 and 14 March 2004.

[13] Both Paul's and James' fathers were still alive, but neither had expressed any interest in the skin. Paul's father, Akumasi, was illiterate, and a little intimidated by the daunting task, and James's father had been seriously ill for years (interview with Akumasi Asana 8 March 2004). Traditionalists argued that "one cannot skip one's father" to become a chief; cynics argued that it would be a better deal for the Bolganaba to enskin somebody old, considering the likelihood of a not-too-distant demise and a new lucrative campaign.

men, Akumasi and James, were carried on the shoulders of their supporters to their respective homes, and both celebrated their enskinment.

A few days later, however, James Azure decided to file a complaint against Akumasi Asana and the Bolganaba for wrongful enskinment.[14] By that time, Paul Atalanga had had t-shirts made celebrating the enskinment of his father, and, to add insult to injury, the slogan in Frafra read, *Ba-Balegasake* (in time they will learn).[15]

The situation was tense, and fights broke out among young men of the competing factions in the market from time to time. It was not until the following year, 2002, however, that "all hell broke loose." People from James Azure's side claimed to be descended from the original earthpriest, and they argued that Akumasi was of a female line and had usurped the chieftaincy as well as the tindanaship. Consequently, they denied Akumasi's followers access to their lands at the time of sowing. The argument from James's followers' side was basically that, although the *territory* of Zaare might technically (though unrightfully and through historical misfortune) be under the political control of Chief Akumasi, the *property right* was less volatile and was not to be transferred like that; it was, rather, the earthpriest's traditional domain. The tindanaship was not subjected to historical events or whims of administrators but was the uninterrupted stewardship of what is sacred – as permanent as the land itself – and postponing the soothsaying ad infinitum by Akumasi and Paul's family would not change that.

After a few days of rioting, a curfew was issued, and James and Paul were taken to Navrongo prison for two weeks. Upon their release, they were forced by the police to sign a bond of peace for twenty-four months. The police commander at the time, Bernard Dery, was a Dagati. This ethnic constellation and the existence of jocular relationships between Dagatis and Frafras allowed the police commander to "tell off" the two Frafras, James and Paul, in public without their losing face. He even blamed the paramount Frafra chief, the Bolganaba, for being at the root of the confusion.

While the conflict was suspended, it remained open-ended.[16] It would seem that James's eyes were already set on the next round and that he was preparing to argue not only in terms of tradition but equally in terms

---

[14] Petition to the Judicial Committee of the Upper East Regional House of Chiefs, Bolgatanga. *James Azure vs. Akumasi Asana and Bolganaba*, 25 July 2001. Material in private possession.

[15] When I discussed the significance of the t-shirt with Paul Atalanga, he insisted: "It is because I'm a traditionalist. It is important for me to protect custom" (interview, 6 March 2004).

[16] In fact, it remained open-ended for several reasons. First, the enskinment form that the Bolganaba was supposed to forward to the Regional House of Chiefs for gazetting of Akumasi Asana, within two weeks of the act, was never processed (Chieftaincy Act, 1971: Act 370 [51(1)]). Second, the case filed by James Azure against Akumasi and the Bolganaba remained legally pending, although, to the Regional House of Chiefs it was definitely "traditionally concluded," thanks to the "Dagati intervention" by the police.

of recent history by creating "established facts." Tax collection was the target. The "basic rate," a nominal tax of 1,000 cedis per adult per year (which does not even cover the cost of its recovery), became an important practical claim to chieftaincy and hence territorial command for James Azure. He thus managed to receive the tax books from the District Assembly through the assemblyman of Zaare and very diligently collected the basic rate from the families behind him in Zaare. Although the district chief executive and his administration insisted that there was no element of formal recognition of James's claim to the skin in Zaare implied in their receiving the taxes through him, they could hardly control popular recognition. By performing small tasks of conflict mediation and collecting taxes for the public, James operated as the chief of one-half of Zaare and tried by the exercise of territorial and political control to create significant historical events for the future.

The conflict in Zaare over chieftaincy and land fed on the past as a source of legitimacy. Although the historiography was not in dispute, it formed the basis for contrasting narratives of legitimate claims. When James's clan had lost out on the chieftaincy, a more spatially oriented strategy was put into operation. First, James's clan claimed the land as the property of the earthpriest by denying Paul's people access to their land. When this failed, James tried to create a territorial and political claim to one part of Zaare by collecting taxes. Thus, rather than fastidiousness, a certain opportunism seems to drive the use of narratives. Words and semantics are not the whole story, however. Violent assertion of claims, physical presence in numbers, and intimidation by youths were also part of a picture of the struggle for political power and land in Zaare. The following case demonstrates how certain notions of space and the past can be operated in dynamic pairs.

Situating Kombosco Lands

The case of Kombosco shows how competing claims over land engage different conceptions of space and, as a consequence, different interpretations of the past. It also shows how different stakeholders' spatial ambitions for the future hinge on government's reading of the past.

Kombosco[17] is a relatively small village some three miles outside Bolgatanga. However, with the growth of Bolga, Kombosco has over the past ten to fifteen years gained increasing interest as a suburban residential area. Thus, the Regional Lands Commission's files show that the interest in acquiring leases there increased over this period (see Table 4.1).

---

[17] The spelling of Kombosco varies between documents. In direct quotations I retain the spelling of the respective authors.

Table 4.1. *Entries for Kombosco in the*
Regional Lands Commission File Book on
Land Documents in Upper East Region
(no data exist before 1996)

Year	Land Documents
1996	5
1997	8
1998	17
1999	24
2000	74
2001	44
2002	33
2003	29
2004 (January–March)	7

Even before the recent interest in Kombosco arose, however, the area had been identified for the development of housing. During the first decades after independence, the government wished to promote affordable housing of good quality for the rural population. Through the Ministry for Rural Development, the Department of Rural Housing was supposed to develop pilot projects in all regions, and for the Upper Region Kombosco was selected.[18] In 1975 land was acquired through the Lands Commission, and the recognized allodial titleholder, the Beo Rana of Beo, was also consulted.[19]

The Beo Rana is one of the few customary authorities in the Bolga area who combines the two positions of chief and earthpriest. The Beo Rana thus performs the various spiritual tasks in connection with use of, transfer of, and litigation over land as well as occupying the political role of a gazetted chief with the relevant prerogatives. "I can drink from the calabash and wear the red fez," has been the motto of the successive Beo Ranas, alluding to his double capacity as an earthpriest and a chief. The Beo Rana is Tallensi and owes allegiance to the Tongo Rana of Tongo and, via him, to the Mamprusi king, the Nayiri of Nalerigu.[20] The Beo Rana thus has customary political

[18] Interview with Daniel Agorinya, 30 March 2004. Memo, Update of Development at the Kumbosigo Rural Housing Project Site since 1975, 8 April 2002 (Department of Rural Housing/Upper East Region correspondence no. 6/22/V.3 (123)).

[19] Most of the paper work was done, but as in so many other cases, the proper acquisition was never fully completed. Thus, a report from the Site Advisory Committee was established (20 March 1975), and a site plan was made (ref 1618/4, 16/07/75). This was sent forth to the Chief Lands Officer in Accra for "further action" on 8 August 1975 (Regional Lands Commission correspondence no. UG.59/vol 3/112), but further action was not forthcoming.

[20] In fact, the village of Beo was under the authority of the Ku-naba, one of the Mamprusi kings, the Nayiri's dependencies, until 1910 when it was brought under Zuarungu as a way for the

authority over his subjects in Beo and the allodial title to the land they occupy. However, in addition, the Beo Rana has also historically controlled the land as the earthpriest in neighboring communities – even communities that are not Tallensi and do not depend politically on the Tongo Rana and the Nayiri but rather on the Bolganaba of Bolgatanga. The most significant villages in this particular controversy are Dulugu, Yargabiisi, and Kombosco on the outskirts of Bolga town.

In order to facilitate the task as earthpriest in the large area, the Beo Rana had appointed representatives – *tengapogsigres* – to take care of the smaller tasks of performing sacrifices, overseeing land transactions, and keeping him informed. In Kombosco, the Beo Rana had charged the chief of Kombosco with the responsibility of being his *tengapogsigre*, because he was already an older man whose seniority matched the responsibilities of the task. Consequently, the chief of Kombosco – owing political allegiance to the Bolganaba who had enskinned him – also performed spiritual tasks relating to the land for the Tallensi earthpriest of the area – the Beo Rana. Hence, when the Department of Rural Housing consulted the Beo Rana in 1975, the chief of Kombosco was equally present and also played a role. The Department of Rural Housing managed to construct ten houses, which were handed over to the Rural Housing Society with the pomp and circumstance befitting such an occasion, involving, again, the Beo Rana and the Kombosco chief.[21] Because the Department of Rural Housing did not escape the general economic malaise in Ghana of the 1970s and 1980s, however, it never managed to construct more than the first ten houses out of the planned fifty. Instead, members of the Rural Housing Society were assigned individual plots and had to construct their houses themselves. With the unaccomplished acquisition of land, the unfinished construction at the time of the divestiture of land from the government with the 1979 Constitution, and rising land values on the outskirts of Bolga, problems lay ahead.

Around 1983 the Beo Rana died, and because his successor was gainfully employed in the South and not eager to assume the duties of office immediately, a regent was appointed to fill in for a while – as it turned out, filling in for twelve years until the proper enskinment of the new Beo Rana was performed in 1995. By the time he came into power, things had evolved somewhat. Land in the vicinity of Bolga had gained value as public servants

British to punish the Ku-naba. Later, in 1937, though, a similar maneuver to clip the wings of the Zuarungu chief, Beo was brought under the Tongo Rana and became part of the Tallensi group. Throughout, however, Beo remained dependent on the Mamprusi king and only shifted around between intermediary masters (personal communication and handwritten notes on "The History of Beo and Winkogo" [no date] and "The History of Kumbosego" [no date] from Christopher Asaare, amateur historian of Bolgatanga, 12 November 2002). See also Anafu, 1973.

[21] Memo, "Update of Development at the Kumbosigo Rural Housing Project Site." Material in private possession.

and other "strangers" to the area were looking for accommodation, and after the 1979 Constitution, and in particular after the 1992 Constitution, people had become aware that lease agreements between lessor and lessee required endorsement not by the government in the shape of the Lands Commission, as previously, but by the allodial titleholder. In the absence of the Beo Rana, several of his *tengapogsigre* had endorsed leases on his behalf.

In 2000 the chief of Kombosco died and was succeeded by his son. However, the task of being the Beo Rana's *tengapogsigre* went to an older gentleman from another family. The two offices of chief and *tengapogsigre*, which had been combined in one person, were now split between two families, much to the chagrin of the new chief. However, the new Kombosco chief saw that land was being leased for up to 6 million cedis per plot,[22] and at the same time there were some forty plots claimed by the Department of Rural Housing that had never been fully developed. Land acquired by the government before 1979 but which had subsequently never been put to use was, according to law, to revert to its original owners. The chief was made aware of this by one of the lawyers in Bolgatanga and encouraged the local inhabitants in Kombosco to retake or lease the lands in question. Obviously, this provoked a reaction from the Department of Rural Housing. The regional director contacted the Regional Lands Commission.

The natives fully aware that the land has been lawfully acquired for Rural Housing Scheme in the interest of the society, still lay claim to the land and have gone to the extent of selling out the partially developed plots to some intruders who are encroaching upon that piece of land for development. Despite the on-going discussions with the natives and the chief of the area to find an amicable solution to the problem, they refused to heed the call to refrain from encroaching on the land.[23]

It is worth noting the suggestion of an amicable solution. Informally, the Department of Rural Housing had approached the chief to see if it could acquire the land once more, so to speak, this time by paying some compensation, and a total of 6 million cedis was suggested. The recent history of improperly acquired government property in Bolga and the immense amounts of compensation were undoubtedly looming in the back of the minds of the Rural Housing officials. However, similar thoughts probably occupied the Kombosco chief, and the protest and the suggestion of an amicable settlement were met with self-confident scorn from him and his elders.

It is a fact that the said land was occupied by Government in 1975 without compensation for Rural Housing purpose. The said land contained 14 acres (which

[22] Plots are generally 100 by 70 feet.
[23] DRH/UER/6/22/V.3, 6 February 2002.

can be about 60 plots) but the Department of Rural Housing itself were only able to develop 15 plots . . . since then to date. In the early 90s a group of people including the Foreman of the department called Society of the Development hijacked and distributed the undeveloped land to themselves to the detriment of the land owners and put up houses that are not designed by Department of Rural Housing. However, the land owners have taken back plots that are not yet developed by them. . . . I want to remind the Department of Rural Housing that the 1979 and 1992 Constitutions of Ghana has provided for the compulsory return of undeveloped lands occupied by Government without compensation to the owners and also compensate lands that are used up without compensation, so for the Department of Rural Housing to call the land owners encroachers . . . amount to intimidation because it is our RIGHT to re-occupy the undeveloped plots and *claim compensation* for the developed plots. We however wish to state that the plots are sold for at least six million (c 6.000.000) Cedis, an amount of at least three hundred and thirty million (c 330.000.000) Cedis is our demand as compensation for the land.[24]

At this stage, the ambition nurtured by the chief of Kombosco (and encouraged by his lawyer) was to secure the land, or compensation for it, for the allegedly dispossessed villagers.[25] The final section of the letter indicates as much.

We also wish to state the ownership or titles to the undeveloped plots be it either propriety [should probably read "property"] or absolute is our BIRTH RIGHT and Department of Rural Housing can not under any circumstance either directly or indirectly course or intimidate us into surrounding [should probably read 'surrendering'] such rights. So it is our PEACEFUL hope that you will use your honorous [*sic*] office to take and effect the necessary documentation for any one who bring legitimate and properly enclosed [should probably read "endorsed"] document by the land owners, the chief of Kumbosigo and the Beo-Raana.[26]

Though not entirely clear, the mention of two forms of ownership, "property" and "absolute," and the mention of the Beo Rana as landowner suggest that the chief of Kombosco recognized split ownership and the Beo Rana's allodial title. Upon sending the letter, the Kombosco chief sued the Department of Rural Housing for compensation, but for some reason, the Beo Rana

---

[24] Letter from Kombosco Chief to regional Lands Officer, 8 March 2002; Rejoinder to Department of Rural Housing Letter on the Subject Issues Arising from Land Ownership Kumbusigo Rural Housing Scheme Bolgatanga District. Material in private possession.

[25] The financial compensation for government acquisition is to go to those who have lost the possibility of using the land, that is, the villagers. The establishment of allodial ownership with the traditional authorities was an unanticipated, but major, side effect of the SSNIT and GWS cases (see Chapter 3).

[26] Letter from Kombosco Chief to Regional Lands Officer, 8 March 2002; Rejoinder to Department of Rural Housing Letter on the Subject Issues Arising from Land Ownership Kumbusigo Rural Housing Scheme Bolgatanga District. Material in private possession.

refused to support the suit.[27] The Kombosco chief was left hanging, with the case still pending. However, new opportunities to vindicate his claims and even upgrade them soon materialized.

In October 2002 President Kufuor had come to Bolga on an official visit, and during a speech he announced that two new districts were to be created in the Upper East Region. Garu-Tampane was to be carved out of Bawku District, while Tallensi-Nabdam was to be carved out of Bolgatanga District.[28] This outcome was the culmination of a very long struggle for a district by the various political forces in Tongo and Nangodi – in particular, the hometown associations, Tallensi Rock Union and Nabdam Literates' Association.[29] This situated the struggle over the lands in Kombosco in a larger arena with more powerful actors and more comprehensive agendas. Only weeks after the president's speech in Bolga, the chiefs of Kombosco, Dulugu, and Yargabiisi, supported by the Bolganaba, sent a petition to the Regional Lands Commission for a change in the processing of land leases in their respective areas.

The change to be Beo Rana [who endorses leases] around 1998 has hampered significantly law and order in the sale of land in these areas and leave the Chiefs with little or no room to play their supervisory role on land matters. . . . The Beo Rana politically and traditionally belong[s] to Tongo which is distinct from us and should *not* be principal signatory to leases and take royalties from one traditional area to another area. These three villages' chieftaincy is older than that of Beo-chieftaincy and chiefs of these three areas are *not enskinned* by the Beo Rana. Villages that are being ruled by Tindaanas *do not have Chiefs* and the Tindaana is *not contested for*, but in the case of Beo Rana the Tongo Rana enskins him as a Chief. So Beo Rana is sub-Chief of Tongo and we can not allow a sub-Chief of another traditional area to rule over us.[30]

Compared to the previous claims for compensation, this petition signi-fies a change in approach. First of all, the petition neatly shifts land matters

---

[27] The department of Rural Housing had recently successfully defended itself against a similar suit in Navrongo, which could have influenced the decision. Interview with Kombosco Chief, 16 March 2004.

[28] Local Government Act 462 (1[2]) of 1993 confers the powers to sign executive instruments to this effect on the president. Executive instruments must later be confirmed by Parliament.

[29] The Tallensi area had previously been an *administrative* entity: Tallensi Native Authority (1940–58), Tallensi Local Council (1958–60), and Tallensi District Council (1960–66), until it was absorbed into the Frafra District (1966–88) and finally Bolgatanga District (since 1988). In 1983, however, the Bolgatanga District was divided into three *electoral* areas (Bolgatanga, Tallensi, and Nabdam) with a member of Parliament for each. For an account of "district making" in the Upper East, see Lentz (2006b).

[30] "Petition for the Change of the Processing of Lease of Land in Kumbosigo, Yargabisi and Dulugu Residential Area." Signed by the three chiefs and sent from the Bolganaba's Palace, 14 October 2002. Material in private possession.

to the chiefs. As chiefs, both village and paramount chiefs, the authors of the petition would prefer to see the Beo Rana as a chief also. It would be evident that a Tallensi chief from Tongo, drawing his authority from the Tongo Rana and ultimately from the Mamprusi king, the Nayiri, could not claim any authority over chiefs from the Bolgatanga Traditional area drawing their authority from the paramount Bolganaba. Since the Bolganaba's emancipation from the Nayiri, the village chiefs of Kombosco, Dulugu, and Yargabiisi did not "share overlord" with the Beo Rana. Moreover, the petition plays the ethnic card in anticipation of the new district: Tongo is "distinct from us." The Beo Rana did not delay his rebuttal. In a petition to the Regional Lands Commission he argued that

... the Beo Rana has from time immemorial been the Tindana (Landowner) of all Beo Traditional lands before the advent of the institution of Chieftaincy in the Beo Traditional Area of authority.... That the conferment of chieftaincy ... did not operate to vest in such individuals paramount or Allodial title to lands settled on by the inhabitants of the said areas. That the Beo Rana was similarly conferred with Chiefship in addition to his already existing customary office of Tindana in which office was and is as at date vested with the Paramount or Allodial title to all lands of the Beo Rana.... That the Beo Rana acquired the entire large stretch of land which includes Dulugu, Kumbosgo, Yargabisi, and [others] by virtue of first settlement and occupation and exercised unrestrained and uninterrupted rights of allodial ownership of Beo Rana's lands and particularly of late over the lands settled on by the people of Dulugu, Kumbosgo and Yargabisi as at date.[31]

There was no immediate written response, but soon land leases were being endorsed by the Kombosco chief without consultation with the Beo Rana's representative. The Kombosco chief argued that he (or his father) had previously endorsed leases for land in Kombosco. Leases do, indeed, exist, signed by the Kombosco chief; however, the capacity in which he signed is unclear – whether as *tengapogsigre* representing the Beo Rana or as the chief and the allodial titleholder. By the end of November of that year, the Beo Rana had sued the chief of Kombosco "for and on behalf of the entire people of Kombosco."[32] From that day, the processing of land leases from Kombosco was suspended.[33] While the Beo Rana's claim was essentially based on his identity as earthpriest and his origination in the first

---

[31] Re: "Petition for the Change of the Processing of Lease of Land in Kumbosigo, Yargabisi and Dulugu Residential Area." Signed by the Beo Rana. 13 November 2002. Material in private possession.

[32] Writ of suit between Tindana of Beo and Chief of Kombosco, 26 November 2002 (suit no 17/2002) High Court of Bolgatanga; Statement of Claim, 14 April 2003; Summons for Directions, 27 May 2003; Amended Statement of Defence and Counter Claim, 6 November 2003; Reply to Amended Statement of Defence and Counter Claims, 23 December 2003; and Notice of Additional Issues, 2 March 2004.

[33] People could still enter the File Book for Land Documents (see Table 4.1), but the effective processing of leases was interrupted.

settlement, the Kombosco chief's defense was based on different categories of identity, namely ethnicity, which had recently been introduced with the imminent creation of the Tallensi-Nabdam District. The chief and his solicitor wanted a trial to determine "whether or not ethnicity is a criterion or factor in the determination of allodial title ownership of land under customary law."[34] Whereas the Beo Rana argued in terms of a tradition from "time immemorial," or at least well before the creation of chiefs, the claims of the three chiefs and the Bolganaba were more complex. They not only argued that the concerned villages' chieftaincies were senior to that of Beo but also alluded, arguing in terms of ethnicity, to some of the historical events that separated the Tallensi from the other Frafras, namely the Bolganaba's emancipation from the Nayiri.

This attempt to resituate the area of Kombosco and Beo in terms of traditional authority, land jurisdiction, and administrative areas was not the first. As early as 1931 when closing down Zuarungu as an administrative station was proposed, the commissioner of the Northern Province suggested that the Nabdams would go into Bawku District, the Nankannis into Navrongo District, and the Tallensi into South Mamprusi District.[35] He immediately received a reply from the district commissioner in Zuarungu, who, in addition to an understandable reluctance to be "closed down,"[36] argued that splitting up the area according to traditional areas would be anything but simple.

A more formidable difficulty, however, is the absence of recognised boundaries between most of the chiefdoms which is the cause to-day of many disputes. I had certainly hoped to devote much time after Christmas to demarcating the boundaries and deciding the extent of the domains of the various chiefs, but even if this is satisfactorily done I think your proposal will cause a great deal of confusion and discomfort among the people generally.[37]

The high commissioner of the Northern Province flatly refused this argument, responding in a series of numbered paragraphs:

3. I cannot see why the proposed arrangement should "cause a great deal of confusion and discomfort among the people generally." Only a very small percentage of them

[34] Notice of Additional Issues, 2 March 2004 (suit no. 17/2002) High Court of Bolgatanga.

[35] NRG 8/2/17. No mention was made of a distinct people speaking the Grueni dialect, and Bolgatanga did not figure at all as a town of any importance. See Bening (1974a; 1975b: 127).

[36] He thus argued in terms of the existing administrative collaboration with chiefs; with the fortunate geographical location of Zuarungu, and with the existing infrastructure: "It seems to me that it will be a pity suddenly to close down Zuarungu station; it possesses several quite good buildings, notably a brand new prison with cell accommodation superior, I believe, to any in the province.... I am sending this letter by special runner as I want you to see it before you meet Mr. Mckay." Letter from Zuarungu District Commissioner Page, 10 October 1931. NRG 8/2/17.

[37] Letter from Zuarungu District Commissioner Page to Commissioner of Northern Province, 10 October 1931. NRG 8/2/17.

will realise any change has taken place. 4. I cannot for one moment accept your statement that there are no recognised boundaries. They must be told to settle them at an early date; WE CANNOT DO IT FOR THEM, and they well know what they are. I will discuss this with you later.[38]

The district commissioner must have felt very strongly about his argument, as he ventured to persevere against his superior officer:

With reference to your paragraph 4 I cannot agree either that the chiefs know their boundaries or that they can settle them. I repeat that there are in many cases no recognised boundaries between chiefdoms. There are generally known boundaries between the various tindanas but it is quite common – & permissible since the chiefs have no control over the land – for the tindana following the chief of A to grant land to followers of the chief of B. These people still continue to follow the chief of B, and although the chief of A will probably agree to this in theory, in practice, as is to be expected, it is a fruitful cause of dispute between the chiefs. We are the only people who can settle the boundaries and make rules for the future disposal of the land, I cannot see why the chiefs here should be expected to be capable of settling them for themselves when in the Colony with much longer established chiefdoms these disputes are often taken to the Privy Council for decision.[39]

Aside from the striking actuality of this almost eighty-year-old correspondence, it also falls neatly within the Lugardian-Guggisbergian debate on how to deal with development and custom (see Chapter 2). Much more contemporary competing maps had, however, seen the light of day in the process of lobbying for the Tallensi-Nabdam District.[40] In 2001 the Tallensi Traditional Council, regrouping village chiefs of the Tallensi area and the paramount chief, the Tongo Rana (supported by Tallensi Rock Union), the member of Parliament for the Tallensi electoral area, assemblymen, and opinion leaders forwarded the latest in a series of petitions for the creation of a district to President Kufuor.[41] In order to qualify for a district, the government, through the Electoral Commission, had to assess a number of criteria. *Population size* and *existing infrastructure* are quite straightforward, whereas *ethnic homogeneity* and *land mass* are somewhat more open for interpretation.[42] The petition from Tallensi Traditional Council included

[38] Letter from Commissioner of Northern Province to Zuarungu District Commissioner, 13 October 1931. NRG 8/2/17.

[39] Letter from Zuarungu District Commissioner Page to Commissioner of Northern Province, 22 October 1931. NRG 8/2/17.

[40] The Nabdam Literate's Association was formed in 1962 (NRG 8/2/138). Tallensi Rock Union was founded in 1992 ("A Brief Report on Tallensi Rock Union," no date). Material in private possession. Both associations lobbied for the creation of the districts and the development of their respective areas (see also Lentz, 1995).

[41] "Petition for the Creation of Tallensi District," forwarded by Tallensi Traditional Council, 15 September 2001. Material in private possession.

[42] Interview with Regional Director of Electoral Commission, Bolgatanga, 29 March 2004.

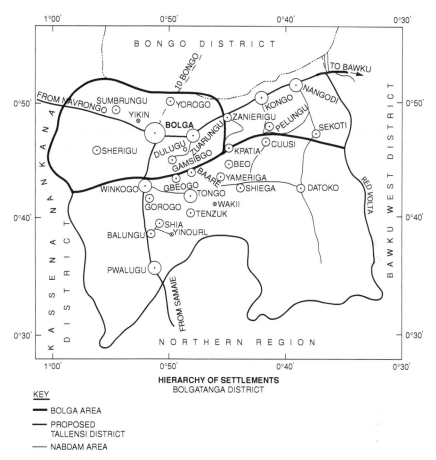

Figure 4.1. Sketch of New District Boundaries. *Source*: "Petition for the Creation of Tallensi District."

a few maps, one of which proposed the geographical outline of a future Tallensi District. This proposal was based roughly on the existing electoral areas established in 1983 (see Figure 4.1).

As Tallensi Rock Union stated, these were the most innocuous boundaries and just served the purpose of "getting" the district. Later, when boundaries were to be established concretely, the government would use "natural boundaries."[43] When President Kufuor announced the creation of the district in 2002, the fine lines of the boundaries remained to be settled. By "natural boundaries" the Tallensi petitioners – and, in particular,

---

[43] Interview with the President of Tallensi Rock Union, John Zoogah, 8 November 2001 and 27 November 2004.

Tallensi Rock Union – meant land "controlled by the Tallensi people." This area could include land in Dulugu, Yargabiisi, and Kombosco, as well as other villages in the area, notably Gambibgo, the village of the then district chief executive. The intention of the Tongo-Beo protagonists thus seemed to base future political territorial claims on existing recognized property rights. These rights were, in turn, based on a notion of the past as an inveterate source of mores, interrupted only by the invention of chiefs and their fabricated claims to land. If this line of reasoning was to prevail, however, it meant that the court case over the allodial title in Kombosco would be crucial. The dispute between Beo and Kombosco was already common knowledge, and as the various ideas about possible interpretations of "natural boundaries" for the new district percolated through Bolgatanga, big men with interests in what would become the decimated Bolgatanga District reacted.

Attack is the superior defense. Instead of merely insisting on the electoral boundaries dividing the current Bolgatanga District into the Bolga, Tallensi, and Nabdam constituencies, the district chief executive and other dignitaries began to lobby with communities in the Tallensi Constituency to get them to join the new Bolgatanga District, and thus reduce the size of the future Tallensi-Nabdam District. Efforts were particularly directed against people of Gono, the northernmost section of Beo, bordering Gambibko, Yargabiisi, Dulugu, and Kombosco.[44] When Beo in 1938 was transferred from Zuarungu to Tongo, Gono was part of the package and had become part of Tallensi Constituency. Though speaking the Grueni dialect, its people had subsequently engaged in Tallensi festivals and celebrations. However, for the past six years the people of Gono had resumed the observance of the festivals of the Gruei-speaking people of Bolga as well. The people of Gono had taken advantage of living in a border zone by ensuring their adaptability to both sides, keeping options open in the event of opportunities.

The district chief executive's choice of Gono was in all likelihood motivated by more than its plastic ethnic compatibility with Bolga, however. A fair amount of government infrastructure is situated in Gono, and although much of it is redundant,[45] the remunerative activities of filing for compensation for nonlegal acquisition of land with the government were promising in the area. The chief and elders of Gono were in favor of the plan and expeditiously organized an "emergency meeting" on 27 December 2003. Here, a petition against the inclusion of Gono community in the new

---

[44] Thus, when members of a party from the DCE's office were "intercepted" in Beo, it caused a stir as it was believed that they were effectively marking out the boundaries in the landscape. They argued that it was merely a routine visit, but the atmosphere of the day did not favor this kind of interpretation. Interview with District Coordinating Director, Nong-Inga Nsor N'yabir, 29 March 2004.

[45] Such as the old Agricultural Station, the meat factory, etc.

Figure 4.2. District Chief Executive's Map for the Future Bolga District. *Source*:
Town and Country Planning, Bolgatanga.

Tallensi-Nabdam District was prepared and sent to the district chief executive for his lobbying with the Ministry of Local Government.[46] The petition suggested that the new district boundary should separate Gono from Beo, placing Gono and its infrastructure in the future Bolga District.

Apparently, this just furthered the ambition and appetite of the district chief executive. Hence, during a meeting with the representatives of the new district in early 2004, another map was produced by the executive and his administration, situating not only Gono but even Beo proper comfortably within the future Bolga District.[47] This map did not go down well with the participants, and the meeting ended inconclusively (see Figure 4.2).

[46] "Petition against the Inclusion of Gono Community in the Newly Created Tallensi/Nabdam District," 29 December, 2003. Sent from the Gono Chief Palace and signed by the chief, elders, heads of families, and representatives of The Gono Youth Association. Material in private possession.

[47] The map also placed the Nabdam village of Dachio within Bolga District.

The spatial strategy of the Bolgatanga-based litigants was virtually the opposite of the Tallensi group. Here, the ambition was to base property claims on recognized territorial divisions. If the territorial divisions would separate Beo from Kombosco, Yargabisi, and Dulugu, the Beo Rana's claim could be seen as an unwarranted, and hence weak, territorial vindication. This argument, of space as territory, depended on the notion of the past as history, where the fortunate event of the establishment of a new district combined with the historical and much deserved emancipation of the Bolganaba from the Mamprusis and the subsequent sequestration of land rights from the Beo Rana. For this line of argument to be successful, a favorable settlement of territorial boundaries was crucial.[48]

Thus, while the creation of the Tallensi-Nabdam District was now a legal and political fact, the exact geographical contours and their territorial and property implications were still for some time to come dependent on the performance of political and legal acts, and how the past was most successfully invoked.

Conclusion

The contemporary construction of the past and, as a frequent corollary, the representation of cultural identity have been crucial for the successful vindication of political rights in Bolgatanga. However, more than a single past has proved potentially valid as a claim for land and office. When arguments of the past, confronting *tradition* with *history*, intertwined with competing projections of legitimate forms of control over space, complex combinations of claims have emerged.

While the competition over chieftaincy and land depends on the framing of the past, success has equally hinged on fortuitous or clever readings of the structures of opportunity. Strategic, or open, moments have arisen from time to time. Changes of government, adoption of a new constitution and tenure reforms, decentralization policies and the creation of new administrative boundaries, and government policies relating to taxation or chieftaincy have all, in isolation or in combination, created openings for a rearrangement of political rights and positions. The competition can be quite intense in such moments. The contestants seem to be aware that, while rights and offices are essentially negotiable, certain moments are highly propitious for change, whereas other times seem to favor reproduction. Consequently, "socially constructed" does not necessarily mean ephemeral or weak. Once successfully constructed, the past, identity, and rights become markers for

---

[48] In case the "maximum option" presented by the DCE, including Beo in Bolgatanga District, was to be endorsed, the Beo Rana as a Tallensi would be in a difficult political position to defend his claims in an overwhelmingly Grueni-dominated district.

the future negotiation of society. Such settlements may stick for some time, and the "stickiness" of certain structured situations is related to the institutions involved in the competition. Whether the past was argued in terms of history or tradition, and whether space was seen in territorial terms or as property, legitimization was sought through a validation of claims by the state, the government, or other official institutions.

The analogy between space and the past may at first sight not seem entirely satisfactory. Unlike the two pasts, both territory and property are, in principle, clearly bounded, and both are ultimately political in the sense that their existence rests on the exercise of power, by a state or some other controlling agency. However, the tensions between the two strategies and between political and legal institutions demonstrate that, while both are ultimately political, they are not identical modern forms of controlling space. Moreover, the boundedness of territory and property by a state or other controlling agency presupposes their control. As the chapter demonstrates, such control is sometimes precarious. This distinction can become blurred by constitutional provisions and social practices that link allodial title chiefly to jurisdiction. The categories can slide into and even become one another: territory may be a step toward ownership of land while ownership of land may be a step toward territorial control. Governors may indeed claim to own, and owners may very well pretend to govern.

The present validation of the past and the preferred projection of legitimate spatial control represent debate, friction, and competition between various institutions of public authority and interest groups. The Traditional Council, the House of Chiefs and the tindambas' association (see Chapter 3), the Regional Lands Commission and the Electoral Commission, hometown associations and the district chief executive and his administration, and the High Court all provide a functional semantic terrain for time and space. Command over this terrain is coveted by individuals such as chiefs and earthpriests and by people with ambition to gain access to their offices, as well as by the very institutions that provide the conventional elements of how to debate time and space. Although neither the past nor space seems to be distinguished by *infinite* plasticity, there seems to be sufficient semantic scope for *fluidity* to characterize them. Opportunities will in all likelihood continue to emerge. To seize the day, one must be able to seize yesterday, preferably in a form that resonates with tomorrow's spatial ambition.

5

Settled Facts or Facts to Settle

Land Conflicts under Institutional Uncertainty

I sat upon the shore
Fishing, with the arid plain behind me
Shall I at least set my lands in order?
T. S. Eliot, *The Waste Land*

Introduction

As we have seen in earlier chapters, land claims are often tightly wrapped in questions of authority and the politics of jurisdiction. Few land issues are not also in some way issues of authority. For this chapter, however, emphasis differs as attention is primarily paid to two aspects of everyday struggles over property. First, the chapter demonstrates the relative inconclusiveness and renegotiability of the question of landed property in and around Bolga, as well as the imaginative strategies employed to secure land rights in the area. It shows how political-legal questions about property are negotiated and fought over outside the formal legal arenas. Second, the cases demonstrate people's simultaneous contrasting efforts to curb the negotiability. It shows how important it is to create "established facts," however varied.[1]

[1] Moore applies a very useful distinction between two countervailing types of process: processes of regularization, and processes of situational adjustment. Processes of regularization are "processes which produce rules and organizations and customs and symbols and rituals and categories and seek to make them durable.... [They are the result of people's efforts] to fix social reality, to harden it, to give it form and predictability" (Moore, 1978: 50). Formalizing and increasing the predictability of the rules applied, for example, in land tenure disputes thus represent processes of regularization. "The countervailing processes of situational adjustment are those by means of which people arrange their immediate situations ... by exploiting the indeterminacies in the situation or by generating such indeterminacies, or by reinterpreting or redefining the rules or relationships. They use whatever areas there are of inconsistency, contradiction, conflict, ambiguity, or open areas that are normatively indeterminate to achieve immediate situational ends. These strategies continuously reinject elements of indeterminacy into social negotiations, making active use of them and making absolute ordering the more impossible. These processes introduce or maintain the element of plasticity in social arrangements" (Moore, 1978: 50).

90

Contrary to Western legal thought, claims in a rural African context are not forfeited merely because they are delayed. In her work on the Chagga in Tanzania, Sally Falk Moore (1992: 29) points out how such claims rarely perish:

[T]o be worth anything a claim must endure until the obligee has the means to pay it. That may take more than one generation. An in-definitive time frame can be a major economic element in the effectiveness of a claim. As the Chagga say, it is no use claiming a cow from a man who does not have one. But if you wait until the original debtor's son or grandson prospers, your claim may be easier to lodge, your case easier to win in the local arena.... Both debts and assets are heritable, but until there are adequate assets, and the way is socially clear for collection, a debt is not worth very much.

Thus, a debt may not be worth much if the debtor enjoys support or protection from powerful people in the micropolitical arena. "The good news for the creditors," Moore (1992: 30) continues, "is that the politics of the situation can change. If someone dies or emigrates or other changes in local alignments take place, a claim that was socially impossible to bring forward at one time, may suddenly become viable at another. Thus delayed claims have their economic and social rationales." It is my contention that this logic can be extended beyond private debts and thus be found in behavior connected to expectations of claims and rights in a wider sense.

In her seminal book, *Property and Persuasion,* Carol Rose (1994) examines the ways in which narratives and symbols are employed to make particular property claims stick within an overall culture. Rose's central proposition is that property requires some kind of communication to an audience of all others who might be interested in claiming the object in question and to the relevant institutions of authority that may sanction the claim. Stories, allegories, metaphors, and actual possession all contribute to persuade others of the justice of particular claims, and secondary symbols such as deeds and other recordings of transactions may become important props in the competing acts of persuasion. The competition between different claims to property is dynamic and changes through the influence of a number of sociopolitical processes, an important one of which is legislation. Legislation may in general be more or less effective, reach its targets with more or less precision, and result in laws that may be more or less observed. In certain areas, however, legislation has dramatic effects, not least because it influences the political situation for stating a claim. Land legislation is one such area because innumerable claims have built up over time; because they do not perish easily, they remain in "hibernation," ready to be activated as various forms of communication at the appropriate opportunity.

When the state divested itself from the land in the Northern and Upper regions with the 1979 Constitution, it provided an opportunity for reassessing the past and for renegotiating ownership to land. Land values increase with growth and development, and particularly in regional capitals such as Bolga, government acquired a significant amount of land for administration and development. However, in many, if not most, cases, government acquired the land it needed for development without employing the proper legal instruments. As a result, the government usurped the land it decided it needed, while paying less attention to the technical and legal procedures set out by law. As the 1979 Constitution divested the state of its trusteeship over lands in the Northern, Upper East, and Upper West regions that had not been legally acquired, the question of what happened to such government lands became acute.

From 1979, land was no longer held in trust, and it became quite unclear who could actually lease out land and in particular who could endorse such leases. This ambiguity was clarified to some extent by the landmark court decisions in the SSNIT Affordables and Ghana Water and Sewerage cases (see Chapter 3). Although these cases formally raised the importance of the earthpriest in land transactions, they did not necessarily resolve questions of competing uses of the land. They did, however, alert people to the possibility of renegotiating earlier settlements in a new politico-legal context. This chapter presents five microexamples in order to show that opportunities for reintroducing claims arose in different ways and were seized by different means. Although only a few actors controlled the circumstances, their ability to profit from possibilities was quite varied.

Instances of Everyday Renegotiation

Healthy Planning

Urban planning plays an important role in land politics in Bolga and the translation of policies into practice. However, practices also transform urban planning from grand design to damage control.

Bolgatanga has enjoyed the status of a statutory planning area since 1974. In practical terms, such status means that various areas in Bolga have been laid out for residential purposes, industry, and public facilities like hospitals, clinics, schools, stadiums, and churches by the Town and Country Planning Department. Other areas have not yet been planned for. For the latter areas, no leases are supposed to be granted. In planned areas, though, the Town and Country Planning Department must approve all leases to make sure that development is taking place according to plan. Many people thus find themselves in a rather peculiar situation where they have property in unplanned areas and are thus unable to get official documentation of their tenurial position; others find that their land has been reserved for a future school, clinic, or another facility. These latter landowners are allowed to lease the land only to someone who will develop it according to such plans. Due to the nature of the planned facilities, government itself is the obvious potential buyer; in light of the state of the public coffers, however, it is less than likely that recommended development of such lands is imminent. People are thus practically unable to sell or transfer their land rights within the parameters set out by Town and Country Planning.[2] These predicaments produced somewhat contradictory strategies from people with respect to planning; nonetheless, a common feature has been to go ahead, despite regulations. As Gough and Yankson (2000: 2488, 2496) argue for Accra, "Most development on stool land remains unapproved," and while "Town and Country Planning department officials are charged with developing land-use plans and plot lay-outs . . . development is occurring at a far faster rate than they can produce plans." With some resignation, the regional director of Town and Country Planning in Bolgatanga noted, "development is ahead of planning – and this is very unfortunate."[3]

People who had land in the unplanned areas and wished to sell their property rights by leasing the land often had lease documents drawn up in town by an ordinary typist, had it validated by a lawyer, and then – and only then – submitted it to the Town and Country Planning Department and the Lands Commission for official approval. Meanwhile, the future leaseholder had often begun construction, and the administration faced a fait accompli and had the choice of either allowing it or, the more cumbersome alternative, removing it.[4] Such actions are negotiations of property. People hoped to formalize actual situations in order to enjoy the protection of the law by its recognition of their interests as rights. People thus acted to extend government sanction of rights to unplanned areas of Bolga. As such actions occur, however, complementary actions of unraveling government jurisdiction and state property were just as significant.

As the cases of compensation began to be the talk of the town in the 1990s, people whose land had been taken for government purposes began to see their chance to gain a windfall. Also the people of Zorbiisi – a neighborhood in Bolga – saw an opportunity to be compensated for the land they had lost to the hospital grounds in 1950. The acquisition of the land for the hospital was, however, done according to the rules and processes

[2] The 1969 Constitution removed rights to freehold, but land may be held and sold as leasehold (Gough and Yankson, 2000: 2488). The 1986 Compulsory Land Title Registration Law reintroduced freehold, but the cumbersome procedure has in practice reserved this option to Accra and Kumase.

[3] Interview with Director of Town and Country Planning in Bolgatanga, Mr. Ayevi, October 2001.

[4] Such situations are likely to foster corruption and the bending of rules. See Blundo and Olivier de Sardan (2001a and b). Although this was not investigated systematically, most respondents concurred that predecessors of the current staff were not unknown to have made such transactions official for a fee ex post.

of the time. Before 1962 no compensation was due, and a Certificate of Allocation (290/50) had been issued. The hospital grounds were legally acquired government property.

Not discouraged by such nuances and emboldened by the recent legislation and the cases of successful vindication, local people began to look for ways to get compensation just the same. As in many other cases, the local inhabitants still occupied some of the land on the hospital area that had not yet been used by the hospital, and the boundaries between hospital grounds and the unacquired land were not demarcated in any clear way.

One of the hospital employees, identified here as Mr. K, was also somewhat of an entrepreneur and, like many others, he had a small kiosk in the blurred boundary area of the hospital grounds serving as a pharmacy or drugstore. In 1997 he had received a permit to establish a temporary structure by the Town and Country Planning Department.[5] Mr. K's business was successful but was in violation of the government regulation that all drugs must be sold from permanent structures. This regulation applied especially to those pharmacists who handle class A and B drugs, the most profitable segment of the market. Because Mr. K, as a pharmacist, was qualified to dispense such drugs, he decided to erect a more permanent structure. Having consulted a local resident of Zorbiisi, whom he considered to be the owner of the land, Mr. K began to lay concrete and build a structure. No lease was issued, but a not-altogether-clear arrangement between the owner and Mr. K was made; since that time, Mr. K paid the school fees and medical expenses for the landowner's family. Not surprisingly, the hospital administration was against the construction of the pharmacy on what it considered to be hospital grounds, not least because it would expose the hospital pharmacy to stiff competition. Hence, the director of the hospital contacted the regional director of health, who ordered verification from the Department of Survey of the building's location. The director of the hospital also requested that the regional minister have construction stopped. The latter asked the Town and Country Planning Department to take action, and Mr. K was given a clear sign of its intentions, as red paint on the walls of his business soon read: "To be demolished by 4/2/2000."

Mr. K was not inclined to see his efforts wasted and his prospects dwindle, however, and as a member of the District Assembly of Bolga, he was reasonably well versed in the workings of local politics. Mr. K thus insisted that the matter could not be taken up by the regional minister before it had been dealt with at the lower – district – level. The District Assembly was a not altogether hostile arena for Mr. K. The aspect of providing drugs

---

[5] The Town and Country Planning Department was not very restrictive about allowing temporary structures on what they see as "not yet developed government land" because such structures, in principle, could easily be wiped away in case need arises (interview with Town and Country Planning Department, November 2001).

within the vicinity of the hospital and at a competitive price compared to that of the hospital's own pharmacy weighed in Mr. K's favor. This was not unimportant because the Town and Country Planning Department after the Local Government Law (Acts 207 and 462) had become a decentralized department in 1988. Thus, although it could insist that regulations be kept to the letter, it could hardly go against the District Assembly to which it now answered. The verification of location requested by the regional director of health seemed not to have been conclusive. Mr. K still claimed to be outside the hospital grounds and also claimed to be supported by the Lands Commission,[6] while the Town and Country Planning Department as well as the staff of the Lands Commission insisted that his proposed site was within.[7]

In the meantime Mr. K roofed his pharmacy, hoping to establish a fait accompli. The whole affair raised a number of still unsettled questions: Could more land within the hospital grounds be effectively privatized? Could the resident of Zorbiisi (and hence Mr. K) eventually get a lease on the land and formally undo state property? Could the Ministry of Health successfully reclaim the land for a possible extension of the hospital? Could Town and Country Planning enforce a demolition? Could the long-term occupancy by Mr. K and other people doing business out of temporary structures eventually become prescriptive acquisition? Would the government eventually have to pay compensation, even for land that has been properly acquired but for which no compensation had been due at the time? These and other questions were left hanging – maybe for good, or maybe just until political circumstances, administrative procedures, or economic opportunities would enable one or more of the stakeholders to renegotiate the situation. Meanwhile, as late as 2007, the pharmacy ("to be demolished by 4/2/2000") continued to thrive.

Modernity Undone?

TIME (turn in text)

If one happens to take the road out of Bolgatanga for Tamale and turn right just at the edge of the town, one soon finds oneself in quite rural surroundings – round thatched huts in fields and women and men going about their business. Pushing a little further ahead, however, one enters an Upper Regions Agricultural Development Programme (URADEP) village built to accommodate the staff of the URADEP, which was financed by International Foundation for Agricultural Development (IFAD) in the 1970s. Nicely aligned identical bungalows with tin roofs signify a modern project – not only was the URADEP going to lift the region out of abject poverty, but the village itself heralded change.

---

[6] Letter to District Chief Executive, no date but probably February 2000. Material in private possession.
[7] Interviews, November 2001 and March 2002.

When the Ministry of Agriculture (MOFA) initiated URADEP in 1978, its land was vested in the government. To some extent, the ministry informed the Bolganaba and the local population of its plans and negotiated with them. The local inhabitants were led to expect jobs, the extension of public utilities such as the power grid and piped water, and even amenities such as a health clinic, a school, and a marketplace. Moreover, URADEP would plan a completely new settlement for the population as it vacated the site selected for the URADEP bungalows.[8] Eventually twenty bungalows were built. However, the economy of Ghana was in dire straits around 1980 (Chazan, 1991; Rothchild, 1991), and what should have been a model village ended up as a few rows of bungalows "without as much as servants' quarters." Public utilities and institutions were put on hold and gradually turned into dashed hopes.[9] This state of affairs continued until the landmark cases between the people of Tindanmolgo and SSNIT Affordables and the Ghana Water and Sewerage Corporation.

The earthpriest and leading members of the community of Tindansobliogo contacted the same lawyer and began procedures for a lawsuit against MOFA to seek compensation for the land lost to the URADEP village. This suit was accompanied by other measures as well. First of all, the farmers began to cultivate the land around and within the URADEP compound right to the doorstep of the bungalows. Whatever had been there in terms of a garden or a courtyard was annihilated, and in the growing season all that could be seen of URADEP village – the beacon of agricultural development – were twenty metal rooftops peering out over the millet stalks. Second, as Bolgatanga was growing, peri-urban dynamics embraced the URADEP village, and land values began to rise. It became tempting for the owners to sell land to people who could not afford land within the town of Bolgatanga. This was not uncomplicated, however. The first step in establishing a lease is to have the land surveyed. With the temporary receipt and map from the Department of Survey, the owner would then go to the Town and Country Planning Department for the establishment of a site plan and, thereafter, to the Lands Commission for the drawing up of

---

[8] Minutes of a meeting held on 24 December 1977 between Dr Assibi Abulu (Programme Manager, URADEP) with URADEP consultants and contractors on the one side and the Tindana inhabitants of Tindansobligo (URADEP staff housing site) on the other side. Material in private possession.

[9] This did not prevent the district chief executive from inviting the Tindana of Tindansobliogo to a meeting with the Bolgatanga Resettlement Committee to discuss the resettlement (letter of 2 October 1980). The response clearly reflects the new situation established after the 1979 Constitution. "[I]n view of [the] short notice I regret to bring to your information that I can not attend this all important meeting without sufficient knowledge of the issue at stake by my subjects who are the true owners of the land. I further wish to draw your attention that there is no legal instrument any where showing the acquisition of my land which therefore gives the said committee the power [it should, no doubt, read *no power*] to resettle my people" (letter of 9 October 1980). That was the end of the correspondence between the two. Material in private possession.

the lease. Subsequently, a building plan had to be approved by the Town and Country Planning Department. In many cases, however, construction commenced as soon as the surveyor's map was produced and the temporary receipt was issued.

In the URADEP village, the local population had a survey made by the Department of Survey measuring out plots of 100 by 100 feet between the bungalows, with the intention of selling land strips between the houses.[10] The further processing of leases was stalled by the Town and Country Planning Department. The URADEP bungalows do not officially exist in terms of plans and property; "no records at all," it laconically reads on the Lands Commission's list of acquisition of government lands.[11] Nonetheless, Town and Country Planning Department was as well aware of the existence of the twenty government staff homes as everybody else. Processing leases as if the bungalows were, in fact, not there would hardly have constituted good planning. Moreover, one cannot dismiss the impression that the idea of the URADEP village – however irregular its implementation – was closer to the ideas of proper development of the Town and Country Planning Department than other more common breaches of planning procedures. Nonetheless, some of the local inhabitants began construction of houses on the measured-out plots between the bungalows.

All this put pressure on MOFA to find an amicable settlement. However, considering that plots like the ones in URADEP village went for 3–6 million cedis as early as in 2001, the question still remains whether the government would have the means to reach an agreement that required buying the land. Though passed over by some of the promised material accoutrements of modernity, the local inhabitants of Tindansobliogo now challenged the ministries and public administration by the modern means of planning and lawsuit along with the insistence of cultivation and construction. Time, at least to this moment, seemed to be working for the local inhabitants, in one way or the other.

Negotiating the Wall

In addition to time, timing also appears to be crucial in claims for property. The dispute between the Tindana of Tindansobliogo and one of Bolgatanga's famous, politically influential and wealthy personalities, identified here as Madam B, is a case in point.

In 1977 Madam B bought a small hotel and about seven acres of land in Bolga. She bought it from a Mr. Gyamfy, who had been given the land

---

[10] Interview with Bernard Dery, MOFA 29 October 2001, and with landowners of Tindansobliogo, Ettibla Dampore, Anmare Ayimburia, and Anaba Attiah, 31 October 2001.

[11] Proposed Acquisitions by the State in Upper East Region, note prepared by Regional Lands Commissioner. No date, but approximately 2000. Material in private possession.

by the government as compensation for land he had had to give up when the dual highway was constructed in town. Initially, Madam B walled but a small part of her property, letting the rest lie undeveloped. This land was cultivated by the local inhabitants of Tindansobliogo and had been so for as long as anyone could recall. Over the years, the Royal Hotel and Madam B prospered, and at one point in the late 1990s she decided to wall the entire property in view of developing it further.[12] This caused great discontent with the local people, who saw themselves as illegitimately dispossessed. To them, the initially walled compound was tolerable, though essentially squatting on their land – land they had never ceded with consent. Moreover, since 1979, land seized by government without proper acquisition was to be handed back to its owners. To Madam B, the opposite was equally clear. She had a ninety-nine-year lease signed by the – at the time – appropriate authority, the Bolganaba; she had paid land rent for the seven acres; and she had a site plan.

The Tindana of Tindansobliogo invited Madam B to discuss the issue, but no settlement was reached. The situation remained the same for a few years. The earthpriest and the population found it futile to pursue the matter as long as Madam B was the regional treasurer of the ruling party, the National Democratic Congress (NDC), and a large-scale patroness of the party, who was well connected to the establishment of the town. To resign is not to acquiesce, however. Hence, on the day following the defeat of NDC in the national elections in May 2001, the youth of Tindansobliogo mobilized and knocked down the wall shielding the seven acres and the Royal Hotel. Cultivation was resumed the same rainy season, and only debris now marked Madam B's claim.

Whether Madam B's lease is still valid is unclear. Competing claims to property are not disputed in a political vacuum, and a "mere" lease document is apparently not of fixed validity. What counts as a valid and legitimate proof of property in one situation may be less of an accepted assurance of rights in another. Property need not necessarily change hands outright at the change of political constellations, as in this case. But the underpinning of property ownership does not necessarily remain settled facts over time. In Bolgatanga the institutionalization of property has met with significant reversals over the years, and small events may just tip the balance and unsettle established facts.

Sign Language

Rent seeking appears to be a major motivator for people's efforts to institutionalize control over land. However, the symbolic significance of identity

---

[12] Interview with Madam B, 6 March 2002.

and belonging embodied in claims to land and "place" may well help to perpetuate competition – even when economic stakes are low. The story of Bolgatanga Senior Secondary School – Big Boss – is instructive in this respect.[13]

Approaching Bolgatanga on the road from Tamale, some seven miles before reaching the town, one reaches the small village of Winkongo and the biggest educational facility in the Upper East Region, Big Boss. No signboard tells the visitor, the student, or the teacher that this is Bolgatanga Senior Secondary School. The school was inaugurated in 1975, but the signboard was burned by the people of Winkongo, and since then, every time a new signboard was erected, it was removed, burned, or otherwise vandalized.

Secondary schools were an important issue for Kwame Nkrumah in the early 1960s and remained a significant mark of development for most governments since then. However, it was not until 1970 that the Zuarungu Middle School at the outskirts of Bolgatanga was converted into a secondary school that Bolga could boast such an establishment.[14] The school was soon too small, however, and the government acquired a piece of land (one square mile) in Winkongo with the consent of the population. Buildings that had to be pulled down within the grounds were valued and marked "WIST" (Winkongo Secondary Technical), and people were paid compensation. When the school opened, the headmaster had "Winkongo Secondary Technical" written on the school bus and on a sign at the wayside. However, within a few weeks, he was called to order by the Regional Administration and forced to "correct" the name to Bolgatanga Secondary School. Immediately after, the new signboard was burned for the first time. The people of Winkongo were led by a group of the village's intellectuals, Winkongo Youth.[15] They authored a petition to the regional administration, pointing out that Winkongo was not part of Bolgatanga (as it is situated in Tongo traditional area), and that the authorities had broken a promise because recognition of the name was the only price to pay for the land (no lease had been prepared and no formal acquisition was ever made – only "unexhausted structures" were compensated). The school used to be called Zuarungu Secondary School when it was located in Zuarungu, and even the University of Ghana, Legon, was named after the specific locality it inhabited. The

---

[13] I am indebted to the late Petro Bumbie for alerting my attention to this case.

[14] The first two regional ministers during Nkrumah's time, L. Abawana and A. Asumda, diverted the allocated funds to build secondary schools in their respective hometowns, Navrongo and Bawku. Both tried to obscure the fact of the "mislocation" by not naming the schools after the towns but after the contractor (Kasajan Secondary School in Navrongo) and the local chief (Azoka Secondary School in Bawku), respectively.

[15] For an account of Youth Associations in northern Ghana, see Lentz (1995).

school in Winkongo should therefore also bear the name of the locality, it was argued.

The paramount chief of Tongo, the Tongo Rana, initially supported the population of Winkongo in its claims. As his support weakened, however, a member of the Winkongo chief's family, popularly known as Chief Paul, declared that Winkongo did not belong to Tongo but was an autonomous chieftaincy. Chief Paul styled himself as a chief and refused to vacate his house, which was still standing inside the school compound. Several attempts to negotiate a solution to the problem were made, but all failed. In 2001 the school won the Science and Math Quiz sponsored by the brewery Amstel Malta, and the prize was, of all things possible, a lit signboard for the school. The headmaster had to refuse it because it would only reignite the conflict over the name. Since then, the situation remained locked. The Regional Administration in Bolga would not "cede" its grand school to a village, Chief Paul continued to inhabit the grounds, no signboard reads Big Boss, and Winkongo Youth remained firm in its demand not to "hand over Winkongo to Bolga."[16] As a postscript to this affair it can be mentioned that in 2003 the squatter, Chief Paul managed to sell a piece of land next to Big Boss to the Ghana Tourist Board for 3 million cedis. The Ghana Tourist Board trusted Chief Paul's credentials as a proper chief and landowner, but it would appear to be a costly mistake. Although Chief Paul had made a vigorous defense of his claims, he was unable to produce any written documentation of ownership, just as he was later unable to produce any of the 3 million cedis. While he failed to prove his ownership, he managed to establish sufficient evidence long enough to make a quick profit.

Though almost anecdotal, the story illustrates how the complete state acquisition of land was obstructed because its public announcement was seen to deny the local inhabitants the name of their place in the world. While accepting the state's request to cede the land to development, the Winkongo community was not willing to forfeit its name to the town and its administration. The school had to tolerate the odd squatter and the inconvenience of anonymity to the passerby. The controversy may not have been a dispute over property in a strict sense, but it testifies to the importance of legitimacy when property claims are signaled to a relevant audience.

Meyer Fortes, Granites and Marbles Company, and the Crocodile

In 2001 a large group of people from Tenzuk marched to the regional minister of the Upper East Region to hand in a letter of protest written by the Tenzuk Unit Committee, titled "Petition to Save the Tenzuk Hills from Further Destruction." The petitioners wished to draw the attention of the

---

[16] Moreover, the member of Parliament from Tongo supported the Winkongo Youth's stance as infrastructure in his constituency might help to establish it as a district in future.

minister to the operations of the Granites and Marbles Company Limited, which allegedly were destroying the natural beauty of the Tenzuk Hills. The petition stated that the Granites and Marbles Company, whose quarrying activities had hitherto been limited to portions of lands within the Wakii community based on an agreement it had with the Wakii people, had moved uphill to Tenzuk lands. This relocation, according to the petition, was illegal because Tenzuk had no agreement with the company for such operations. In a separate letter addressed to the Tongo Rana, the Bolgatanga district chief executive, the regional director, Museum and Monuments Board, the police regional commander, the inspector-in-charge of the Tongo Police Station, the director of Tongo Quarry, the president of Tallensi Rock Union, the minister of Tourism, and the member of Parliament of the Tallensi Constituency, the Youth of the Tenzuk communities threatened to use all available means, including bows and arrows, to drive away the company from their lands.[17] This was the culmination of a long-standing friction between the Tenzuk and Wakii communities about their respective uses of the natural resources of the Tenzuk Hills.

Tenzuk Hills in Tongo has enormous sacred power for both Tallensi and other ethnic groups in Ghana because it contains numerous important sacred shrines. It was the site of intense controversy between the local population and the colonial administration in the first third of the twentieth century. Historically, it has been viewed by the Akan in southern Ghana as a site of potential ritual power. Allman and Parker (2005) argue that the importance of the shrine to groups from the South grew with the colonial imposition in southern Ghana. In 1932, the colonial anthropologist, Rattray, observed the presence of wealthy Asante businessmen at the shrines (Rattray, 1932).[18] Tongo Hills was also the starting point for the renowned British anthropologist Meyer Fortes's research from 1934 to 1937. Hence, "pilgrims of anthropology" now also visit the hills. The area is among the most renowned tourist attractions in the entire Upper East Region of Ghana and figures in the country's 1999 UNESCO World Heritage Tentative List. Its fame has even earned it mention in the *Bradt Travel Guide to Ghana*, which also secures many additional secular and nonprofessional tourists.[19]

---

[17] "The Destruction of Tongo Hills with Bulldozers and Other Equipments Must Be Stopped," authored by Tenzuk Community signed by Community Secretary, 28 May 2001. Material in private possession.

[18] Rattray (1932: 262) notes about his visit to the Tensuk shrines, "[o]n the morning of the ceremony I reached the rocks below the first cave about 8 a.m. and I was the first arrival. The chief of Tenzugu and the Ten'dan' had not yet appeared. From then onward until about 9 a.m., groups of pilgrims began to arrive. To my wonder and astonishment I saw well-dressed Africans, men and women who I later discovered, had motored hundreds of miles from Kumasi, Kwaku and Mampon. Among these were several of my Ashanti friends of old days, and never shall I forget the look of amazement on their faces at meeting me in such a place."

[19] The actual annual number of pilgrims and tourists is not known because there is no systematic registration. However, spiritual and tourist visits put together amounts to several thousands annually

In addition to the pilgrim and tourist economy, Tenzuk Hills offers possibilities of quarrying. Since 1979, Granites and Marbles Company Limited has operated in the area, and in 1984 it obtained its first concession.[20] As early as 1979, the company approached the communities in and around Tenzuk Hills, but the chief and earthpriests refused it access. The Tenzuk community rejected quarrying in the area because its gods are in the stones, and blasting the rock would prevent rain and destroy harvests.[21] Moreover, tourists and visitors would cease to come if the scenic beauty and the sacred shrines and rocks were ruined. In the neighboring village of Wakii, however, the company received a warmer welcome. The chief of Wakii summoned the eight earthpriests of his area, and it was agreed to let the company operate. Then, at a gathering in 1979, the Wakii representatives thumbprinted a declaration allowing the company to operate freely.[22] This was done to the tune of pasquinades composed by the people of Tenzuk. Thus, tension between the two communities was established from the outset.

In 1984 Granites and Marbles Company obtained a formal concession, and in addition to the rent paid to the National Lands Commission, the company occasionally handed out envelopes to chiefs and earthpriests containing 200,000 to 500,000 cedis. This was meant as a compensation for the performance of the necessary sacrifices and other services. These moneys were distributed by the company's public relations officer. Monetary support for festivals and small donations of stationary to schools were also offered by the company. In addition, it constructed and repaired the road from the national highway to Tenzuk Hills, primarily to facilitate the transport of rocks, but it meant a general improvement for communication within the area. Finally, the company also donated some ninety poles for the electrification efforts in the area,[23] and it sometimes offered to desilt dugouts used for watering cattle and other purposes. Common for all these efforts to build up legitimacy around its operations was the company's informal and ad hoc nature. The mineral concession obliged it to pay the government

(personal communication with Andy Murphy, Nature Conservation Research Centre, 2003). See Briggs (2001: 325–26).

[20] The company was not too diligent in obtaining and renewing its concessions. In fact, it was operating outside government regulations from 1989 to 1993 and again from 1999 until around 2002 (Regional Minister/UER, "Report of the Committee on Alleged Encroachment and Destruction of Tenzuk Hills within the Tallensi Traditional Area in Bolgatanga District").

[21] Colonial attempts at destroying the symbolic – and potentially political – significance of the shrines in the Tenzuk Hills had also included explosives (Allman and Parker, 2005: 75–78). Quarrying, no doubt, seemed to echo this destruction to the local inhabitants.

[22] Establishment of Quarry. Wakii/Gbeogo Hills, Tongo. 13 July 1979. Signed by Tongo Rana, Chief of Wakii, Chief of Gbeogo and 8 tindambas. Material in private possession.

[23] Unfortunately, the ninety poles were pilfered while the project awaited the extension from the main line.

a fee, but no lease agreement was established with the local population. The thumbprinted agreement from 1979 merely stated the consent of the local authorities of Wakii to Granites and Marbles Company's operations. No counterpayment was ever spelled out. This was in contrast to the company's meticulous recording of donations and letters of thanks received from beneficiaries.[24]

Through the 1990s tension prevailed between Tenzuk and Wakii, and petitions went to the District Assembly and the regional minister. The people of Tenzuk primarily complained that Granites and Marbles Company destroyed the environment, which was sacred as well as a source of income to them. There was also some disgruntlement about not receiving adequate development compensation because they were inconvenienced by the quarrying. In fact, as the consequences of the 1979 Constitution and the landmark court cases were realized during the 1990s, the Tenzuk community was encouraged to state its interests despite the fact that the quarrying license had been issued by the state. The people of Wakii, on the other hand, systematically denied the people of Tenzuk ownership to the land in question in their petitions.[25]

Events were brought to a head, however, when Granites and Marbles Company wanted to extend its area of operation. Its public relations officer managed to persuade the Tindana of Tamboog situated between Tenzuk (to which it belonged historically) and Wakii to thumbprint one of the Wakii petitions, thus changing his allegiance. As a sign of gratitude, the company provided him with an "envelope" and offered to desilt the village dugout. This was to have rather unfortunate results. In the process of desilting the dugout, the workers came across a crocodile, which they killed and later enjoyed as a meal. What they did not realize at the time was that the crocodile was sacred to the inhabitants and the totem of the earthpriest's clan. The position of the people of Tamboog vis-à-vis Granites and Marbles Company changed instantly, and Tamboog realigned with the Tenzuk community. The incident caused uproar among the Tenzuk community, which marched to the regional minister, as described earlier.

A committee was set up to investigate the validity of the competing claims. However, while the committee members were busying themselves with the intricacies of overlapping claims and trying to come up with constructive recommendations, Granites and Marbles Company short-circuited the process and went directly to the Ministry of Mines and Forestry in Accra. Here, the company successfully brought about a renewal of the mining

---

[24] "Report of the Committee on Alleged Encroachment and Destruction of Tenzuk Hills."

[25] For example, "The Destruction of Tongo Hills with Bulldozers" and "False Allegations against Granites and Marbles Company Operations on Wakii Hills," authored by Wakii Community and signed by the Chief and 9 tindambas, 6 June 2001. Material in private possession.

concession without any cumbersome involvement of the local population or institutions.

Seen from the perspective of negotiability, it would appear that Granites and Marbles Company over the years was quite successful in negotiating informal – and quite cheap – arrangements securing access to the mining resources. With the impending constitutional change in 1979, it even managed to secure the written support from the Wakii community – a community that would have a much stronger claim to the land and compensation, once the divestiture of land was a fact. While the compensation process thus tended to be informal, Granites and Marbles Company was very careful to have it recorded. This served to establish evidence of an understanding between the communities and the company.

Such evidence, however, would appear to be closely related to its institutional context. As long as the tension between Granites and Marbles Company and Wakii on the one hand and Tenzuk on the other was limited to the local arena and did not involve formal committees and the regional minister's office, conspicuous charity and sponsorship were sufficient for the operation to go on. Eventually, the growing awareness of tenure rights among an increasingly outspoken population and the unfortunate killing and eating of the Tindana of Tamboog's god caused a change in the institutional arena. The dispute moved from an informal, nonlegal arena to one where settled facts were of a different, more formal nature. Granites and Marbles Company could either undertake negotiations with the committee and the regional minister to engage in written agreements with the communities to settle facts, or try to move the problem to another, less complicated arena. The latter option was evidently preferred. This case is a good example of the limitations imposed on weaker parties when negotiating in contexts of inequality. While the population of Tenzuk was able to organize and mobilize interests in its favor on the local scene, it was unable to prevent Granites and Marbles Company from organizing and activating interests from outside the locality and to keep wider influences at bay.

Conclusion

For more than a century, questions of property and the authority to determine the answers have been negotiated in words, law, and action in the Bolga area, as in Ghana in general. Property rights have changed radically and dramatically in Bolga and the Upper Regions, not least during the past three decades. While chiefs and earthpriests have schemed, acted, and debated to vindicate the allodial title and the ensuing benefits, the government has reduced or extinguished these rights at various points in time, at least on paper. In practice, however, the government has often had to allow the customary officials to exercise some authority. Government policy has been full of contrast. Over time, different state institutions have had more weight than others, and different priorities have dominated.

During the colonial period, the administration seemed to dominate as administrative expediency had priority (see Chapter 2). When the colonial administration took control over the land, its reasons for doing so were several. The government, for example, wanted to reserve its access to possible riches and to prevent landlessness of the rural populace. During the first decades of independence, an alternation between party dominance and military administration prevailed, with social control as a primary objective (Konings, 1986; Ladouceur, 1979; Ninsin, 1989; Rathbone, 2000). Hence, the postindependent governments largely continued colonial policy for two decades – for one thing, it made urban planning much easier, at least in theory. Since the 1979 Constitution and the gradual emergence of democratic institutions, no single institution would appear to have dominated. Structural adjustment policies and the ensuing disengagement of the state, and hence the opportunity for more privatized ownership of land, opened the field for several interpretations of who should control it. Thus, when the state divested itself of land in 1979 and left it to be debated who the allodial titleholders were, a "perpetual" competition was reanimated. The potential compensations at stake were huge – and continue to be – as government institutions became squatters at the stroke of a pen. In addition, planning was upset, as people aspired to reclaim past entitlements. The court system made some important rulings and offered a renaissance to certain claims from earthpriests and past land users. The emerging controversy between earthpriests and land users based on their competing claims might still be only at an embryonic stage, however (see Chapter 3).

The reclaiming of past entitlements demonstrates one of the dominant features about land rights in northern Ghana, in the country of Ghana, and at least to some extent Africa in general. There appear quite often to be rival claims to land and property, and the plurality of norms and the often-times ambiguous legislation afford several legitimate claims – or, rather, offer legitimation of several competing claims. When a particular claim is favored as a right, and the competing claim as a consequence does not come to fruition as a right, this latter claim is by no means extinguished. In fact, the contextual and political support for a particular claim seems rather less durable than the claim itself. Hence, the political, economic, and organizational context may well change to a more advantageous constellation for a particular claim at a later stage. Thus, Mr. K's claim to the plot for his pharmacy, and the population of Tindansobligo's claims to the land in URADEP village and the undeveloped lands of the Royal Hotel, gained currency due to the 1979 Constitution and the landmark court cases. The contestation of Granites and Marbles' operations was definitely also emboldened by a changing context. The prospects of changing circumstances are prominent in the Ghanaian and African context and explain why claims endure. However, prospects of change do not explain why some of the claims are successfully transformed into property rights and others remain in hibernation.

A particular constellation of legitimate claims does not transform land claims into rights. It is a necessary but not a sufficient condition. The negotiation of property described in this chapter as well as in the preceding ones, demonstrates that to make rights out of claims, organization is crucial. The improvisation in the face of opportunity and risk, the linking up with other groups, the creation of temporary or enduring alliances with resourceful actors, the choosing of fora for vindication of claims, and the orchestration of expression of interest are essential to success. Obviously, not all are equally capable of organizing at the moment of opportunity. The obvious images of organization include the union of earthpriests (Chapter 3), the intimidating vandalizing of signboards, the collective march to Bolga by the people from Tenzuk, and the destruction of the wall of the Royal Hotel. These are examples of how numbers in a coordinated or more spontaneous effort are effective. Equally powerful, however, is the organization of interests within institutions.

When Mr. K was able to entrench himself and successfully ignore the hospital management and the Town and Country Planning Department, his success can be attributed to his seat in the District Assembly. Equally, Madam B's immunity to the neighbors' protestations derived from her central position within the NDC apparatus. As soon as this affiliation was no longer a connection to central government, her adversaries were no longer mute and could organize on their part. Similarly, Granites and Marbles Company was sufficiently powerful and resourceful to draw on influences from outside the locality and thereby managed to offset even relatively well-organized resistance to its operations. Earlier chapters equally demonstrate how chiefs' institutional linkage with the state administration historically provided them with the upper hand in dealing with other customary authorities. Claims and claimants do not operate in a vacuum. While land claims often relate to the past and to past claims (see Chapter 4), claimants relate to institutions, some of which enable them to assert claims with success. While state institutions would appear to be very important, it is worth noting that they constitute a plurality of sometimes, and not altogether, congruent entities.

Thus, when addressing the issue of property in Bolgatanga and in Africa more generally, two aspects must be assessed simultaneously. First, the legitimacy of property varies over time. What constitutes a good claim at one moment may be less rewarding at another and may not resonate with what is generally or politically accepted. Second, what is an auspicious institutional organization of interests at one point in time may hold less value or be outright impossible at another – Madam B's connections with NDC and the effective reclaiming of the land taken by MOFA for the URADEP village being cases in point. Local actors may master neither the general legitimacy of property nor the larger institutional constellations. From a local point of view, these appear to be structural circumstances to which one has to conform or adapt. Government policy influences such structural conditions but does not wholly control them. Hence, many of the local actions, conflicts, and negotiations related to the question of property appear to frustrate government policy. However, it is not a frustration at random. The ability to read and act on the opportunities of the moment seems to be a prerequisite for success in everyday negotiations of property, and this ability is generally, though not exclusively, in the hands of local people who are well connected and well informed, and well-heeled.

6

"Bawku Is Still Volatile"

Ethnopolitical Conflict and State Recognition

The intention is to make sense, not discredit.
It's true that things aren't always what they seem,
but what they seem is always part of what they are.

Louis Menand, *American Studies*

Introduction

Ethnopolitical clashes have marred northern Ghana for decades (Brukum, 2001; Drucker-Brown, 1988, 1994). Bawku in the Upper East Region has been the scene of repeated confrontations – some very violent, others less so – between Mamprusis and Kusasis. The latest violence occurred in 2001 and 2002 in relation to local elections and the appointment of a local district chief executive. This chapter analyzes the *longue durée* of this ethnopolitical conflict and the role and idea of the state in this connection.

Ethnopolitical violence and competition, it is argued, are increasingly challenging the African state. The inability to put communal violence definitively to rest, or deal with it in appropriate institutional fora, is threatening the central state authority. Scholars of African, and indeed Ghanaian, politics often see the unruly politics based on the rhetoric of ethnicity (chiefly pedigree), firstcomers' rights, autochthony, and historical rights and injustice as testimony to the incapacity of the modern, secular, nation-state based on universal citizenship and equality (Akwetey, 1996; Skalník, 2002). Akwetey argues that the absence of adequate democratic institutions is to blame for the recurrent outbreaks of violence; there are simply no channels for expressing interests and demands. While it is dubious to *explain* one phenomenon (e.g., violence) by the absence of another (e.g., democratic institutions), Akwetey has a point when he argues that pent-up claims

This chapter was previously published in a similar form as "'Bawku is still volatile': Ethno-political conflict and state recognition in northern Ghana," *Journal of Modern African Studies* 41, no. 4 (2003): 587–610.

by suppressed groups have burst out as authoritarian regimes have been replaced by democratic ones and as patronage politics with "rewards" and "punishments" has become the dominant mode of operation by the politically powerful (Akwetey, 1996: 106). The system of reward and recognition by the central state dates back to the very genesis of the state in Ghana. As Ferguson and Wilks (1970: 326–28) point out for northern Ghana, "by the nineteenth century, systems of lesser chiefships had come into being within which position was in some sense achieved rather than ascribed. . . . within such organizations appointment to office was usually the prerogative of the king." This prerogative was later assumed by the colonial and independent state (see Harvey, 1966: 71–88). The powerful instrument of nomination gave rise to intense competition for office and politicization of chieftaincy in Ghana as well as elsewhere (Berry, 2001; Peel, 1983; van Rouveroy van Nieurwaal, 1999).

Admittedly, communal violence and ethnically based politics do not figure in the Weberian notion of the ideal-typical state, and the incapacity to prevent violence can certainly be seen as a "governance deficiency." However, despite the immediate and conspicuous challenge to the state (in particular when local politics turn violent), there is also a, perchance more subtle, recognition of the state as competition unfolds. Ethnicized political competition can be seen, at least partly, as an attempt by various groups to solicit the recognition of rights and status by national and other levels of government. As Akwetey points out, efforts at protest and vindication of rights are often directed at civil servants and other representatives of the state. Hence, the *idea* of the state is, if not entirely clear, quite powerful despite the incapacity of government institutions. And local political appreciation of the state is implicitly significant, despite public expressions of disappointment with concrete acts.

The so-called Bawku skin affair that has unfolded in the Upper East Region provides an instructive example of these paradoxes. The competition over the chieftaincy, symbolized by the skin, between Kusasis and Mamprusis is now into its fifth decade at least, despite many efforts to resolve it. The skin is the symbol of chiefly authority in northern Ghana, equivalent to the stool in the South. It symbolizes the chieftaincy and the throne. When a chief is enskinned, he is seated on the skin of an ox sacrificed for the occasion. In normal parlance, chiefs who are forced to abdicate are destooled, not deskinned. Lentz (2002) argues that there is no clear link between party affiliation and ethnic or regional divisions in Ghana. In general, her assertion may well be true. However, a significant reason for the longevity of the Bawku conflict is that the issue has acquired the character of a "pattern entrenching conflict." Not only do the various conflicts follow a pattern; they are reproducing and entrenching the pattern as they are played out. Thus, arguments explaining and reading confrontations along the lines of what is considered the fundamental divide between Kusasis and Mamprusis are often more easily propelled than more complex and contradictory readings.

Many of the most significant actors actively attempt to canonize the ethnic interpretation as it is instrumental in mobilization. Therefore, the point is not that this particular conflict is so deep-seated that it cannot be resolved or reconfigured; the point is rather that there has been a confluence of elements of reproduction that seems to have reinforced each other over the years. A wide range of political – including party-political – and economic competition over chieftaincy, land, markets, names of places, and other issues are thus cut to fit the ethnic distinction, as conflicts over rights and prerogatives have been constantly rekindled. These competitions have been played out through a variety of political practices, ranging from legal procedures, through party politics, administrative exclusions, hometown association activity, cultural festivals, and symbolically charged and well-choreographed receptions of dignitaries, to bloodshed, as this chapter shows in detail. The ambition of this chapter is not to display a petrified and deadlocked situation, but to account for the *process* of its reproduction and entrenchment. The fact that the conflict is pattern-entrenching does not mean that loyalties do not sometimes cut across the ethnic divide. But it means that such movements are easily denounced and considered invidious. Obviously, internal rivalry among Kusasis and Mamprusis, interethnic marriages, and political alliances *contre nature*, all occurring as opportunities arise, do not easily conform to the entrenched pattern. However, as long as they are seen as "abnormal," in a sense they confirm the pattern. Most political activities fitting this pattern are directed toward the state as the source of distinction – that is, toward the institution that can qualify claims as rights or discard them as illegitimate.

The Political Background

The context in which the Bawku skin affair became a political issue combined impending independence, regional competition, and politico-administrative transformation. During the colonial era, the Northern Territories had suffered from poor development of infrastructure and education. Until 1948, when a delegation of politicians from the Northern Territories Council met with the Coussy Committee on the future constitution of the Gold Coast, the North lay on the periphery of national politics, merely reacting to changes produced by confrontation between nationalism and colonial government. It was only from that time, and with the introduction of universal suffrage in the mid-1950s, that the region became actively involved in national politics, and political parties involved themselves in local affairs (Ladouceur, 1979; Staniland, 1975: 117). During the 1950s independence was gradually approaching, amid profoundly different visions for future political and administrative arrangements. One group, led by Kwame Nkrumah, claimed immediate independence for a strong, unitary, and energetic state. This call was inspired by various brands of socialism and saw the chieftaincy as an inherently unjust social and political institution. The other group was more diverse, with J. B. Danquah and Kofi Abrefa Busia as prominent representatives. It promoted a liberal democratic orientation and saw a prominent role for the chieftaincy in a future Ghanaian polity (D. Apter, 1968; Austin, 1970; Boahen, 2000 [1975]; Rathbone, 2000; Ray, 1996, 1999).

Nkrumah's Convention People's Party's (CPP) ever more intensive political campaigns during the early 1950s called for a new organization of "northern interests," and the Northern Peoples' Party saw the light of day in 1954. Leading figures in the Northern Territories Council began to organize and mobilize for the party. The active involvement and support of the chiefs appeared to be a key to its political success, and the appeal to the chiefs was helped a great deal by the CPP rhetoric of giving power to young men and "verandah boys" (Ladouceur, 1979: 114; Staniland, 1975: 140). One important supporter of the Northern Peoples' Party was the paramount chief of the Mamprusis, the Nayiri, resident in Nalerigu. Ladouceur (1979: 118) argues that the most important aspect of the 1954 campaign was the relationship between the candidates and the traditional authorities; and among the most actively campaigning chiefs was the Nayiri in a strong coalition with Mumuni Bawumia, one of the principal political characters of the day.[1]

One way for the CPP to secure political control in the North was to undermine the power of the Mamprusis chief, the Nayiri, and hence the Northern Peoples' Party. Consequently, the CPP began to mobilize among potential supporters in the areas controlled by the Mamprusis, notably among the Frafras and the Kusasis. In the mid-1950s the Mamprusi Traditional Area comprised three subdivisions, South Mamprusi, Frafra (around Bolgatanga), and Kusasi (around Bawku). As Ladouceur (1979: 124) relates, "there was a growing dissatisfaction in the early 1950s among the Frafra and Kusasi young men over what they felt was Mamprusi control and domination over affairs in their areas. For some, references in current affairs to 'colonialism' and 'imperialism' meant not only British rule, but also subjugation to an alien African ruler – the Nayiri – and his representatives. . . . For many Kusasis and Frafra young men, it appeared as though the Mamprusis were employing the new politics, through the chiefs, as another means of dominating the Frafra and the Kusasis." Proposals for dividing the Mamprusi

---

[1] The 1954 result was that NPP and its allies controlled seventeen out of twenty-six seats, and CPP a mere nine, in the Northern Territories (Ladouceur, 1979: 121).

Traditional Area, aired by CPP as early as 1954, were implemented in 1958.[2] When the CPP triumphed in government elections, the northern opposition ranks were slowly thinned as members of Parliament defected one by one to the government (Ladouceur 1979: 176). It was in this context that the Bawku skin affair was to become a political issue.

The Quest for the Bawku Skin

Bawku District (or Kusasi District, as it was known when it, and the Frafra District, were carved out of Mamprusi District in 1958) is a densely populated area with Bawku town as the unrivaled commercial center (Chalfin, 2000, 2001; Eades, 1994; Webber, 1996). In terms of population, the Kusasis are the majority. Only in Bawku town is the proportion of Kusasis rivaled by that of the Mamprusis, Yorubas and Hausa,[3] and Mossi (who largely control trade and transport). It is worth noting that intermarriage is not and has not been uncommon. Even within the political elite, people of "mixed descent" exist. However, ethnic identity is derived exclusively from the paternal line. Thus, despite the potential for ethnic amalgamation, the distinction between Kusasis and Mamprusis is cultivated and reproduced in political rhetoric. The political control of the town and the area had historically been in the hands of the Mamprusis for perhaps 150 years until 1957. The chief of Bawku, the Bawkunaba, was historically Mamprusi, appointed (enskinned) by the Mamprusi king, the Nayiri.[4] Canton and village chiefs were a mix of Mamprusis and Kusasis, all receiving their title from the Nayiri.[5] From 1931 the Nayiri was forced by the colonial administration to delegate this power to the Bawkunaba.[6] From this point in time, a hierarchy among chiefs in the Bawku area was established. In a report from 1931, District Commissioner Syme relates how a chiefs' conference was organized by him with a view to elevating one of them to a higher status. The chiefs decided that the Bawkunaba was to be their tribal chief (a title with no formal significance). Despite the fact that he was Mamprusi and

---

[2] This was only the latest of a long series of administrative splits and amalgamations. The North Mamprusi District was an amalgamation of the Zuarungu, Navrongo, and Bawku Districts in 1921. With the inauguration of the native authorities in 1932, North Mamprusi and South Mamprusi districts were amalgamated (Bening, 1975b: 121, 129).

[3] In fact, many of the "Nigerian" traders are of Yoruba descent, but their lingua franca is Hausa. Hence, they are generally referred to as Hausa in the area. See Eades (1994).

[4] A state council meeting organized by the British in 1931 decided that Kusasi subdivision was to be established in Mamprusi Traditional Area. The Bawkunaba was elected by an electoral college of canton chiefs and subsequently enskinned by the Nayiri as the principal chief of the area (Bening, 1975b: 123).

[5] The term "canton chief" is no longer officially used and has been largely replaced by "divisional chief."

[6] Letter from District Commissioner's Office, 30.3.1931 NRG 8/2 (ADM.56/1/198).

enskinned by the Nayiri, questions about payment and transfer of tributes and taxes from Bawku to Nalerigu began to arise. Thus, some modest moves for emancipation from the Nayiri even by a Mamprusi Bawkunaba could be noted at this point.[7]

In 1957 the Bawkunaba died and a successor was to be enskinned. Four families, or so-called *gates*, used to compete for the chieftaincy in a tentative rotational order, all trying to curry favor with the Nayiri. However, while the Nayiri eventually enskinned Yerimiah Mahama, the Kusasi community of Bawku had taken the matter into its own hands and selected the Kusasi, Abugurago Azoka, as Bawkunaba. This received support from various Kusasi chiefs and earthpriests, the Kusasi Youth Movement,[8] Kusasi veterans of the two world wars,[9] and Kusasi members of Parliament, notably Ayeboo Asumda, who was later to become the first regional commissioner of the Upper Region on its creation in 1960 (Ladouceur, 1979: 174, 191).[10] This led to a very awkward situation, in particular because the new chief began to replace Kusasi and Mamprusi chiefs in the different cantons with people loyal to himself.[11] A series of petitions from both parties reached the government,[12] and the political unrest made the governor-general establish a commission of inquiry to investigate the matter.[13]

Two contrasting claims to the chieftaincy were evoked. The Kusasi Bawkunaba, Abuguragu Azoka, claimed to descend from those who first settled on the land. He produced a letter dated to 1954 from the government agent stationed in Bawku recognizing him as the earthpriest of the area. In addition to this letter, an unpublished report from around 1932 by District Commissioner Syme, "The Kusasis: A Short History," was introduced as a historical source underpinning the Kusasi claim of first occupancy.[14] The

---

[7] Letter from District Commissioner's Office, 30.3.1931 NRG 8/2 (ADM.56/1/198).

[8] Later to be known as the Kusasi Youth Association.

[9] Interview with John Ndebugre, 3 November 2001.

[10] The Northern Territories of the Gold Coast on independence became the Northern Region of Ghana, which in 1961 was subdivided into Northern and Upper Regions. In 1980 the Upper Region was subdivided into Upper East and Upper West Regions.

[11] Interview with Bob Toya, 15 November 2001; John Ndebugre, 3 November 2001.

[12] NRG 8/2/132.

[13] "Report of the Committee Appointed by His Excellency the Acting Governor-General to inquire and report its findings on the claim of Abugurago Azoka to have been elected or appointed and installed as Chief of the Kusasi Area" (1958). See also *Ghana Gazette*, 2 November 1957, 1 March 1958.

[14] One might expect this report to be rare, but I have seen half a dozen meticulously typed copies with Kusasis in Bawku and Bolgatanga. The importance of the document has meant that many with an interest in the affair seem to have a copy. However, the report seems less unequivocal on the issue of the first occupancy by the Kusasis than some stakeholders would impart. Syme's report is archived as NRG 8/2/214. J. K. G. Syme resided in Bawku from 1929 to 1939, with a few interruptions when he served in neighboring districts (Roncoli, 1994: 54).

claim was, furthermore, that the Mamprusis had only arrived in the area together with the "whiteman" and, preferred by the latter to the Kusasis, had been installed as chiefs. To questions about the role of the Nayiri, Abugurago Azoka maintained that the "Kusasi chiefs" were not *appointed* by the Nayiri, but that their election by their own people was *blessed* by an official visit to the Mamprusi paramount chief.

The Mamprusis, on the other hand, claimed that they established the town of Bawku as a military post to protect trade routes and that the chieftaincy had been with them since its creation 150 years earlier. Moreover, the Mamprusis pointed out that they brought peace to the area, allowing the acephalous Kusasi communities to cultivate the land under the protection of the Mamprusis. Yerimiah Mahama, the Mamprusi Bawkunaba, furthermore denied any claim that his opponent, Abugurago Azoka, and his family had been earthpriests owning the land. The land belonged to the Nayiri, and Abugurago Azoka's father had, at best, been the caretaker of the *dawa-dawa* trees for the Nayiri.

Eventually, the commission of inquiry found in favor of the Kusasi claim that the chieftaincy had been imposed on existing, if rather weak, political structures. It also found that the general attitude of the Mamprusis as overlords over the Kusasis, with its implications of maltreatment and disrespect, was out of step with the values of citizenship in present-day Ghana. The commission saw the election of Abugurago Azoka as "part of the general struggle among the Kusasis to throw off the Mamprusi ruler and possibly anyone who opposes the move." Hence, it concluded, the Kusasi Bawkunaba had been customarily elected and installed as chief of the Kusasi area.[15] In 1958 the Bawkunaba was elevated to a position of paramountcy, ranking alongside the Nayiri. This was a further move in terms of emancipation following the first elevation of the Bawkunaba in 1931.

On 1 August 1962 Nkrumah barely escaped an assassination attempt in the village of Kulungungu, north of Bawku. There was widespread suspicion that the assassination had been orchestrated by the Mamprusis, who bore a grudge against the president. Following this attempt, a large number of people were detained in barbed-wire compounds. "Most of these detained were Mamprusis and Mossi, many of the detained Mamprusis were former chiefs and their families who had been destooled following the take-over

---

[15] When the commission's decision was published in *Ghana Gazette*, it read that "Abugurago Azoka was customarily elected and installed as chief of *Bawku*," and not the *Kusasi* area as had been the object of the investigation. The Mamprusis took the matter to the Divisional Court and won on the grounds that the two were not identical. This ruling was seen as hairsplitting and was overturned in the Court of Appeal on Abugurago Azoka's appeal (see *Ghana Gazette*, 2 November 1957, 1 March 1958, and Court of Appeal, 21 October 1958). This was not the last time the question of the name of the area came up. In fact, it was later to become a much thornier issue.

of the traditional structures in Kusasi district by the Kusasis in 1958"
(Ladouceur, 1979: 207). The leaders of the Northern Peoples' Party were
forced into exile along with the Mamprusi Bawkunaba, Yerimah Mahama,
who due to the Chiefs Removal Order had to remain twenty-four miles
from Bawku.[16] Yerimah Mahama died in 1962.

In February 1966 President Nkrumah and the CPP were overthrown in
a military coup and the National Liberation Council took power under the
leadership of Colonel A. A. Afrifa.[17] Immediately after the coup in 1966,
CPP cadres held meetings with chiefs in the Bawku area to rally support
for Nkrumah's return. CPP cadre Azonkor Assibi thus addressed the chiefs
in April:

I address you in confidence and no part of our discussions here should be exposed to
outsiders. You know Nkrumah installed you as chiefs. You were loyal to him and I
believe you will still be loyal to him. A section of the Army has deposed Nkrumah
during his absence from home. I want to assure you that Nkrumah still enjoys the
support of the country and will surely return to the country. I want you to realize
that without Nkrumah you will lose the positions and titles you now hold. It is
therefore our duty to help the rest of Nkrumah's friends in the country to make his
return possible. Therefore those of us in Bawku have thought over the matter very
carefully and the Bawku-Naba (Abugurago) has approved that every canton chief
should contribute 4 cattles [*sic*] and village chiefs should pay £5 and a sheep each.
These animals shall be sold and the proceeds shall be directed to channels that will
help Nkrumah to return here.[18]

This and a similar report[19] show how closely people connected chieftaincy to government policy. As we know, Nkrumah did not return to power.
Rather, Dr. Kofi Abrefa Busia, the former leader of the banned United Party,
was soon to become an adviser to the military government. He was later
elected prime minister in 1969 as leader of the Progress Party.[20] Mamprusi
leaders – many of them old Northern Peoples' Party cadres – returned
from exile and were released from prison, and some were restored to office.
People like Adam Amande became deputy minister and Imoro Salifu

---

[16] Interview with Ambassador (former Colonel) George Minyilla, 17 March 2002.

[17] Colonels A. A. Afrifa and E. K. Kotoka took power in 1966. Kotoka was later assassinated under
suspicious circumstances in April 1967. Afrifa became the strongman of the National Liberation
Council and maneuvered General J. A. Ankrah out of the position of its chairman (Akwetey, 1996:
118).

[18] CPP Chiefs in the Kusasi Area Plan to Help Nkrumah to Return, Evidence by: Indebugri-CPP
Chief of Nafkolga within the Binchuri Canton (mimeo). Material in private possession.

[19] Meeting at Kongo-CPP Chief and Canton supporters about 15 April 1966. Material in private
possession.

[20] The Progress Party was initially built around old United Party cadres (Ladouceur, 1979: 224).

regional minister (regional chief executive), and they managed to lobby for a change of name from Kusasi to Bawku District and from Kusasi to Bawku Traditional Council when the traditional councils were reintroduced in 1971.[21] This group also appealed to the government to rectify what it saw as the wrong decision in 1958 of enskinning the Kusasi Bawkunaba. Thus, in the Chieftaincy Amendment Decree of 1966 (NLCD 112), the Bawkunaba, Abuguragu Azoka, was destooled and the Mamprusi prince, Adam Azangbeo,[22] was enskinned, following the official funeral of Yerimiah Mahama, who had passed away four years earlier. The same decree lowered the rank of the Bawkunaba to divisional chief, and the suzerainty of the Nayiri was reestablished. The new Bawkunaba destooled all chiefs enskinned by his predecessor and reenskinned either chiefs who had been destooled when Abugurago Azoka had come into power or new chiefs who proved fealty to him.[23]

The peculiar result was that throughout Bawku District two chiefs would claim authority, each often with the national flag, the Black Star, waving in front of his house. In most cases, each contending family had its own regalia (a staff and a drum) ready for the happy event of their enskinment. The red cap and the skin of a freshly slaughtered animal are personal items invested with authority for the occasion and granted by the enskinning chief. The situation was peculiar for two reasons. First, the Mamprusis do not have a procedure for destoolment of chiefs; hence a chief, once enskinned, can be removed from office only by death or by elevation to another office. Consequently, the administrative and political destoolment ordered by law did not sit well with Mamprusi political thought (Drucker-Brown, 1981; Schlotner, 2000). Second, it might at first sight seem odd that political pacesetters of the acephalous Kusasi society would frame their plight in terms of a chieftaincy structure, instead of going against chiefs generally. In light of the political and institutional weight of chieftaincy in Ghana in general, however, it would have appeared an appealing strategy, uniting community aspirations and personal ambition. The situation with two chiefs led to violent clashes where new and reenskinned chiefs claimed back the regalia from the demoted chiefs. The Bawku skin remained with the Mamprusis until the death of the Bawkunaba, Adam Azangbeo. However, just as the Mamprusi community had done at the downfall of Nkrumah in 1966, the Kusasi community filed petitions to change governments, when the new military government of Acheampong overthrew Dr. Busia in a coup

---

[21] Chieftaincy Act 1971, Act 370, and Local Government Act 1971, Act 359. Also interview with John Ndebugre, 16 March 2002.

[22] Adam Azangbeo was "regent," that is, the son of the deceased chief until formal enskinment of a new chief.

[23] Interviews with Bob Toya, 15 November 2001; Adam Amande, 10 March 2002.

in 1972. The secretary to the Supreme Military Council, G. B. Boahene, responded to one such petition:

[M]y investigations into your allegations have revealed that the area in question is called Bawku District Council and not Mamprusi District Council. This alone is evidence that the area belongs to the Kusasis. Be that as it may, you might have realised that for some time now, there has been so complete a fusion of the tribes in the area that it is difficult to distinguish between Mamprusis and Kusasis. It is observed that, [only] very few of the 18 Canton Chiefs in the district are Mamprusis. And once nearly all the 18 Canton Chiefs are Kusasis and have been properly enskinned, it is the desire of this Office to let sleeping dogs lie.[24]

Thus, the divide was not clear-cut between Mamprusis and Kusasis. Rather, it separated Mamprusis and the few Kusasis who recognized the Mamprusi overlordship and the authority of the Nayiri from the Kusasis who were demanding a Kusasi Bawkunaba.

The latter had no intention of "letting sleeping dogs lie" and petitioned government again at the first opportunity, namely when Flight Lieutenant Jerry Rawlings seized power in a coup in 1979.[25] The change of regime marked a change of fortune in the Bawku skin affair and an increasing intensity of the confrontation. Thus, when Adam Azangbeo died in 1981, no official funeral was, or has since been, authorized for him, and hence his direct successor could not be enskinned. The son, Alhaj Ibrahim Adam, would act in the deceased Bawkunaba's place as a regent, and until 1983, there was no Bawkunaba. Nugent explains that since the late 1940s, Ghanaian politics had swung between two tendencies – Nkrumaism and the Danquah-Busia tradition. In 1969 the Busia Progress Party had won "when many Nkrumaists were debarred from full participation. Ten years later, victory went to the avowedly Nkrumaist, Peoples National Party, led by Dr. Hilla Limann. . . . After more than a decade in the cold, the politicians who belonged to these defunct parties perceived a golden opportunity to recapture the political Kingdom" (Nugent, 1995: 221; see also Akwetey, 1996). Rawlings's regimes represented, in particular in the early years, a break with the Busia and Progress Party philosophy, and "most PNDC [Provisional National Defence Council] stalwarts, with the significant exception of Rawlings himself, venerated Nkrumah as the spiritual grandfather of the revolution" (Nugent, 1995: 51; see also Chazan, 1983).

---

[24] SCR-29/10/V.2, 10 October 1977. Material in private possession.

[25] Rawlings's government from June to September 1979 under the Armed Forces Revolutionary Council was interrupted as Rawlings handed power to the democratically elected Hilla Limann from 1979 to 1981. Rawlings took power again from December 1981 under the Provisional National Defence Council and later from 1992 under the National Democratic Congress (NDC). See Nugent (1995).

One important political figure in the Bawku affair was, and has continued to be, John Ndebugre, a Kusasi intellectual, a lawyer and at one point regional secretary first for the Northern Region and later for the Upper Region, and a cabinet minister (agriculture). One of Ndebugre's main achievements in the Bawku skin affair was the successful lobbying for the reversal of the NLCD 112 decree of 1966.[26] The Chieftaincy (Restoration of Status of Chiefs) Law 1983 (PNDCL 75) destooled the eighteen divisional chiefs and the Bawkunaba Adam Azangbeo (the latter posthumously), and (re)enskinned the chiefs or their successors who had suffered destoolment in 1966. Ironically, even Abugurago Azoka I was reenskinned posthumously. He died in September 1983 and was reenskinned by PNDCL 75 in December of the same year.[27] This was not only the occasion to once more replace the Mamprusi loyalists with Kusasi; even within Kusasi lineages, old accounts were settled and opportunities grabbed.[28] Such squabbles obviously went against the grain of the overall pattern of the Kusasi-Mamprusi conflict. It illustrates that not all conflicts follow the pattern, but such conflicts have never been *represented* by the political leaders as more than mere squabbles and "noise" blurring the bigger picture.

PNDCL 75 was preceded by lawsuits and different petitions, in particular from Abugurago Azoka, who also filed a legal suit to be reenskinned, and by the Bawku Traditional Council (consisting of Mamprusi loyalists), hoping

---

[26] As a regional minister, Ndebugre drew up a memorandum arguing the Kusasi cause, and he organized a meeting for the other regional ministers on the matter. He also actively prevented the funeral of the Mamprusi Bawkunaba from taking place, disallowing a delegation from Bawku to bring the skin regalia to the Nayiri's court in Nalerigu to complete the ceremony. See Provisional National Defence Council Memorandum by PNDC Secretary for the Upper Region [John Ndebugre] Subject: "The Kusasi Mamprusi Conflict in the Bawku District of the Upper Region" (undated but probably late 1982, after 19 October). Material in private possession. See also UCR.01/31 Memorandum from PNDC Secretary of Upper region [Issaka Tinorgah] Subject: "Chieftaincy Problems in the Upper Region," 2 April 1982. Material in private possession. Also interview with John Ndebugre, 21 November 2002.

[27] Letter from Bawkunaba's Palace, "Funeral Announcement: The Death of Abuguragu Azoka, Bawkunaba," 22 September 1983, and PNDCL 75 of 21 December 1983. Announcing Abuguragu Azoka as Bawkunaba as early as September, before official enskinment, indicates that people had anticipated the turning tides. Material in private possession.

[28] Some divisional chiefs used the confusion to reshuffle their political base, contrary to Regional Minister John Ndebugre's recommendations. See "Petition on the Matter of the Confusion Let Loose upon the Zebilla Sub-District and the Arbitrariness of Destoolment and Enstoolment of Disqualified Chiefs in the Area" (25 June 1984) by thirty-one chiefs in Bawku West addressed to the PNDC chairman, Rawlings. "A good example of such was chief of T . . . assitrarily [*sic*] and capriciously enskinned a chief at M . . . even though the committee re-installed the pre-1966 chief who was still alive and had committed no crime against the skin." Material in private possession. See also, Resolution by Bugri Youth Association held on 25th March, 1984. "It is hereby resolved by the entire youth of Bugri that the position held by A . . . as chief of Bugri be nullified and void [*sic*]." Material in private possession.

for the support of the National House of Chiefs in Kumasi.[29] Emboldened by the change of regime and impatient for the return of the chieftaincy, on 25 February 1983 the Kusasi Youth Association raided the Bawku Traditional Council and collected all its official documents, stationery, rubber stamps, the typewriter, the register of chiefs, minutes, and court books, and paid and unpaid vouchers, including unclaimed chiefs' allowances.[30] The stolen goods were allegedly taken to the Bawku District PNDC office as the association declared:

Resolution of the Kusasi Youth Association on the Closure of the Bawku Traditional Council. We members of the Kusasi Youth Association exercising our civil responsibilities and rights have today, Friday February 25th closed down the Bawku Traditional Council and given its property and office keys to the District Administration for safe keeping until further notice.[31]

Among the Kusasi Youth Association's claims were a change of the name of the council to Kusasi Traditional Council, removal of the registrar as he was seen as a Mamprusi partisan, and suspension of allowances paid to the chiefs in the district until the chieftaincy matter was cleared. The argument put forth for a change of name was that other traditional councils took names after the group of people whose tradition the council protects (e.g., Frafra, Mamprusi, Wala) and that Bawku was an exception. The motivation was obviously that such a change of name would compound Kusasi political power. The raid led to a very tense situation for many months, when all the effects removed from the council remained under the control of Kusasi Youth. Later, toward the end of 1983, violent clashes broke out between Kusasis and Mamprusis, and it was alleged by the Mamprusi Traditional Council, led by the Nayiri in the Northern Region, that the PNDC regional secretary of the Upper Region, John Ndebugre, had incited the Kusasi uprising. Ndebugre emphatically denied this allegation and did not miss the opportunity to point out to the Nayiri that since the Upper Region had been carved out of the Northern Region, no citizen of the latter (implying the Nayiri) had any jurisdiction over citizens in the former (implying the Kusasi community and Bawku town). If the Nayiri was concerned with the fate of the Mamprusis, he could just resettle them in his

---

[29] See Resolution by the Bawku Traditional Council Members against the False Claims of Abugurago Azoka as a Royal in the Bawku Chieftaincy Dispute. Bawku Traditional Council 070/26.

[30] Letter from the Bawku Traditional Council Registrar to the Principal Secretary, Chieftaincy Division, Accra (Bawku Traditional Council/TJ/1-1983), and Resolution of the Kusasi Youth Association on the Closure of the Bawku Council. Material in private possession.

[31] Resolution of the Kusasi Youth Association on the Closure of the Bawku Traditional Council. Kusasi Youth Association, 25 February 1983. Material in private possession.

and their own place, the Mamprusi District in the Northern Region.[32] The violence had occurred in connection with a festival, *Samanpiid*, a celebration of the harvest among the Kusasi. Customarily, it is held as a private small-scale celebration in the household and is not a major spectacle. However, Ndebugre saw the possibility of turning the Bawkunaba's *Samanpiid* into a rallying point celebrating not only the harvest but also the fruits of politics.[33] A durbar was organized in December 1983 just after PNDCL 75 was passed, and it was seen as sheer provocation by the Mamprusis; confrontation ensued between them and the Kusasis, resulting in casualties on both sides.[34]

The passing of PNDCL 75 was an important triumph for the Kusasi Youth, Abuguragu Azoka II (son of Abuguragu Azoka I), and John Ndebugre, who interpreted the law as correcting the unlawful NLCD 112 decree of 1966.[35] Again, the regalia and, in particular, the Ghana national flag, the Black Star, was seized from all destooled chiefs.[36] However, the victory was not yet complete. Using the momentum, Kusasi Youth and the new Bawkunaba continued to push to change the official name of the Traditional Council and the district. While the Bawku Traditional Council was established by Chieftaincy Act 370 (1971), there was a later legislative instrument (LI 889, 1974) which (in a schedule) made mention of a Kusasi Traditional Council. Whether this was a simple mistake, a political "Freudian slip," or an intended ambiguity by the drafters of the legislative instrument is hard to establish. However, the opportunity was seized by the champions of the Kusasi cause. Pressure was put on the registrar of the Bawku Traditional Council to effectively change its name to Kusasi Traditional Council (a move outside his authority). The registrar complied and changed the name of the council in his official correspondence.[37]

Abugurago Azoka II thus submitted his enskinment report to the registrar of the Regional House of Chiefs in Bolgatanga through the *Kusasi*

---

[32] Letter from John Ndebugre to PNDC Regional Secretary of Northern Region UCR/01/21/1983; Letter from the Nayiri, President of Mamprusi Traditional Council to Regional Secretary, John Ndebugre, Mamprusi Traditional Council/IJ/1/SF.1/17-1984. Material in private possession.

[33] Cultural festivals are as such important cultural and aesthetic arenas for the exercise of political strategies. See, for example, Lentz (2001) and Gilbert (1994) for Ghana, and A. Apter (1999) for Nigeria.

[34] Interview with John Ndebugre, 3 November 2001.

[35] Ibid.

[36] "Report on the Bawku Chieftaincy Affair – Government Recognises Abugurago Azoka as Bawkunaba," 20 February 1984. Kusasi Traditional Council 9/UEHC/SF.2/Vol 3/4.

[37] Change of name Bawku Traditional Council to Kusasi Traditional Council, 16 February 1984, Kusasi Traditional Council/12/PNDC/SF.1, and "Report on the Bawku Chieftaincy Affair. Government Recognises Abuguragu Azoka as Bawkunaba," 20 February 1984, Kusasi Traditional Council/9/UEHC/SF.2. Material in private possession.

Traditional Council.[38] Despite political pressure,[39] this move met with resistance, probably because most chiefs in the Regional House appreciated the potential consequences of an easy change of name in terms of similarly unwelcome petitions in their respective districts and divisions. Hence, the registrar of the regional House of Chiefs of the Upper Region was quite reluctant to accept documents from the "nonexisting" *Kusasi* Traditional Council. At the behest of the Upper Region House of Chiefs, its counsel, lawyer Ambrose Dery, was asked to produce a legal opinion in the matter. His report concluded that the proper name would be Bawku Traditional Council on technical, legal, and political grounds because the name *Kusasi* Traditional Council would omit other important ethnic groups of the area.[40] However, before this particular case died down, a much more violent confrontation had begun to dominate the picture, and the new PNDC regional secretary eventually advised Accra that any change of name was likely to "compound the delicate situation of the area."[41] The issue that brought the situation to a state of violence qualifying for the label "war" was land.

The Issue of Land and Markets

When the rainy season began in June 1984, the Mamprusis learned that in many places – in particular, in the eastern part of Bawku district – their land had been seized by the Kusasi and the newly (re)enskinned village chiefs. Some Kusasis also had their land confiscated, apparently because of their loyalty to the Mamprusi chiefs.[42] In practical terms, Kusasis simply went

---

[38] Abuguragu Azoka petitioned Rawlings to make the Regional House of Chiefs recognize the change of the name: "The reason why I humbly appeal is that, it seems that the Registrar of the Upper East Regional House of Chiefs Mr. . . . has been reluctant to receive my enskinment report forms from the Registrar of the Kusasi Traditional Council, to submit them to the National House of Chiefs for the necessary registration and subsequently gazetting me with the excuse that his office and the National House of Chiefs do not know any Traditional Council known and called Kusasi Traditional Council." "Petition on the Change of Name of the Bawku Traditional Council to Kusasi Traditional Council by Abuguragu Azoka" (24 June 1984). Abuguragu Azoka II was enskinned on 24 April 1984 and the skin was once more elevated to paramountcy (*Local Government Bulletin*, 5 September 1986, 119).

[39] The regional administrative officer of the PNDC thus put pressure on the registrar of the regional House of Chiefs in Bolgatanga to accept what the registrar of Bawku Traditional Council had been coerced into. Letter UG. 66/SF.35/43/ 27/4/1984. Material in private possession.

[40] "Report in the Matter of a Change of Name of Bawku Traditional Council to Kusasi Traditional Council and in the Matter of a Legal Opinion by the Acting Council for the Upper East Regional House of Chiefs, Mr. Ambrose Dery," 21 September 1984.

[41] UG.66/SF.34/196, 29 November 1984. Material in private possession.

[42] The "Report of the Committee to Investigate the Bawku Lands Dispute 1984" (the so-called Minyilla commission) stated that 148 Mamprusis and some 87 Kusasis had land confiscated by the new Kusasi chiefs (Government of Ghana, 1985: 14–15).

to the fields hitherto cultivated by Mamprusis or Kusasis loyal to them and sowed the fields and physically prevented the users from accessing their property. These lands, like lands in the Bawku area in general, had been family-owned for a long time and could be transacted as a commodity. In reality, land was leased by families with customary freehold (see Chapter 3) without interference from the chiefs.[43] No unused land is available, and if people are denied access to their plots, their livelihood options are curbed dramatically (Roncoli, 1994; Webber, 1996). The PNDC Law 75 restoring the chieftaincy to the Kusasis had given them the courage and opportunity to wrest the land from the Mamprusis and to punish Kusasis who had been loyal to them. It led to many violent confrontations, with houses and other property burned down and the loss of several dozen lives. An additional problem was the eviction of Mamprusi, Yoruba-Hausa, Mossi, and Asante traders from the central market in Bawku. The local government owns the market stalls and leases them to traders. Hitherto, the market had been dominated by the previously mentioned groups, but now the Kusasi-dominated District Council ejected all the storekeepers. The reason advanced was to put an end to various irregularities (viz. unauthorized subletting).

A committee set up to unearth the facts found that the ejection from the fields was an organized and orchestrated action, and in their report the authors suggested that the Kusasi Youth Association might have instructed people to all venture the same explanation for the reclamation of the land from the Mamprusis (viz. that their relatives had returned from Kumasi in the Asante region in the South and needed it for cultivation). In some areas, Mamprusis were asked to pay 60,000 cedis to the Kusasi Youth Association not to have the land taken. At various hearings, the conflicting Kusasi and Mamprusi versions of the settlement history were evoked, and documents such as District Commissioner Syme's "The Kusasis: A Short History" and a report on landownership in north Ghana[44] were produced in support of the Kusasi claim that they, as autochthones, were merely reclaiming what they had lost to the Mamprusi usurpation in the first place. The Mamprusis brought forth the myth of Na Gbewa, the founding father of the Mamprusis, and his settlement in Pusiga, close to what later became Bawku, long before any Kusasi settlement.[45] The Catholic Church of Ghana came out with a small booklet on *Intertribal Conflicts in Ghana*, which in general agreed with the cause of the Kusasis. The predominantly Muslim Mamprusi community

43 Interview with Mr. J. B. Atogiba, 15 November 2001.

44 The so-called Allassane Commission Report, produced prior to the divestiture of state lands in 1979.

45 See A Script on Na-Gbewaa written by Mr. J. S. Kaleem (Zobogu-na) and read by Mr. Ziblim Andan (Executive Director – Cotton Development Board), undated. Material in private possession.

interpreted this work as a partisan contribution and claimed that the church had forfeited its potential neutrality.[46]

The outcome was a temporary setback for the Kusasi cause. The confiscation of the agricultural land was deemed illegitimate and illegal, and the land was returned to its former owners, the Mamprusis or Mamprusi loyalists. With regard to the market stalls, it was found that the irregularities in their rental were exaggerated and often the result of poor management on the part of the district administration. Moreover, the eviction orders had been forwarded in a "clandestine manner... without passing through normal and accepted channels of communication in the civil service and administration."[47] As a result of the disturbances and the report, John Ndebugre was "re-assigned to the Office of the President" (a euphemism for suspension),[48] and two laws directly aiming at the Bawku were passed: PNDCL 98 (Prohibited Organisations [Bawku District] Law 1984), prohibiting the Kusasi Youth Association and other ethnic organizations, and PNDCL 99 (Bawku Lands [Vesting] Law, 1984), vesting all lands in the Bawku District in the government.[49] But the chieftaincy remained with the Kusasis.

No real, long-term solution to temper the antagonisms was reached, however, and only a year later, in 1985, new violence broke out – this time over the discharging of lorries at the kola nut market. Trucks with kola nuts arrive in Bawku from Kumasi. The goods are off-loaded by bands of strong young men known as *kaya-kaya* (literally "goods" in Hausa). They are organized in groups with more or less flamboyant names: Congo Boys, London, Zingaro (the name of a popular cartoonist), Parliament, and Club 37 (referring to a military camp in Accra). All of these groups are affiliated with what are known as Kusasi and Mamprusi "Parliaments," respectively. These are local "hangouts" for the members of the, now illegal, youth associations, often decorated with posters such as those shown in Figures 6.1 and 6.2. Usually, lorry drivers and businessmen would call on particular groups of *kaya-kaya* to offload their cargo. One day in 1985 a fight occurred between different *kaya-kaya* boys, and violence and unrest spread throughout Bawku, where residences and warehouses were burned down. In a commentary in one of the newspapers,[50] the Bawkunaba deplored the Mamprusi aggressors, while the Mamprusis equally blamed the Kusasis, in

[46] Interview with Adam Amande, 10 March 2002.

[47] The "Report of the Committee to Investigate the Bawku Lands Dispute 1984," p. 22.

[48] Only to become minister of agriculture later, though.

[49] Land had only been given back to its original owners after passage of the 1979 Constitution, after having been vested with the British crown and the State of Ghana since colonization (Bening, 1996).

[50] *Ghanaian Chronicle*, 29 September–1 October 1985.

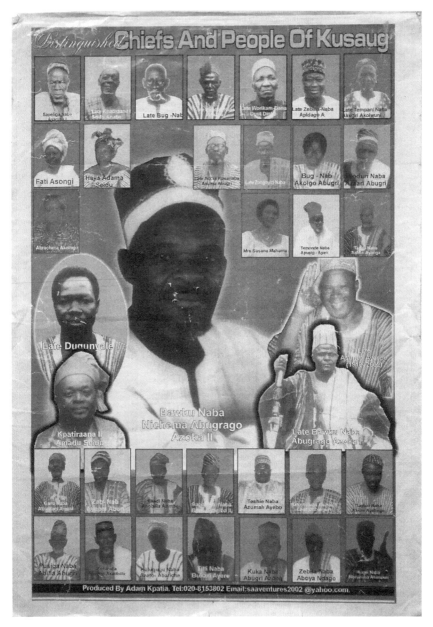

Figure 6.1. Kusasi Poster of Chiefs and People of Kusaug, Posted in Bawku

Figure 6.2. Mamprusi Poster of Chiefs and Elders of Bawku, Posted in Bawku

each case calling on the government to recognize its earlier decision (the 1957 and 1983 decisions for the Kusasis, and the pre-1957 situation and the 1966 decision for the Mamprusis, respectively).

Names and Elections

After 1986, things calmed down. The PNDC (later metamorphosed into the National Democratic Congress [NDC]) and Rawlings were in power, and the status of the Bawkunaba was in no immediate danger. During that time, Kusasi entrepreneurs and businessmen had, as card-holding members of NDC, managed to get contracts with the district administration and were gradually marginalizing the Mamprusi businessmen.[51] Emboldened by the gradually more favorable situation for the Kusasis, the member of Parliament for Bawku West, Cletus Avoka, a Kusasi leader, rekindled the issue of the name of the district. Bawku District had been split in two in a 1988 administration reform: Bawku East and Bawku West, with Bawku and Zebilla as their respective capitals. Addressing the Kusasi Youth Association in Tamale in 1999, Avoka announced that the Bawku West District Assembly in Zebilla had decided by resolution to change the name of Bawku West to Kusasi Toende because it made little sense to refer to Bawku, a town not within the boundaries of the district. He also encouraged the Bawku East District Assembly to change the name of its district to Kusasi Agolle, that is, the names under which the area was known locally when District Commissioner Syme wrote his booklet in the 1930s. This speech was very badly received among the Mamprusi leaders in Bawku, and one of them, Rahaman Gumah, came out threatening "fire and brimstone" in the event of such a change. It never came about but set the atmosphere for the 2000 presidential and parliamentary elections, confronting the NDC and New Patriotic Party (NPP), and giving the latter with a fair chance of winning.

The NPP not only shared the initials of the old Northern Peoples' Party but had also become the hope for the Mamprusis as the party that might topple President Rawlings and the political leaders of the NDC, who had held power for close to two decades. The Mamprusis hoped that if Rawlings (who had enabled the Kusasis to regain the chieftaincy in Bawku) were replaced by NPP, the chieftaincy would also once more revert to the Mamprusis. One important figure in the old Northern Peoples Party, Imoro Salifu, a Mamprusi leader, had become regional chairman of the New Patriotic Party in the Upper East Region, and the Mamprusis were in general

---

[51] The practice of favoring political supporters was not restricted to Bawku, but was a nationwide phenomenon. See, for example, "NPP Members Cry over Contracts," *Northern Advocate*, November 2001.

mobilizing in support of his party. The Kusasis, on the contrary, were in general supporting NDC.

During the campaign, both Rawlings and the leader of the NPP, John Kufuor, came to Bawku. However, only Rawlings paid a courtesy call on the Bawkunaba before addressing the rally. While Kufuor was intending to do the same, some of the local NPP Mamprusi organizers managed to change the program, and to Kusasis and Mamprusis alike, the refusal to pay respects to the Bawkunaba signaled that in the event of victory, the NPP would indeed reward the Mamprusis with the Bawku skin.[52]

There was an increasing tension in town running up to the elections on 7 December 2000. The voting was calm, but during the counting of the ballots late that day, shooting broke out. As votes were counted, some disagreement between NDC and NPP party functionaries developed into a heated argument, and suddenly gunshots were heard. As if prepared for it, Mamprusi and Kusasi youths took to the streets, vandalizing property and firing at each other. Only when a detachment of the Airborne Force arrived from Bolgatanga and a dusk-to-dawn curfew was imposed did things cool down. Sixty-eight people had been killed and more than 200 houses were burned down, leaving more than 2,500 people without shelter.[53] The results of the election were that NPP won, and Kufuor was inaugurated as president with a majority in Parliament. Kusasi anxiety and Mamprusi impatience were the moods of the day.

President Kufuor appointed a new regional minister for the Upper East Region after the elections, Mahami Salifu, a Mamprusi and member of NPP. On his first visit to Bawku, the regional minister paid a courtesy call on the Bawkunaba in his palace, but much to the displeasure of the chief, he also paid a call on Ibrahim Adam, known among the Mamprusis as the regent (still awaiting the official funeral of his father, the late Mamprusi Bawkunaba, Adam Azangbeo).[54] A similar situation occurred when the vice president of Ghana, Aliu Mahama, visited Bawku in July 2001. A large motorcade of taxis, trucks, private cars, and motorcycles awaited the vice president outside Bawku, and he was driven in a grandiose if not entirely streamlined cortege to the town. Here, he was to pay a courtesy call on the Kusasi Bawkunaba, but as they approached, most vehicles peeled off. Having paid the visit as vice president, he was persuaded, as an NPP dignitary, to pay a visit to the NPP headquarters. Here, another grand

[52] See Memorandum to All These It May Concern: "Damongo Consultations Peace Meeting under the Auspecies of Bawku Peace Initiative" (October 2001) by Justice (retired) B. Yabuku. Material in private possession.

[53] Figures provided by the then district coordinating director of Bawku, Mr. J. B. Atogiba (15 November 2001).

[54] *Daily Graphic*, 2 January 2002.

reception was prepared. The vehicles that had abandoned Aliu Mahama had continued to the NPP headquarters near to the house of the Mamprusi regent. The regent was styled as a chief, and all the village chiefs of the Bawku District, who had remained loyal to the Mamprusi Bawkunaba – that is, all those who had lost out with PNDCL 75 in 1983 – were gathered in their finest outfits to greet, and indeed be greeted by, Aliu Mahama, representing not only NPP but, as vice president, the Republic of Ghana. Taken by surprise, the organizers of the vice president's visit were unable to prevent the meeting from unfolding as a virtual encounter between the president's delegate and the "rightful" Mamprusi Bawkunaba.

Previously, the local Council of Churches had produced and circulated a small booklet, *The 2000 Bawku Ethnic Conflict: Its Effects on the Populace and the Church*. While purporting to present a balanced view of events, it caused great acrimony among some Mamprusi opinion leaders. Retired Justice B. Yabuku wrote a virulent memorandum condemning the Kusasi bias of the booklet, stating bluntly his – and many Mamprusis' – position. "I must state that to us Mamprusis, Bawku has no chief, and no-one can coerce us into recognizing any bastard as a chief." Yabuku also condemned the local Council of Churches' misguided attempt to "religiosize" [*sic*] the conflict as one between Christian Kusasis and Muslim Mamprusis. However, Yabuku could not himself refrain from implicating God, as he claimed "God is always on the side of the Mamprusis because they are the rightful owners of Bawku."[55] As a result of the mixed reception of the booklet, the churches were prevailed upon to retract it by the district coordinating director of the District Assembly (the highest ranking nonpolitician in the assembly).[56]

Simultaneously, bad news was forthcoming for the Kusasis in the District Assembly. The president appoints the district chief executive (DCE) of each district in the country, subject to the approval of the members of the District Assembly. Not surprisingly, President Kufuor appointed a local NPP leader, Rahaman Gumah, one of Imoro Salifu's henchmen. However, having been so virulently outspoken in support of the Mamprusi cause in the matter of the name of the district, Gumah was not able to get a vote of confidence. In fact, he did not even get 50 percent of the votes cast needed to qualify him for a second round of balloting. This result notwithstanding, the regional minister, Mahami Salifu, also a member of NPP and a Mamprusi, attempted to go through with the second round of voting. This was aborted as the regional electoral officer boycotted the meeting. Unable to have his candidate nominated, President Kufuor asked the regional minister

---

55 Memorandum to All These It May Concern. Material in private possession.

56 See Executive members of the Local Council of Churches, Bawku: Withdrawal of Booklet on "The 2000 Bawku Ethnic Conflict. Its Effects on the Populace and the Church," 15 May 2001. Material in private possession.

to be acting DCE until an acceptable candidate was found. However, the regional minister immediately delegated this responsibility to none other than Rahaman Gumah, whom he appointed "Special Assistant," housed in the DCE's office and provided with the DCE's car. Once again, the situation grew tense, and it took only a trivial exchange of harsh words in the market between two kiosk owners (allegedly over the sagacity of bombing Afghanistan in the pursuit of Osama bin Laden, of all things) to ignite yet another wave of violence in the beginning of December 2001 necessitating the intervention of troops. The situation in mid-2002 was thus quite tense.

In late 2002 President Kufour came to Bawku. He paid a courtesy call on the Kusasi Bawkunaba and let the Kusasi community know that he would dissolve the District Assembly if Gumah, his appointed DCE, was not endorsed by it. In exchange for this endorsement, the issue of chieftaincy would not be reopened and the Kusasi Bawkunaba could nominate seven of the government appointed members to the assembly. This offer was interpreted by Kusasis and Mamprusis alike as an invitation from the NPP president to the historically NDC-inclined Kusasis to "cross the carpet." A few days later, the veteran Mamprusi and NPP hard-liner, Imoro Salifu, died from a stroke. At this point, the solidity of the Mamprusi position began to fracture. Not only was Gumah, now appointed and endorsed as DCE, physically intimidated by Mamprusi Youth for having struck a deal with the NPP, allowing the Kusasi Bawkunaba to suggest the names of the government-appointed members of the District Assembly. Calls for rejuvenating and hardening the Mamprusi leadership were also made. Thus, in late 2002, a memorandum, Operation Survival, signed by a Mamprusi, began to circulate. This was an appeal for financial contributions for the purchase of arms for the defense of the Mamprusi community, accompanying a denouncement of the old guard's – Imoro Salifu's and Adam Amande's – control over Mamprusi politics. Thus, while the Bawku skin affair appeared to be settled for some, it appeared unsettling for others. Or, as the *Northern Advocate* had stated, "Bawku Is Still Volatile."[57]

Conclusion

The preceding outline of the Bawku skin affair suggests that it has been perpetuated by a number of factors. Moreover, the past twenty years have been more violent than the preceding twenty, despite efforts from governments to "set things straight" through legislation, or to resolve the conflict with various peace initiatives. Such efforts have at any one time been interpreted as partisan by at least one of the two groups. Therefore, what Akwetey

---

[57] *Northern Advocate*, January 2001.

(1996) and Skalník (2002) observe is plausible; the challenge of providing an institutional setup for peaceful negotiation of politics has at times proved too huge a task for the Ghanaian state. Or, maybe it was merely a task of inferior priority.

While the conflict was made up of many issues, there seemed to be a firm and institutionalized pattern to them. When the political parties were introduced, the tension between chieftaincy and commoners was one of the lines along which the CPP tried to mobilize support. This form of mobilization drove a wedge between nobility and commoners within particular ethnic groups in most of the country, but in Bawku district, the chieftaincy structure was also cleft along ethnic lines, as the Mamprusis would identify with the chieftaincy, whereas most of the Kusasis could identify with a commoner position and their aspiration to establish a chieftaincy of their own. Ethnic identification was more effective than that of "class," so that even commoner Mamprusis, who had no realistic expectation to become chiefs, identified with the cause of their nobility. As Lentz (2002: 262) argues, the British principle of a two-party system made it easy to link national party politics with local conflicts. Nugent (1995) suggests that even during the various military regimes, the two-party structure identified who was in favor and who was not. In Bawku, the binary opposition of political parties matched the Mamprusi-Kusasi competition almost perfectly. The British-style two-party system thus exacerbated and helped politicize the conflict.

Some writings aspire to identify the root causes of ethnopolitical conflicts (Bawku Peace Initiative, 2001; van der Linde and Naylor, 1999). Although it can be argued that some causes are more fundamental than others, the outline given here suggests that the various issues combine in a less hierarchical order. For example, while the name of the district hardly qualifies as a "root cause," the partisan debate over the name was crystallized into those who were for and those who were against reproducing the binary distinction. Likewise, the ejection of one group from the market and the threat of replacing it with another, and the systematic destoolment of divisional and village chiefs at the occasion of the change of Bawkunaba, are not just inert effects. They are effects that in turn reproduce the political fault line. The cumulative and reproductive character of politics in Bawku has had the effect that most issues are interpreted within this binary opposition, and once actions, visits, moves, vote counts, speeches, and the like are interpreted to fit this mold, then responses, ripostes, and retaliations further confirm it. Even minute disagreements – such as school yard fights, or squabbles in the marketplace – are configured by the conflict and in turn confirm it as the fundamental organizing principle of opposition and political competition in Bawku.

The processes of exclusion encountered in the context of violent conflicts in Bawku are accompanied by rather absolutist metaphors such as "full restoration" and "annihilation" of rights. Moreover, "history" provides ample justification to both sides to never relinquish demands or yield. However, this should not obscure the fact that the conflict is indeed reproduced through a multicolored fabric of big and small controversies. Akwetey (1996) and Skalník (2002) are quite right to state that the Ghanaian state has not devised a superior institutional structure for managing local political issues. But it is equally true that national political players – from Nkrumah and CPP, to Busia and Progress Party and NPP, to Rawlings and PNCD and NDC – have instrumentalized the conflict. Handing out factional rewards for political backing from one or the other side has often proved too difficult to resist as a political stratagem for national politicians. And as long as it is likely that government-level political ambition will translate into partisan decisions in Bawku, it seems likely that the pattern at the local level will reproduce.

The state remains the central reference point of the conflict despite a relatively poor record of "good governance." Apart from the overt violence, all other political measures taken in the Bawku skin dispute invoke the *idea* of the state. First of all, no questioning of the state's prerogative to sanction chieftaincy has, to my knowledge, been voiced. Although chiefs and chieftaincy are considered traditional artifacts of society, they require the invigorating authorization and recognition of the state to operate with validity. Despite the fact that the 1992 Constitution formally separates chieftaincy affairs from matters of state, the importance of the recognition that "men of the state" and its institutions can bestow upon such claims seems not to have faded. While the Kusasis' seizure of the skin in 1957 represented "emancipation" from Mamprusi domination and the suzerainty of the Nayiri, it was provided and assured by even more powerful authorities – the Ghanaian central state with the ruling party, a governor-general-appointed commission, and the judiciary, all in agreement. Likewise, when the skin was reconquered by the Mamprusis in 1966, this was done along administrative, political, and legislative avenues – all considered the terrain of the state.

This is not to downplay the violence and atrocities committed, which are real and mark the seriousness of the issue, but the efforts were in many ways directed at the state and were more sophisticated than brute force alone. Thus, while letters to the editors of newspapers have played a role in the continued competition to relate the "true story,"[58] petitions to changing governments seem to be important ways of seeking redress for grievances, however dated. Nor did it suffice for the names of popular descriptions of

---

[58] See, for example, *Daily Graphic*, 7 and 19 December 2001, 2 January 2002: "The Bawku Jigsaw Puzzle" (by Sydney Abugri); "Sydney Abrugri Is Spreading Falsehood and Lies"; and "Abugri Is Spreading Lies ... a Rejoinder."

areas to be assigned; to have consequence, state recognition was required. While the skin has changed back and forth with changing governments, changing governments have not proved a guarantee for a change of the Bawku skin. Sometimes, the group "out of office" did not manage to convince the new government of either the justice of its cause or the benefits that would accrue to a particular government from supporting its position. It would appear that certain contingent constellations of people and places of influence were necessary for turning opportunities into gain. In particular, Adam Amande's and Imoro Salifu's political positions in the 1960s and John Ndebugre's comparable position in the PNDC in the early 1980s suggest as much.

It is useful to pay attention to the reverence expressed for certain symbols in order to assess the import of the state in the local context. The raid on the Bawku Traditional Council in 1983 identified some of the significant symbols of authority of the council and its president, the Mamprusi Bawkunaba. Official documents, stationery, and rubber stamps, as well as registers and court books, are all items that signify central-state recognition of the Traditional Council's public authority; they are the administrative regalia. The symbolic salience of documents and writing is crucial in local politics and has been so for at least half a century (see Hawkins 2002). In the same vein, the Black Star is a potent symbol of authority delegated from the state to the chief entitled to hoist it. It was obviously important that the symbols of state were not left in the hands of "impostors." In contrast, "traditional" regalia such as the skin itself, the drum, and staff, were not systematically looted. It suggests that these items were devoid of their "political magic" and were regarded as merely personal paraphernalia compared with those that imply recognition by the state.

The legitimacy of claims to the chieftaincy has been bolstered by other symbols. Visits by national politicians such as the vice president provided "photo opportunities" and offered a stage for lodging claims. Again, it is telling what a visiting dignitary may bestow at the time of vindication in terms of recognition. While the vice president's visit may not have transferred the chieftaincy to the Mamprusi camp, it reinforced the claim of benefiting from "state" attendance and approval. The latest visit by President Kufour provides an identical (though opposite) opportunity for interpretation. The affair concerning the name of the area similarly testified to the popular appreciation of the power of the state to authorize and name, nominate, endorse, and acclaim.

In the combination of a conflict that structures the meaning and significance of virtually all disputes, and the idea of the state as the source of distinctions, most public utterances from the political center – Accra, the capital – have confirmed, willy-nilly, the fault line of the conflict. This is not to say that changing governments in Ghana have not had strong interests in their role as the source of distinction. This idea of the state has been used and confirmed by central authorities in Ghana, regardless of regime. The paradox is that the character of the conflict has made policy and intervention from the central state partisan, confirming alliances with one or the other side of the conflict. All the while, there is an unfailing idea of the state as a powerful source of distinction, which may explain why decisions that are contrary to specific interests seem not to call into question the state's general legitimacy.

[handwritten note: key — ethno-political conflict bolsters role or/idea of the state as source of recognition]

7

The Rent of Nonenforcement

Access to Forest Resources

They have committed false report; moreover they have spoken untruths;
Secondarily, they are slanders; sixth and lastly, they have belied a lady;
Thirdly, they have verified unjust things; and, to conclude, they are lying
   knaves.

Shakespeare, Much Ado About Nothing

Introduction

Two apparently contradictory forest policies have been pursued in northern Ghana as in much of West Africa. On the one hand, various forms of
local natural resource management policies, in the form of indirect rule or
newer approaches to decentralization and popular participation, have been
encouraged. On the other hand, colonial and postcolonial administrations
throughout West Africa have frequently usurped local rights to woodland resources as state laws restricted or suspended customary communal
use rights, which were regarded as being inconsistent with rational forest
management (Elbow and Rochegude, 1990; Ribot, 1995, 1999). Despite
policies of decentralization, Ribot (2001) points out how government agencies have often maintained their influence through the continued exercise
of state-granted privileges and management by restriction, exclusion, and
fear.

The literature on law and land in Africa tells us that rules enshrined
in formal law provide only part of the picture (Berry, 2002b; Blundo and
Olivier de Sardan, 2001a and b; Chanock, 1991a, 1998; Comaroff and
Roberts, 1981; Juul and Lund, 2002; Lund, 1998; Mann and Roberts, 1991;
Moore, 1986, 2001). People's practice as citizens and public servants often

An earlier version of this chapter was published as "Governing access to forests in northern Ghana.
Micro-politics and the rents of non-enforcement" (Wardell and Lund, 2006). The article is coauthored
by Andrew Wardell, who generously allowed me to use common work for the present chapter.

differ significantly from what the law(makers) could be held to expect. Law is not implemented or enacted unscathed by everyday negotiations, by more dramatic circumvention, or by manipulation or outright nonobservance. Thus, the meaning and effect of law in a particular place depend on the history, the social setting, the power structure, and the actual configuration of opportunities. This does not mean that laws and regulations do not have an effect. In fact, they constitute significant, though not exclusive, reference points for citizens and public servants enrolled in politico-legal institutions as to what is legal and illegal in their negotiations of access and rights – even if they are not enforced. In fact, laws and regulations may have decisive effects in terms of the opportunities that their *nonenforcement* provides. The formal latitude for discretionary decision making is often extremely limited for public servants in African administrations. However, in practice, the room for local-level rule making may be quite significant. In effect, an administrative culture may develop where certain readings of the law may be technically incorrect, though considered "the law" by the administrators and, in consequence hereof, by the local population. This is crucial because it puts the power of distinction between legal and illegal in the hands of a select group of administrators. As a consequence, what is commonly accepted as the reference point, the law, may in fact be a social construction that differs significantly from the formal law. The rule of law is often rule by those who define it.

The chapter compares the influence of colonial efforts to decentralize access to natural resources in northern Ghana, formerly the Protectorate of the Northern Territories of the Gold Coast Colony, to more recent policies. Despite successive waves of decentralization, laws have become stricter and local peoples' rights ever more circumscribed by the administration's ability to effectively cancel out policies of decentralization and retain crucial powers. This effort is often accompanied by references to certain orthodoxies about man's inherently abusive relationship to nature.[1] The chapter, furthermore, explores the relationship between these contradictory policies and the *actual* governance of access to the forests resources. Underneath the changing waves of policy and the powers of government agencies to limit access, another pattern of governance unfolds. Despite strict laws, this situation is characterized more by nonenforcement than by infliction of severe sanctions against people who circumvent policies of exclusion from access to forest resources. The nonenforcement of potentially strict regulations not only signals that people's access is tolerated, but it also combines with economic and political rent seeking by local public authorities.

---

[1] For discussions of this orthodoxy, see Fairhead and Leach (1996, 1998).

Colonial Forest Policies: Ambiguous Decentralization

Two philosophies of forestry management and policy can be identified in the colonial period. On the one hand, distinct efforts were made during the colonial era to rely on local political institutions, both to register practices and to negotiate future resource use rights in the Northern Territories. Hearings with those who were considered to represent their communities – the chiefs – were undertaken before forest reserves were formally constituted. Legitimate criticism can be leveled against the colonial idea of "indirect rule," and legitimate representation through chiefs, but efforts were exerted to consult with the population. On the other hand, however, ideas of "scientific forestry," centralized planning, and policing also ran through the administrative practice of forestry governance.

Promotion of Local Participation

No reorganization of local systems of government was attempted in the Northern Territories throughout the period 1901–29.[2] Colonial commissioners did, however, consult with chiefs, elders, and their followers to discuss and review disputed elements of customary law and native constitution in 1930–31. These conferences ultimately resulted in the reconstitution of the authority of the native states and, during the period 1932–35, the promulgation of three key ordinances providing for the reorganization of executive, judicial, and financial arrangements in the protectorate.[3] These ordinances established a new system of local government – the Anglophone "indirect rule" colonial model – which revolved around a paramount chief and his traditional council of elders, the "native authority" (Mann and Roberts, 1991).[4]

Early forestry initiatives in the Northern Territories were essentially guided by political officers under the leadership of the chief commissioner of the Northern Territories (CCNT). This guidance was provided after agreement had been reached with the chief commissioner that "all forestry work should be carried out through the Native Authorities" (Marshall,

---

[2] A governor's conference was held on 11 March 1921 to discuss the policy of indirect rule, which requested the "Chief Commissioner to draw up and submit to me in due course a policy for the Northern Territories." Governors' Confidential Diary 1928, 19 October 19. NRG 8/4/62/1.

[3] Native Authorities (Northern Territories) Ordinance (Cap. 84), Native Tribunals Ordinance No. 1, and Native Treasuries Ordinance No. 10 of 1932. See also Native Authorities Ordinance No. 18 (Cap. 111, 1932) and Land and Native Rights (Northern Territories) Ordinance (Cap. 121, 1935), as well as Gold Coast Colony (1928, 1933, 1952).

[4] The Native Authorities Ordinance resulted in the establishment of the Mamprusi Native Authority, which encompassed five Sub Native Authority Areas (Kassena-Nankani, Builsa, Fra-Fra Federation, Tongo Federation, and Kusasi) established under the Native Authority (Mamprusi Area) Order No. 7, 1933, and Native Authority (Mamprusi Sub-Areas) Order No. 8, 1933 (Bening, 1975b: 122–31).

1945: 5).[5] The overriding concern – that of facilitating "indirect rule" – was put to the test and eventually enabled the colonial forestry department in the protectorate to assist in drawing up sets of rules for native authorities.[6] The chiefs and earthpriests, in several cases, believed that forest reservation would bring hardship to their people, and as a result the Forestry Department developed a number of strategies to allay such fears. These included exemption of all existing farms from the proposed reserve area, verbal assurances that exploitation would be permitted after a working plan had been prepared, provision of revenue and certain powers to the native authorities, and education of native authorities on the importance of forestry. In practice, however, shortages of staff, limited capital investment, lack of operational funds, and the transformation of the Forestry Department into a timber supply organization after the outbreak of the Second World War (Brooks, 1947) severely hampered efforts to develop native authority forestry in northern Ghana.

The publication of *Forestry in the Northern Territories of the Gold Coast* (Marshall, 1945) and the resolutions emanating from the North Mamprusi Forestry Conference (Forestry Department, 1947) contributed to the preparation of a formal postwar forest policy for the Gold Coast Colony (Forestry Department, 1951, 1957). The North Mamprusi Forestry Conference held in 1947 rejected any plans to evict and resettle local communities on the grounds of impracticability and the lack of evidence of the beneficial effects of watershed protection. It let to the adoption of a broader land use planning framework, with the aim of conserving soils and protecting forests and water supplies.

The Forestry Department's role in the Land Planning Areas was to establish forest reserves to protect the headwaters of rivers and their catchment area to maintain and improve the natural vegetation in order to thereby minimize erosion. It also included plantations to provide adequate supplies of wood fuel and poles for building to the local communities and plantations to protect river and stream banks. This process let to the constitution of Reserve Settlement Commissions.

The Reserve Settlement Commissions were mandated to identify and protect access and use rights of all communities living in the periphery

---

[5] However, three tour reports influenced the Forestry Department's perception that one of the primary purposes of protecting the savannah woodlands was to safeguard supplies of forest products for local communities. The Upper East Region was selected as the priority area in the Northern Territories due to its high population density (McLeod, 1922; Moor, 1935; Vigne, 1935).

[6] Section 17 (1) of the Native Authorities (Northern Territories) Ordinance (Cap. 84) enabled the native authorities – with the approval of the chief commissioner – to establish Forest Reserve Rules. The rules concerned protection of trees of economic value (1932), control of bush fires over a total area of more than 25,900 square kilometers (after 1936), forest reservation to protect the headwaters of the Volta River (after 1940), and training of Native Authority Forest Rangers (after 1949).

of the proposed forest reserves. The commissioners passed judgment on a schedule of communal admitted rights following consultation with chiefs (but not the earthpriests). The Reserve Settlement Commissions had powers to abolish any right, if it was considered essential that this be done, awarding such compensation as it saw fit for the loss of rights.[7] The admitted rights were often very extensive. However, the process was often a lengthy one,[8] as a result of procedural delays and/or the selection and appointment of qualified and experienced Reserve Settlement Commissioners.[9]

Promotion of Government Control

The greatest hindrance to progress in the Land Planning Areas was deemed to be the "extreme shortage of staff" (Ramsay, 1957: 26). In addition, collaboration between the different government departments proved problematic. Local participation was curbed by more deliberate measures as well, however. Thus, attempts to replace indirect rule by a more modern form of local government were also introduced by the colonial administration during the period Reserve Settlement Commission procedures were applied in the Northern Territories.[10]

By 1944 the chief commissioner of the Northern Territories had informed the native authorities that the government had decided to take over the maintenance and patrolling of reserves. Native authority forestry was increasingly to be superseded by "scientific forestry" managed by a soon-to-be-strengthened Forestry Department.

A postwar preoccupation of the colonial administration in the Gold Coast was the reform of local government along modern lines and the building up of regional administrations (Anon., 1950: 23).[11] The deconcentrated district forest offices in northern Ghana were, however, divorced from the processes of local government reform and continued to be influenced primarily by the office of the chief conservator of forests in Accra. This provided

---

[7] Notes for the Guidance of Reserve Settlement Commissioners and Forest Officers Engaged on Reserve Settlement (no date). NRG 8/11/21.

[8] For example, the Red Volta West Forest Reserve was originally proposed and later surveyed by forest officer Vigne in 1939. The original demarcation of the proposed reserve was undertaken in 1941. A Demarcation and Selection Report was prepared in May 1950. The reserve was gazetted in November 1956 after three attempts to convene the Reserve Settlement Commissions.

[9] Some reserves awaited settlement for as long as thirteen years. See letter from Colonial Secretary's Office to CCNT, Ref: EF.9/25, 5 October 1949. Material in private possession. See also Constitution of Forest Reserves. Procedure to be adopted to expedite the steps precedent to constitution. NRG 8/11/21. See Cox (1943).

[10] This followed the report of the Coussey Committee on Constitutional Reform in 1949 and the promulgation of the Local Government Ordinance in 1951.

[11] This concern was also reflected in the recommendations of the report of Sir Henley Coussey's Committee on Constitutional Reform presented to Legislative Council in December 1949.

a platform to reinforce local manifestations of centralized power and influence, and it meant a distinct and abrupt move away from the native authority tradition. While the Local Government Ordinance No. 29 (1951) provided for the establishment of elected local councils and marked the end of the policy of "indirect rule," it was the beginning of the decline in the participation and influence of the traditional land and forest-holding authorities in woodland management. A distinct effort was made during the colonial era to register practices and to negotiate future resource use rights in the Northern Territories. Hearings with those who were considered to represent their communities – the chiefs – were undertaken before forest reserves were formally constituted.

The modifications to local government introduced in the period leading to Ghana's independence included provision for a greater degree of representation, more local taxation (but still subject to central control), substitution of indirect for direct administrative controls, recognition of the need for more qualified and independent staff, more emphasis on service provision, legislative powers more closely related to functions, and an executive in transition but with a tendency to remain an integral part of the local authority. These changes were matched by a clear shift in policy toward more governmental control of land and its resources.[12] The formalization of forest policy ushered in an era of greater state involvement in the patrolling and protection of forest reserves, the creation of fuel wood and pole plantations, and, most controversially, the gazetting of new forest reserves in the Northern Territories.

New National Policies: Centralization of Administrative Authority

The first decades after independence were characterized by government policies focusing on capital-intensive agriculture and neglecting small-scale farmers; a land tenure policy effectively denying local people a variety of rights to natural resources; and laws prohibiting access to forest resources, enforced by successive authoritarian administrations with little scope for recourse, let alone democratic participation.

State-Modernized Agriculture

During the colonial era, the Northern Territories were considered a labor reserve for commercial, labor-intensive farming – mainly cocoa – in the South. Apart from the construction of small dams for irrigation, agricultural production, as development in general (infrastructure, education, health,

---

[12] Circular Dispatch from Secretary of State, 17 October 1946. Colonial Office, P. & S. file (12). Cited in Agbosu (1983).

etc.), rarely commanded much government attention (Bening, 1975a, 1990; Bourret, 1949; Ladouceur, 1979; Saaka, 2001). Modernization was seen as urgent, and the development philosophy of the Nkrumah regime favored ambitious, large-scale, state-operated projects to develop irrigation infra-structure, agricultural processing, and large-scale mechanized cooperatives (Beckman, 1981; Goody, 1980; Konings, 1986; Shepherd, 1981). These could all be controlled by the agricultural wing of Nkrumah's Conven-tion People's Party. Irrigated agriculture was seen as the vehicle that could modernize the peasantry.[13] At the downfall of the Nkrumah government in 1966, policies (and, in particular, rhetoric) changed in support of private farmers. However, the ambition was still to modernize. An urban elite of bureaucrats, politicians, and army officers formed the core of a small group of capitalist farmers benefiting from state subsidies for mechanized and high external input production (Shepherd, 1981: 172–87). Despite these efforts, the vast majority of farmers in northern Ghana continued to engage in low external input agriculture and many depended on seasonal or longer-term migration to the South to sustain their livelihoods.

Land Legislation

The Land and Native Rights Ordinance for the Protectorate of the Northern Territories provided that land was to be held in trust by the governor but remained the property of the people (Chapter 2, and Bening, 1995: 242–44). At independence, the State Property and Contract Act of 1960 confirmed that in northern Ghana – contrary to the rest of the country – all lands were vested in government, or rather in the president. Only with the 1979 Constitution was land divested from the state.

As I described in Chapter 3, two significant acts were passed in 1962: the Administration of Lands Act and the State Lands Act (Government of Ghana, 1962a and b). The Administration of Lands Act empowered the president to vest any lands in his office if he considered it in the pub-lic interest. The State Lands Act signified the subtle distinction between land being vested in the state and land owned by it. Consequently, land merely vested in the state under the Administration of Lands Act still had an owner. However, as land was controlled by the state, it would appear that government institutions assumed that there would be no prob-lems with their occupancy or management, even if proper legal acquisition had not been completed. In most cases, the government failed to legally

---

[13] These included the Gbidembilise Valley in Builsa District, the Tono irrigation scheme in Navrongo District, and the Vea irrigation scheme in Bongo District. Planning of dams was initiated in 1960, but endless delays meant that cultivation only began in the late 1970s, and development of the schemes never met the planned targets (Kasanga, 1992; Konings, 1986, 256–70).

acquire the land it seized. Eighteen forest reserves in northern Ghana were recently adjudged to have not been properly constituted in accordance with the provisions of either land or forestry legislation (Forestry Commission, 2001).

Political Structures and Administrative Practice

Since 1951, Ghana has seen a variety of local government structures at district and subdistrict levels (Ayee, 2000). However, while the introduction and reform of these structures were always accompanied by rhetoric of participation and local influence, during the three decades following independence, they served more as centers of party organization and political patronage. Successive military and civilian governments have all to a greater or lesser extent been characterized by centralist policies assigning local representatives a role of "assisting" central-government-appointed administrators (Ayee, 1994, 2000; Crook, 1994; Harris, 1983; Haynes, 1991).

The centralization of political authority was accompanied by a fragmentation of the decision-making process at the center. As Harris (1983: 204, 212), commenting on the 1960s and 1970s, argues, "although . . . ministries claimed control over the minutiae of field agency programs their efforts were marked not only by ineffectiveness and lack of accountability, but by an absence of any sense of responsibility of the co-ordinated or comprehensive development of those areas in which their agencies operated. . . . [A]lthough . . . terms such as 'comprehensive rural development' . . . were common there is little evidence that much meaning attached to them."

These trends were reinforced by the initial inclusion of the Forestry Division within the Ministry of Agriculture.[14] For the Forestry Division, this meant that little or no coordination with other agencies was encouraged and no participation by the local population in the management of forest reserves was solicited. On the contrary, the general understanding of the state's prerogative to control land, as its property, meant that all scheduled rights accorded to the local population living close to the reserve (its formal legal owners) were ignored. The patrolling of forests and forest reserve boundaries remained a clear preoccupation, despite the lack of operational funds and limited personnel that plagued the Forestry Division during the 1960s.[15] The detailed schedules of admitted communal rights painstakingly established for a number of forest reserves in northern Ghana during the decade prior to independence was forgotten.

---

[14] See Ministry of Agriculture, Forestry Division 1960–68. NRG 9/4/14.

[15] See letters from the Forest Ranger, Nangodi to Acting Chief Forester, Navrongo, 14 May 1964 (Ref: 80/NR/63–64) and 14 July 1964 (Ref: 98/NR/63–64) District Forest Office, Bolgatanga, correspondence.

The actual dispossession of the local population was compounded by the promulgation of increasingly restrictive laws.[16] These rendered illegal all customary uses of the forest (collection of firewood, fruit harvesting, hunting, fishing, pasturing of animals, cultivation, harvest of timber for building purposes, etc.) and criminalized customary land use practices, such as the use of fire to clear crop debris or to prepare compound farms for planting.

The combination of authoritarian power, no accountability, de facto expropriation of forest land, and outlawing people's access to their property provided opportunities for heavy-handed policing of the reserves, for removal of illegal occupants, for issuing of on-the-spot fines, and for rent seeking. It would appear that the economic crises of the 1970s and 1980s rendered active policing of the reserves more difficult, and local, private, illicit negotiations over access became increasingly common.

The "Second Wave" of Decentralization

A long period of economic decline and political instability was not conducive to the establishment of a new system of local government in Ghana. Popular discontent and economic reforms eventually ushered in a "second wave" of decentralization as domestic political interests converged with the concerns of international finance institutions keen to downsize government.

The most recent decentralization initiatives in Ghana have witnessed a proliferation of actors combined with the maintenance of central government controls. They differ from "colonial decentralization" in terms of institutional fragmentation and the absence of effective fiscal decentralization. This has limited the political and fiscal autonomy of the district assemblies. The implementation of the new forest policy (Government of Ghana, 1994) espousing local and participatory management has been constrained in northern Ghana by the limited autonomy of deconcentrated regional and district forest offices, which remain divorced from the district assemblies.

Economic Decline, Political Instability, and Popular Discontent

Local government in Ghana was described in 1968 as being "in a state of chaos; the reputation of local authorities has reached its nadir."[17] The country was subsequently governed for two decades by different military regimes for all but two years (1979–81). This precluded the emergence of a new local government system, particularly during an era of economic decline. It

---

[16] Forest Protection Decree 1974 (NRCD 243); Control of Bushfires Law 1983 (PNDCL 46); Forest Protection (Amendment) Law 1986 (PNDCL 142); Control and Prevention of Bushfires Law 1990 (PNDCL 229).

[17] Greenwood Commission Report, 1968. Cited in Ayee (1994).

did not prevent, however, repeated attempts to "tweak" local government structures to gain influence through elected or appointed members of district councils. Efforts to reform local government and encourage rational management, planning, and development were largely unsuccessful (Ayee, 1994; Crook, 1994).

During this turbulent era, a number of local land use conflicts emerged between resource users and the Forestry Department in northern Ghana (Wardell, 2002). These concerned notably the management of the forest reserves and encompassed requests, inter alia, to release farmland within forest reserves;[18] to grant permits to fish;[19] to prevent elephant raiding of croplands bordering (and sometimes inside) the forest reserves; to investigate repeated outbreaks of fire;[20] and to allow seasonal grazing by transhumant herders inside the forest reserves and on peripheral farmlands. In several cases, these conflicts either have persisted to date[21] or have been exacerbated by the reversal of earlier agreements reached with the Forestry Department.[22]

Proliferation of Actors and Increased Dependence on External Funding

The current local government system in Ghana developed after the 1987 initiative to reintroduce district assemblies, a Local Government Law in 1988 (PNDCL 207), the 1992 Constitution, and the promulgation of a

---

[18] These were systematically rejected by the Forestry Department on the grounds that such requests were not in the "public interest." See, for example, "Appeal for release of portion of the FR for farming." Tallensi Youth Association letter, 25 November 1973, to the Conservator of Forests I/C, Northern and Upper Regions, Tamale (Ref: G.119.V.2/158, District Forest Office, Bolgatanga, correspondence).

[19] These were invariably granted subject to a number of restrictions. Permission was given, for example, to residents of Sekoti, Bongo-Bio, and Catholic Missions by the senior assistant conservator of forests throughout the period 1972–87. Ref: R.18/623, District Forest Office, Bolgatanga.

[20] Bush fires often damaged plantations established within forest reserves. Forestry Department reports have consistently viewed them as acts of arson, although the "offenders have not yet been found." See, for example, letters dated 19 March 1965 and 4 December 1975 from the Forest Ranger, Nangodi. District Forest Office, Bolgatanga, correspondence files (no ref. numbers).

[21] For example, a formal request to graze 1,500 cattle in the Kologo-Naga Forest Reserve (Navrongo District) submitted to the chief executive of the Kassena-Nankena District Assembly in February 2002 was rejected by the District Forest Manager on the grounds that "no suitable grazing areas remained within the FR."

[22] For example, "approved" farms within forest reserves were subject to confiscation by the Forestry Department as land outside demarcated plots was being cultivated "illegally" by farmers. "Rehabilitation of all forest lands cleared under the taungya system is the priority of the Department presently. No obstruction from any quarter (farmer or group of farmers) will thus be tolerated.... [T]he ... farms you have operating in the Red Volta West FR have been declared out of bounds to farmers retrospective from 1 January 1986 ... Anyone who contravenes this directive will be prosecuted under the P.N.D.C.L. 142." Letter from the district forest office, Bolgatanga to the Tongo Chief, 30 May 1986. See also letter from the district forest office, Bolgatanga to the Headman, Kanyonga, 16 July 1987 (Ref: R.18/378). District Forest Office, Boltaganta, correspondence.

new Local Government Act in 1993 (Act 462). This shift from a centralized state started as part of political reforms within, and in response to external pressures from without. The instruments promised pluralist political representation at the district level. However, as Ayee (2000: 147–49) argues, there has been a tendency of the district assemblies to centralize within their own boundaries and for assemblymen to usurp the power and functions of the area and village councils. During the virtually one-party reign of NDC (National Democratic Congress) in the 1990s assemblymen had decisive clout in many villages.

In practice, district assemblies are still characterized by being administratively deconcentrated; the decentralization process has "hollowed out" political authority at the local level. This has been exacerbated by the lack of effective decentralization of fiscal authority and, hence, the increasing reliance of local government on central government and/or external funding. District assemblies are now more dependent on central government assistance and/or external funding to meet their recurrent expenditure than they were in the 1960s.[23] This situation has left local authorities increasingly vulnerable to the vagaries of a large number of external "change agents," which have tended to channel support through centralized technical line ministries, such as ministries concerned with forestry and irrigation in particular.

The 1980s and 1990s witnessed a proliferation of externally funded forestry projects and programs in Ghana, born primarily out of concern for the "dwindling" timber resources in the South (Kotey et al., 1998). Many projects included components addressing forestry and land-related issues in northern Ghana. Most have been, and continue to be, centrally controlled by the Ministry of Lands and Forestry in Accra.

Maintaining Central Government Controls

Central government influence on local authorities remains significant. The exercise of *control* functions provides central powers with opportunities to monitor compliance by local authorities with national policies and development plans and programs, to promote the respect for minimum-defined standards, and to equalize taxable capacity and shift tax burdens. A number of different mechanisms are still employed to maintain central government control of Ghana's local government system (Eriksen, Naustdalslid, and Schou, 1999). These include the overwhelming dependence on central government for funding (staff salaries, ceded funds, and the District

---

[23] Estimates of the proportions of local authority recurrent expenditure met by central government (grants-in-aid and ceded revenues) vary from 40 percent (Greenwood, 1962) to 85 percent (Crook, 1994).

Assemblies Common Fund), staff and administrative controls, the complementary legislative doctrines of *ultra vires* and "statutory duties," and the exercise of oversight functions by the Regional Co-ordinating Councils. Civil servants, both centrally and locally, are often reluctant to acknowledge the authority of the assemblies. Ambiguities continue to influence the performance of both district chief executives and technical personnel deployed within the districts. Political autonomy has been grasped by the administration rather than by the elected councils. In essence, decentralization has been "imposed from above" without any significant local influence on policy making (Nugent, 1995).

Despite various institutional restructurings since 1980, the Forestry Department has maintained central government controls (first introduced during the colonial era) by continuing to issue standardized guidelines for the preparation of forest management plans (Forest Services Division, 1998; Rural Forestry Division, 1992) and prescriptive financial controls (Forestry Department, 1997). In addition, there have been isolated incidences of the Forestry Department's recourse to military intervention to evict illegal occupants of forest reserves following the resurgence of interest in artisanal mining of gold – so-called *galamsey* mining – in the 1990s.[24]

Notwithstanding the provisions of the Local Government Act in 1993 and the new Forest and Wildlife Policy adopted in 1994,[25] the relationship between the administratively deconcentrated Forest Services Division and the district assemblies remains contentious. Civil servants who are formally integrated in local government have continued to be part of nationally integrated bureaucratic hierarchies (Crook and Manor, 1998).

A New Breed of Forest Managers?

A number of significant political changes have taken place in Ghana since 1992 when the country returned to civilian rule and democratic elections were held for the first time since 1979. In 1996 a second peaceful election was held when the opposition won a substantial number of parliamentary seats. The ruling National Democratic Congress was ousted by the ballot box in December 2000 (Nugent, 2001). These sweeping political changes were supposedly matched by the scope and extent of the forest sector reforms implemented at the dawn of the new millennium. A Northern Operational Directorate in Tamale has overseen the operations of a new breed of regional

---

[24] Small-scale gold mining occurred in Nangodi, North Mamprusi (present-day Upper East Region) during the 1930s (Hunter, 1966; Wardell, 2002).

[25] The new Forest and Wildlife Policy of 1994 "promotes public participation in the share of benefits and responsibilities in forest management" (Government of Ghana, 1994: foreword, sections 3.2.1, 3.3, and 5.5).

and district "forest managers" representing the Forest Services Division in the three northern regions of Ghana. A clear preoccupation of the new government was to improve service delivery and to secure greater integration of technical line ministry personnel within the district assemblies.

In practice, however, organizational "cultures" have tended to prevail (Grindle, 1997) and forest management proposals either are contemporary repetitions of colonial interventions[26] or have been externally generated by central government and/or international financiers.[27] These generic state control initiatives may ultimately influence but have not to date fundamentally changed local governance systems and patterns of access to and use of woodland resources. This highlights the burgeoning gap between the "world on paper" (Hawkins, 2002) – with clearly discernible historical precedents – and the "unseen" world of local resource users. Resource users living in communities peripheral to the forest reserves continue their long-established land use systems (such as dry season vegetable and tobacco cultivation along riverbanks) and resource-extraction practices (e.g., collection of grasses for thatching, rafters, honey, medicinal plants, and bushfire-group hunting festivals).

Contemporary Decentralization and Participation

The more recent decentralization initiatives in Ghana have resulted in district assemblies that remain weak. They have little influence over the policies of the ministries now formally placed under local government. The district assemblies differ from the district, urban, and local councils established under "colonial decentralization" in terms of institutional fragmentation and the deteriorating conditions of fiscal decentralization. The promulgation of the Local Government Act in 1993 was fueled by the convergence of international and national interests in downsizing government and promoting decentralized, local natural-resource management. This culminated in a form of diffuse political authority within the district assemblies. It has also resulted in a proliferation of actors at all levels of government while maintaining (or reinforcing) central government controls. The implementation

---

[26] For example, a draft "Mini-Strategic Plan for Red Volta West Forest Reserve" presented to Andrew Wardell and myself in February 2002 by the district forest manager in Bolgatanga District includes verbatim, the Reserve Settlement Commission's Proceedings and Judgement, 7 June 1955 (Schedule II: Communal Admitted Rights). Draft in private possession.

[27] The Forestry Commission introduced three proposals to develop management of forest reserves by promoting private-sector investment in plantations, particularly of "degraded" areas; comanagement for nontimber forest products and watershed management, and contracting out for mining and other land uses (Forestry Commission, 2001). The recently launched Northern Savanna Biodiversity Conservation Project includes proposals to manage forest reserves as "corridor biodiversity reserves" along, for example, the Red and White Volta Rivers (World Bank, 2001).

of the new forest policy espousing local and participatory management has been constrained by the limited autonomy of deconcentrated regional and district forest offices, which remain divorced from the organs of local government.

The two waves of decentralization (colonial and contemporary) have both been characterized by externally driven interests, the substantive role of central government institutions and the dependence on "external" funding. The Forestry Department (now the Forest Services Division) has maintained its distinctive identity as part of a nationally integrated bureaucratic hierarchy. This has, furthermore, been underpinned by the symbolic and repeated preparation of "scientific" management plans prepared and owned by the state. These plans have, nevertheless, neither served as tools of management nor provided entry points to facilitate consultation with resource users.

Some skepticism has, understandably, been expressed about recent changes in forest policies in West Africa that aim to promote the transfer of the management of forest resources to different user groups without specifying what is to be transferred and how (Ribot, 1995). It has been suggested that the management of dry tropical woodlands in West Africa often remains marked by a paralyzing dualism – an "official system" versus several "traditional systems" – due to the decreasing level of responsibility of the local resource users themselves (Onibon, 2000). However, a number of recent studies have also started to question the long-standing assumption that exclusive management by a single entity (either the "expert authority" of a national forest service or the "indigenous wisdom" of a local community) will necessarily assure sustainable management of the forest resources (Abraham and Platteau, 2001; Dubois, 1997).

Forestry departments throughout West Africa have been instrumental in constructing the conceptual dichotomy between the realms of the "modern" and "scientific" approach to forest management and the "traditional" and deemed "destructive" use of a broad range of woodland resources. This dichotomy has veiled complex historical, ecological, sociocultural, and local government realities, however. Ordinances, bylaws, regulations, the judgments of Reserve Settlement Commissioners, management plans, and "public awareness" campaigns have not significantly changed the behavior of rural communities with regard to their modes of access to and traditional uses of savannah woodlands in northern Ghana, but they have conditioned their interactions with public authorities in this domain.

Actual Governance of Forest Resources

The actual governance of resources of the forest reserves in northern Ghana differs significantly from declared policies. Not only do the newer policies of the 1990s so far have limited impact on the ground in terms of actual activities as well as in terms of instilling trust between the local population and the Forestry Service. The actual governance also differs from the policies of the previous decades where control, exclusion, and punishment were the declared order of the day. In reality, a much more subtle, negotiated, and politically sensitive form of arrangement has prevailed and prevails today. The following section briefly outlines the role of the main stakeholders, and a case illustrates how access to the forest reserve areas is governed on the margins of the law and in the heart of local politics.

Stakeholders to Forest Resources in Upper East Region

As we have seen in the preceding chapters, the customary offices in the Upper Regions (East and West) comprise the two complementary institutions, the chief and the earthpriest, the office of custodian of the Earth. The chief is the political authority, and while his consent is required for strangers to settle in his territory, land cannot be allocated to the stranger without the consent of the earthpriest. In theory, the earth priest allocates unused land to a new settler. However, little land in the Upper East has not been cultivated, and to access land thus possessed by a family, the family must agree and the earthpriest must approve of the transfer.

The land along the Red and White Voltas, now reserved as the Red Volta East, Red Volta West, and White Volta reserves, is not pristine forest. In fact, before reservation in the 1950s some of the land was used for cultivation and, in particular along the riverbanks, tobacco was grown. Also, land was not without owners. Throughout what is now the reserves, one finds abandoned dwellings and shrines to which earthpriest and family heads used to sacrifice and continue to perform various rites to this day (Wardell, Reenberg, and Tøttrup, 2003). The land in the reserve is not an inert space but a place dotted with signifiers of meaning, and it constitutes a mosaic of traditional areas within the "protected area." Apart from the concrete pillars put in place by the Forest Service demarcating the reserves, other markers testify to historical use and property rights. One set of markers does not necessarily neutralize the other. The history of land alienation to create the forest reserves remains very much a part of the local social memory.

While considered illegal by the Forestry Service and the public administration in general, the use of forest resources has throughout remained tempting, in particular to the communities that used to control them. Hence, over the years many opportunities of use have been seized, negotiated, tolerated, contested, disrupted, and denied according to circumstances. Informants generally concurred that, though penalties were high, the risk of being caught, fined, and denied rights outright seemed to decline along with the economic crisis from the mid-1970s. Consequently, today access to forest resources follows a pattern that combines traditional customs and situational adjustment to local politics and power games. Cultivation of cereals or tobacco inside the reserve thus requires that the landowner – that is, the person or family who historically has owned the piece of land in question – as well as the earthpriest give consent. However, as the operation is considered illegal, the chief of the nearest village is also systematically approached. "Approach" is generally a euphemism for a customary payment for a granted audience, and payment is made according to the risk of "being discovered" by the Forestry Service and the protection the chief may provide.

In the villages studied, another political figure – the assemblyman – was equally, systematically, involved in land allocation. During the 1990s when NDC had a firm grip of the district assemblies, the NDC assemblymen wielded considerable power. Consequently, he also had to approve of the use of the forest land for cultivation. As he was able to mobilize or pacify the staff of the Forestry Service, he could not be left out of the equation. During the 1980s and 1990s, illegal fishing with the use of DDT became a problem.[28] It was debated in the district assemblies, and it was suggested that the assemblymen together with the chiefs should appoint local overseers to keep watch over the rivers. Obviously, these people would have to be already operating close to the rivers within the reserves to be effective, either cultivating tobacco on the banks, cultivating cereals nearby, or indeed fishing themselves. The various assemblymen had small "Authority Notes" typed, authorizing the holder to "keep watch" (Figure 7.1). Strictly speaking, these informal notes did not authorize anybody to do anything they were not already, as citizens, allowed to do – keep watch. However, the local understanding of the meaning of this note was that the holder was authorized to cultivate or fish within the reserve.[29]

Thus, forestry officers were presented with such notes when apprehending people, and while refusing the formal validity of these notes, they generally recognized their political currency. Consequently, rather than fining and evicting people risking a confrontation with the assemblyman and the political party in power, forestry officers would often turn a blind eye while lining their pockets. This system of access seemed to function only if, from time to time, someone was indeed fined, evicted, and had his temporary dwelling in the reserve destroyed and his crop burned down by the forestry officers (see, e.g., Asare, 1993). This would remind people of the illegality of their undertaking and the necessity of negotiating deals of access. What is striking is that this "system" was generally acknowledged by all respondents – farmers and people in authority alike.[30] They would thus, independently of each other, describe the tolerated access interrupted by

---

[28] DDT, bought from cotton farmers, is put in the water. The fish die indiscriminately and are scooped out and sold.

[29] Such "authorization" could also cover collection of firewood on a smaller and larger scale.

[30] Villagers, assemblymen, other politicians, chiefs, earthpriests, and forestry agents all concurred in painting this picture while, carefully, referring to themselves as the odd exception.

AUTHORITY NOTE

Upon·ˈauthority given to the chiefs by the District
Assembly in connection with the polution of rivers,
I authorise Mr.:................................
to keep watch over the ....

.................river(s) against any polution.

   Notify the chief on activities of the above as
well as (galamsey) operators within ~~your~~ jurisdiction.

                     ....
                     CHIEF NAWABU ANYORIGI
                     AKURUBILLA.
                     (KUSANABA TRADITIONAL AREA).

WITNESS:-

....
FRANCIS ATINDOGO
  ASSEMBLYMAN,
(KUSANABA ELEC. AREA).

Figure 7.1. Assemblyman's Authority Note

momentary high-profiled enforcement as collusion or a shared understanding among authorities.

   An indication of the general knowledge, acceptance, and even some
degree of approval of ordinary people's access to the forest reserves was
when the district chief executive of the Bawku East District managed to
convince the Agricultural Support Project of the district to equip a group
of illegal tobacco farmers with a diesel pump for irrigation in preparation
for his campaign to run for Parliament in the district in 1998. This also
points to an element of popular accountability that developed with democratization. Attempts to crack down on farmers, and in particular on chiefs or
assemblymen, became an increasingly untenable option for authorities with
political ambition. Normally, fines to chiefs or notables are not considered
personal but are passed on to community members, who can hardly refuse
to show loyalty but see it as an unwelcome taxation. Therefore, the district
chief executives and the members of Parliament were eager to intervene to
iron out contentious issues. The following case illustrates the operations of

the actual governance of access to the forest reserves along the rivers in the Upper East Region.

A Case of Tobacco Farming

Along the White Volta tobacco has been grown as long as people can recall. Land is allocated by the local earthpriest to a trusted person, a so-called tobacco chief, who then allocates the plots to the interested villagers. After harvest, the earthpriest receives a small portion of the produce and channels some of it to the chief of the area. The farmers do not pay much because, as locals, they have a legitimate claim to access the land. This was, however, what triggered a conflict in 2000. The chief's ploy was to facilitate cultivation of land by "strangers," and concomitantly to cut out the earthpriest, thereby increasing "his own" fees. He then dismissed the earthpriest and his "tobacco chief" and settled people with a weaker claim for a higher rent. What encouraged the chief to take this step was, first, the rising value of the crop. Second, however, the state divestiture of land following the 1979 Constitution was not very clear about to whom land was restored – chiefs, earthpriests, or actual land users – and the vagueness could possibly be exploited by the literate chief against an illiterate earthpriest. However, the change in land allocation caused a fight between old and new tobacco growers, someone fired a gun, and someone was wounded. Suddenly, the police became involved, and it was no longer a small matter but something public authorities had to deal with. The dilemma for the police, as well as the Forestry Service and the local politicians such as the district chief executive, was that it would not be possible, officially, to evict one group while letting the other group stay because the presence of either was illegal. On the other hand, evicting all was equally out of the question considering the political implications. Hence, a series of informal negotiations was undertaken.

The first thing to deal with, apart from the man who was arrested for the shooting,[31] was that the earthpriest had reported the chief to the police for having caused the disturbance. To report this to the police, the earthpriest had first passed through the paramount chief of Bawku, the village chief's superior. Subsequently, the police contacted the district chief executive and, encouraged by the paramount chief, offered to view the matter as a civil rather than a criminal offense providing that the district chief executive would engage personally in conciliatory efforts. The earthpriest was not inclined to relinquish his complaint, but the district chief executive persuaded him to drop a formal suit if he could sway the paramount

---

[31] He was later released, but it was impossible for Andrew Wardell and myself to ascertain what the legal consequences may have been.

chief of Bawku to summon the village chief. This would dent the prestige of the latter because the relevant public would interpret this outcome as an official reprimand. The village chief was indeed summoned, and later meetings were held in the village with the participation of the chief, his elders, and the earthpriest, some of his trusted associates, the district chief executive, and the assemblyman of the area. The immediate result was that the earthpriest's "tobacco chief" was restored on the land, while the chief's "strangers" were denied access in 2000. During the cropping season of 2000, however, consultations continued at odd intervals between the earthpriest and the chief, with the brokerage of the assemblyman and the district chief executive. Hence, in 2001 the earthpriest found space to accommodate the chief's "strangers" in addition to his original ninety farmers.

In conclusion, the earthpriest retained his prerogative to allocate land; the chief failed in his attempt to usurp it; the paramount chief, the district chief executive, and the assemblyman all furthered their image as sagacious and constructive men of office. The police exited from the affair at an early stage, and while the Forestry Service was not ignorant of the affair, it was effectively cut out from its management. Meanwhile, the number of illegal farmers increased.

The Micropolitics of Access

Access to land and resources in the forest reserves does not come close to the prescriptions enshrined in either law or the policies concerning their management. However, the laws and policies are not insignificant. The restrictive laws and powers of the Forestry Department have provided a context for monetary and political rent seeking for other political agents when protecting or shielding the exercise of rights that people were granted by customary authorities and which were formally recognized by the colonial administration through the "Proceedings and Judgments" prepared by Reserve Settlement Commissioners in the 1950s.

Extraction of rent is not a simple matter, however. Although access to land in the reserve is considered illegal, the nonetheless tolerated access is not unstructured. The extraction of rent follows a complicated pattern. On the one hand, the contours of a customary land tenure system with land users and the land-allocating earthpriest are quite clear; they mirror the tenure system outside of the forest areas. However, as access to land in this area is not *considered* a right but considered a tolerated delinquency, legality, legitimacy, and propriety are intensely negotiated – negotiated between unequals, that is. Thus, as recourse to police or formal and recorded treatment of the affair would jeopardize the economic interest of many and upset the relative political calm, it has been dealt with informally at the margins of the law. Here, the legitimacy and power of the various political authorities and the propriety of the committed acts were important for the outcome. The cultivation of tobacco was considered improper by no one; it was quite normal and accepted. That was not the issue. Obviously, there existed two opposing lines of argument concerning the access to the forest. However, some actors, particularly local politicians and government officials, would alternate between the two arguments according to circumstance and audience. On the one hand, state authorities (the Forestry Department, assemblymen, and the district chief executive) were all familiar with the idea that the forest must be preserved to secure the waterways and ultimately the production of hydroelectric power at the Akosumbo dam in the south. Thus, people should be denied access to the resources in the higher interest of the nation. This line of argument is freely rehearsed in the offices of the Forest Department, in speeches by politicians, and by nongovernmental organizations, which give it a "wild-life preservation" twist. On the other hand, farmers, chiefs, and earthpriests, as well as the very same assemblymen and administrators who condemn people's presence in the reserve, share the opposite line of argument – namely, that people who accessed the reserve were not criminals but ordinary folk in honorable pursuit of a livelihood. While lower-ranking agents of the Forest Department never were heard using these arguments, it is interesting that other officials would argue along those lines in certain circumstances. Thus, there was not a neat separation of discourses between state and nonstate actors but rather an adjustment of argument to circumstance.

When the local chief challenged the authority of the earthpriest to allocate land, however, it was a serious breach of established practice and etiquette. Thus, within the realm of illegality there is a need to distinguish between what is proper and what is not. While the intervention of the district chief executive and the paramount chief relied on and reconfirmed their legitimacy, their range of options was not unlimited. They had to "rule" in concordance with what was commonly accepted (namely, that people could access the reserve) in order to contain the affair within an informal realm and hence their reach. Otherwise, they would have appeared incompetent and might have forfeited whatever economic and political rent they could harvest from the tobacco farmers. Thus, these authorities could not insist on the enforcement of the formal rules, but had to stay within a legitimate discourse to maintain future political and economic rent.

Social processes are not solely significant for change; they are equally significant for the reproduction of status, rights, and sociopolitical structures. This particular case falls into the latter category. Thus, when we look at the outcome of these local tribulations, it can be argued that nothing changed. However, the entire process – from the local chief's challenge of the earthpriest's authority to the informal involvement of local politicians and paramount chiefs and the subsequent negotiations to accommodate "new" farmers – constitutes an active reproduction and reconfirmation of effective rights of access and circumscribed positions of authority. In fact, it is exactly through such continuous, repeated negotiations that the actual tenure system is constructed and reconfigured. Thus, while the rules are negotiable, the system is not necessarily unstable. It may, as in this case, be reproduced, reconfirmed, and institutionalized as roles and rights are rehearsed.

It is worth noting that this case by no means is unique. During the research, cases also emerged concerning collection of thatching grass, maize farming, charcoal burning, hunting, and (not least) *galamsey* gold mining, where access was negotiated informally. For the latter, several sizable informal mining towns with colloquial names such as Kumase and Soweto can be found within the reserves. Interviews with a retired district magistrate with more than thirty years of service underscored the system of tolerated illegality as he let out that only three cases concerning the illegal use of forest resources had actually been formally conducted by the court system in the area of the Upper East Region since independence. Moreover, all three had been dropped before a formal court settlement was ever made.

Conclusion

Much of the recent policy literature advocating decentralized, local natural-resource management in northern Ghana tends to ignore that decentralization is not new in the area and has interesting precedents. Although the progenitor of the "second wave" of decentralized governance differs from its colonial antecedent, it is still distinguished by being externally driven. The justification for decentralization has in both instances been a combination of ideal and economic considerations. Ideas of public hearings for the Reserve Settlement Commissions (then) and participatory management (proposed now) combined with efforts to compensate for lack of staff and other resources (then and now). On the receiving end, the local actors have had to adapt to these changes.

A significant difference between the two waves lies in the context. Contemporary decentralization is accompanied by increasing central government and line ministerial control, hollowing out local people's participation and control. Complementary political efforts have over time strengthened central government and line ministries. This has provided the Forestry Department with the means of offsetting local people's ability to enjoy the rights with which they have been enfranchised. Thus, in a peculiar convoluted way, the Forestry Department through the establishment of forest reserves first managed to exclude people from access to their property. It is worth remembering that the reserves were never formally expropriated and hence have remained the property of their original owners. The operations and practice of the Forestry Department in the 1960s and 1970s furthermore meant that the remaining limited rights to access, established in the "Proceedings and Judgments," were denied people. Thus, despite rights enshrined in reserve settlement agreements, the Forestry Department was capable of effectively making rules to the contrary. This did not mean effective exclusion of people from the forest, but it shifted their access to the realm of illegality (see also Thompson, 1975).

The actual governance of access to forest resources reserved by public authorities puts the ambitions of past and future governments into perspective. Laws, regulations, and policies do not determine access and use of resources as such, but erect a structure of opportunities for negotiation of these rights. In such a context, government institutions do not necessarily operate in unison but often constitute complementary and competing actors. They may use central government policy and directives to bolster their authority locally or employ their local clout or knowledge to undo them. The result is neither a coherent policy implementation nor a complete disregard of law and policy. The discretionary and capricious enforcement of laws and regulations provides possibilities for economic and political rent seeking. This depends on the possibility of invoking severe rules and punishment, the relaxation of which must be paid for. Thus, it depends on the commonly perceived illegality of people's resource use. People's ignorance of the extent of their property and use rights provides scope for local authorities to define current practices as illegal despite what is enshrined in official reserve documents. In the concrete case of northern Ghana, it would seem that a tacit understanding between certain public servants and local politicians prevails; access should not be prevented but should be kept illegal in order for various rents to be extracted.

New policies suggest that the current mode of governance should be reversed, but it remains to be seen whether local authorities will relinquish their privileged positions and whether local people will trust the declared changes.

8

Small Dams and Fluid Tenure

Well, I happen to know that whenever you feel agitated and ambivalent, then you do indeed have something to write about.

Philip Roth, *Deception*

Introduction

Local communities and land tenure arrangements do not operate autonomously from the wider political structures of the state (see Mosse, 1997). Government schemes create junctures for people to reassert or to challenge the situation according to interests. Government regulation thus plays an important yet subtle role in the local production of land rights and wealth; although much policy is frustrated by circumvention of rules and regulation, it may well influence and entrench the social stratification. In other words, it affects the forms of property and the production of social classes and stratification.

Public and private interests compete for resources in various ways in northern Ghana. People's struggles to establish and solidify rights and rules are constantly challenged by others' efforts to remake or replace them. The result is that particular resources are negotiated into a texture of composite property relations that defy simple public-private distinctions. The dynamic tension between reproduction and change in this negotiation intensifies when the stakes go up. Small dam schemes present particularly tense situations. The construction of the irrigation infrastructure increases the value of property, and the very operation involving public investment occasions a renegotiation of land rights in ways in which government has only partial control.

Obviously, one of the issues at stake is what policies on irrigation mean to ownership. Ownership is never absolute or stable (see Chapter 1). Hence, when in this chapter reference is made to "the owner," it is a shorthand for the person who has hereditary rights to a piece of land, who can bequeath it to kin, and who can let others have temporary-use rights through either a formal lease or an unwritten agreement. Normally all such transactions will be overseen and accepted by the earthpriest.

The construction of small dams in small valleys for off-season irrigation by the government in the Upper East Region sparked intense micropolitical competition as well as significant changes in land tenure. Most dams were constructed from the 1950s to the 1970s in order to provide alternative income for otherwise rain-fed agriculture dependent communities. During the time of construction, the state was still the custodian of all land. This meant that the government could place dams where it found it technically suitable, without much consultation with landowners. Land was virtually expropriated by government for the placement of the reservoir, the dam, and other infrastructure. State control over land was assumed by most people, and any protest by disfavored landowners was brushed aside by the Ministry of Agriculture. Government agents redistributed land according to their plans.

With the divestiture of land to its original owners after the 1979 Constitution, however, small dam projects now required the creation of Water Users' Associations (WUA). Land could be leased from the owner by the District Assembly, and then from the District Assembly by the WUA. The paradox is that before, when land was *not* legally acquired by government, government *in fact* attempted to control it. Owners had little formal control over who got access to an irrigated plot on *their* land, so they used a number of strategies to compensate. After divestiture following passage of the 1979 Constitution, a formal legal structure was set up for the leasing of land from owners through the District Assembly to the user. But landowners were able to evade leasing their land to the government and to allocate to themselves considerable irrigated plots and access to the public infrastructure. This conundrum of government control over private land before 1979 and the more recent private control over public infrastructure can be understood only if the transactions are seen in the broader context of general government control over land before 1979 and private control after divestiture. Any policy that may have worked to the contrary effect was either ignored or diluted.

The political struggles over access play out in a number of ways. The controversial issues of land control between landowners and other land users affects all sites of small dams in the Upper East, and the chapter first offers a general template for the issue at hand, and how efforts to develop small-scale irrigation had implications for the tenure system and social stratification. However, local circumstances as well as economic and political opportunities set the stage for the actual negotiations. The ensuing two cases illustrate the breadth of such micronegotiations and how development efforts were frustrated in the encounter, as multiple actors attempted to adjust to a situation and make the most of their options.[1]

Private Property and Public Infrastructure

From the mid-1950s to the mid-1960s, a series of small dams was constructed in villages throughout what is now the Upper East. Population density and hence increasing land shortage in the area made dry-season irrigation a welcome opportunity to increase productivity and offer income possibilities.[2] At the time of the initial allocation, land was officially distributed by the agricultural officer from the Irrigation Development Authority (IDA) under the Ministry of Agriculture. Each of the landowners of the fields that were now to be turned into irrigated plots or given up for the reservoir was allocated some three to four plots. The remaining plots of twenty-five by twenty-five yards were distributed among other villagers according to the agricultural officer's estimation of who would be able to cultivate it properly. In reality, however, most of the land was allocated to relatives of the landowners. Thus the status of the plots was somewhat ambiguous; whereas the landowner would consider land allocation an internal family matter, the new beneficiaries would consider the land theirs, granted them by government. In order to demonstrate his control over the land, the landowner would collect the money for water levies among his "tenants" and pay them to the IDA. This way, no direct relation was established between the land user and the government agency. Often the fee would be paid by the landholder to the owner in kind (generally onion seeds), further obscuring the linkage between the landholding, the government agency, and the monetary fee.

Land users, however, often resisted giving up their plots in the rainy season. In principle, when a plot holder had harvested his crop, the land would revert into an ordinary rain-fed field to be cropped by the landowner. But, as the fertilizer used on the irrigated crops still has a residual effect on the rain-fed crops, dry-season farmers had an interest in using the small plot for rain-fed crops as well. Obviously, not all tenants were in a position to secure the year round utilization of their plot. In general, family members

[1] This chapter is based on case studies of fourteen villages and small dams in the Upper East Region from late 2001 to early 2004. Interviews were conducted with chiefs and earthpriests, with groups of landowners and groups of tenants, with agricultural field officers and superior staff, with representatives of nongovernmental organizations and the Diocese's Development Office in Bolgatanga, with opinion leaders and local politicians, and with staff from the Regional Lands Commissioners Office. Dams and dugouts are used for watering cattle and for fishing in addition to irrigation, but this chapter focuses on the latter activity and the related issues.

[2] From 1950 around 220 small dams have peppered the region (Andanye, 1995).

of the landowner would better resist handing over the land in the rainy season, which led landowners in general to prefer "strangers" over family as tenants at the later extension of the dams in the 1990s. Not only were "strangers" willing to pay more than kin; they would actually pay something to the landowner, because "they are easy to sack from the plot" in case of default.[3]

As land was vested in the government, the government, through the IDA, was responsible for land allocation. The general principle laid out was that allocation should take place annually. No plot holder could expect to farm the same plot year after year. However, reallocation of plots by the IDA took place only in cases where water levies were not paid – and even then, only rarely.[4] Thus, in the dam sites investigated, the initial land allocation overall had remained the same; although tenants paid their water levies through the landowner, they considered their rights to the plots as permanent and irrevocable. It is considered "government land," and the idiom of "government land" made any individual owner's attempt to reclaim his property inconceivable. The landowners, however, considered it an undue appropriation of rights by tenants to whom the owners had provided access to land on a less permanent basis. Thus, for the tenant *getting access* to a plot depended on the acceptance and choice of the landowner, while the *endurance* and *expansion* of the right from something temporary to something virtually permanent seemed to be secured by the fact that land was in principle vested in government and landowners had no practical recourse to challenge this.

The benefits of small-scale irrigation were short-lived, however. Poor maintenance, and in many cases a complete lack of it, resulted in a state of disrepair as evidenced by eroded dam walls, inoperative spillways, and siltation of the dams. Thus, in the 1980s virtually all small dams in the Upper East were underperforming. Siltation of the reservoirs meant that the water retention capacity was reduced, as were the irrigable area and the cropping season as a consequence.

In 1992 the Ministry of Agriculture engaged in a Land Conservation and Small Holder Rehabilitation Project (LACOSREP) funded by the International Foundation for Agricultural Development (IFAD). Some forty-four dams and dugouts throughout the Upper East were selected for rehabilitation. This included desilting of the reservoirs, repairing and often extending

---

[3] Interviews with villagers in Binduri, 3, 5, and 8 November 2002; Paga Nania, 12 and 15 March 2004; Baare, 1 November 2002; Zanlerigu, 4, 6, and 11 November 2002. For an analysis of owner-tenant relations and the aspect of kinship in small-scale irrigation in Burkina Faso, see Saul (1993).

[4] Interviews with Regional Director of the Ministry of Agriculture, Roy Ayariga, 12 March and 12 November 2002; 16 and 30 March 2004.

the dam walls, repairing the canals, protecting the catchment area. The philosophy was one of participation in and "ownership" of the project. This last element turned out to be more than mere development rhetoric.

With the 1979 Constitution, in all instances where government had not legally acquired the land according to the State Lands Act (Act 125, 1962), land was to be returned to the owner. None of the land seized for the construction of small dams in northern Ghana was ever legally acquired, and therefore the public infrastructure was, legally speaking, sitting on private lands.[5]

Consequently, the Ministry of Agriculture was no longer entitled as a government agency to allocate land to producers or even to repair infrastructure sitting on someone's property without his consent. In addition, the ministry was disinclined to make huge investments merely for the benefit of owners, who would no doubt lease out plots with a considerable profit. Legal advice was solicited, and a new institutional arrangement was developed. Local government in the form of the district assemblies would enter into a leasehold agreement with the landowners, thus taking over the land for a definite period of time. The district assemblies should then, in turn, lease the land registered as cooperatives to members of the Water Users' Association, who were granted legal status to engage in contracts. In most cases, the landowners would be members of the Water Users' Association and thus would lease land from themselves, as it were, but all members of the association would in principle enjoy equal protection of their use rights whether owners or not (Dery, 1998).

This arrangement appeared very neat to the Ministry of Agriculture and to the district assemblies. However, there were only rather modest incentives for the landowners to relinquish their newly "returned" lands to the District Assembly and subsequently to the Water Users' Association. In fact, it would appear that the landowners could be motivated only if leasing of the land was a condition for the rehabilitation of the dams, reservoirs, and other infrastructure. With no lease agreement, the dam would not be repaired, and no one would benefit. Yet because of the huge funding available from IFAD, the Ministry of Agriculture did not have the patience to settle the paper work of lease contracts before physical activity could be demonstrated to the donor. Consequently, rehabilitation was initiated with the hope of rearranging the property questions along the way.[6] However, the very reason that such complicated lease arrangements were necessary was the divestiture of land from 1979. Consequently, few landowners were inclined

[5] Interview with Regional Lands Commissioner, B. S. Nyari, 5 March 2002 and 9 March 2004. See also Dery, 1998, section 2.4. (See also Chapter 3.)

[6] Interview with Regional Director of the Ministry of Agriculture, Roy Ayariga, 16 and 30 March 2004.

to surrender newly acquired rights enshrined in the Constitution to anyone. In some cases, leases were prepared between the District Assembly and the earthpriest as the landowner, but this was generally considered something of an oddity by villagers. While the earthpriest may be respected as the allodial titleholder, nothing seems to empower him to lease land already occupied to someone else. Such lands can be transferred only at the behest of the landowner and with the approval of the earthpriest.

The result of the repair and rehabilitation of the dams was the emergence of various tenure arrangements in the dam areas, with a notable difference between the land made irrigable during the *first* land management scheme and land that was included into the schemes only *after* the LACOSREP project. In the first areas, the following system emerged. Without a leasing agreement, landowners and their "tenant relatives" who had cultivated the initially irrigated land simply took up farming the same lands as before, reviving the tension between owner and tenant over whether the latter should pay rent for the land to the former or merely the water levy to the Water Users' Association. Landowners, now having ownership restored with the 1979 and 1992 constitutions, had an interest in having it recognized, but tenants insisted that the land had been given to them by the government when it was "government land." However, in most cases, this tension was overcome by the groups' common interest in not relinquishing any land to the newly formed Water Users' Association and hence other farmers. Consequently, the concerned lands had been apportioned to their respective users once and had since then been held permanently, and with time such lands had developed into hereditary property for the tenants.

In the newly developed areas the situation was different but equally muddied. In some cases, the owners of the land connected to the extension of the project – often the same landowners as in the first section – flatly refused to formally hand over full land control to the Water Users' Association. But because the association was promoted by the Ministry of Agriculture, some form of compromise was reached. Repairs and extension help depended, after all, on amicable relations with the authorities. In general, landowners would agree to hand over land and land allocation provided that they themselves were ensured substantial plots. In fact, in this way most of the owners were granted plots large enough for them to sublet. This time around, however, the landowners I talked to all preferred to sublet to non-kin and "strangers," that is, people from outside the village. In practice, this arrangement was ensured by a tacit understanding with the Water Users' Association executives. The landowner would come up with a list of five to ten names for land allocation, letting the executives understand that allocation to these "strangers" would be the "price" for peacefully ceding the rest of the land for allocation among other WUA members during the dry season. The new tenants would equally be made to understand that their access to a plot hinged on the recommendation of the owner, and without it, the Water Users' Association would probably allocate the land to someone else. Moreover, water levies were to be paid through the owner, who also made sure that the farmer did not cultivate the same plot for many years, thus building up a claim. Hence, the new tenants found themselves in a rather precarious situation, with weak claims to the land they tilled. The rest of the land was allocated to villagers through the Water Users' Association.

The competition between landowners and the Water Users' Association is often more formal than real. A survey shows that 44 percent of concerned landowners were members of the associations and 20 percent were members of the executive (Nyari, 2002). Moreover, as the members of the association shared an interest with landowners in tenure security, a consensus about the "folly" of rotation of plot access soon developed in many dam sites. As land users were able to hold on to the same plot year after year over the past decade, landholding gradually transformed from annual to permanent rights, exactly as in the early irrigation areas. The degree of control grew to encompass the right to rent out and bequeath the land, while long-term leases and outright sales remain to be seen.

The development of the actual and practical property relations is ironic. In the initially managed areas, land, while the property of landowners, was allocated to others through government intervention. And the general understanding of land as "government land" meant that the new land users managed to hold on to it. The process amounts to expropriation and reallocation of land to new landholders with permanent and transferable rights. However, the government idea of rotational landholding stumbled on the united interests of all land users – owners and tenants alike – to build up enduring rights through permanent use of the same plot.

Land in the areas of extension, on the other hand, was supposed to be leased to local government, the District Assembly, and further to the Water Users' Association. However, most of the leases were never established, and the land remained under the control of the owners. Nonetheless, in most places the owners conceded to relinquish some of their land to the association on the condition that they had portions reserved for themselves that were sufficiently large for them to sublet. Thus, the owners could secure some land for themselves, while keeping formal their ownership as a bargaining chip to preserve actual use rights to some of it. Here again, the mutual interests of landowners and the other villagers to build up rights through permanent use made rotational plot allocation rare. The only exception was the second group of tenants of the landowners – strangers to the village – who so far have failed to build up stronger rights. Thus, this weakest group remained marginal, although policies had been designed to give it a relatively better deal. The role of the Water Users' Association became restricted to the allocation of water in the irrigation system and to the collection of water levies.

The small-dam schemes demonstrate that tenure systems transform in nonlinear ways. Although government interventions have significant effects, seemingly trivial actions by individuals can undermine state policy, as people pursue their interests with whatever institutional opportunities are available. The irony is that the frustration of government policy was done by a social group – landowners – recently "reenfranchised" by constitutional change to exercise property rights in ways that were prohibited prior to 1979. Thus, government control of land before the 1979 Constitution led to de facto expropriation, and land allocated to new users during that period was not recoverable by the owners after divestiture. On the other hand, infrastructure that was to be awarded equitably to villagers was de facto privatized, as land – crucial for accessing the benefits of the infrastructure – was returned to and remained under the control of landowners after 1979.

As I studied the overall development of property relations in the areas of small-scale irrigation in the Upper East, I encountered numerous instances of conflicts where political processes outside the village played a significant role in the outcomes. Villagers would engage with political forces of another magnitude, and political players in Bolga or other centers would have an important area in which to manifest their influence.

Landowners, Stranger-Farmers, and Locals in the Village of Pongo

In the village of Pongo, some ten miles from Bolgatanga, a dam constructed in 1960 was repaired and extended in 2000.[7] In connection with this, a Water Users' Association was formed, and a set of bylaws was established prohibiting stranger-farmers.[8] When the dam was first repaired, the village chief – the most prominent member of the Water Users' Association – wanted to reallocate the recovered sixty plots as well as the some of the extra land, which was now irrigable. Moreover, he wanted "allocation fees" for his service, claiming to be the traditional landowner of all lands in the village. The chief had recently been enskinned following a protracted and

---

[7] Names of places and persons in this section are changed for the sake of anonymity. To my interlocutors, acknowledgment by name would be an embarrassment. Moreover, some of the most conspicuous features of the two cases have been modified in order to make identification of actual places, persons, and events difficult.

[8] Excerpt of bylaws: "Plots shall be allocated strictly for ONLY farmers within the project catchment area. Any farmer who shall lease out his/her plot of land to someone else for monetary gains shall loose the plot for re-allocation" (Bye laws for Pongo, no date but probably 2000). Material in private possession.

costly campaign, and this request for fees appeared as a welcome opportunity
to recover some of his expenses.

The farmers who used to cultivate the plots did not have the patience
for this kind of operation, though, and just went back to the plots they
used to cultivate, leaving some few new plots for allocation. Villagers, and
in particular those belonging to the gates that had recently lost out to
the chief, saw the idea of an "allocation fee" as an undue claim effectively
symbolizing the chief's appropriation of their land, whereas the chief saw
it as his prerogative to allocate his property to his subjects – what else
would be the purpose of having a chief as the chairman of the Water Users'
Association?[9] During a meeting at the dam site just before the dry season in
2001, the issue was debated. The leader of Pongo Youth Association, Philip
Anaho, pointed out that many villagers had put in labor for the dam repair,
and these villagers should be given access to the land without paying any
extra fees. Pongo Youth Association was mainly made up of the villages'
few intellectuals working in Bolga or other towns, such as Tamale, Kumase,
or Accra, and the young men in the village. Philip Anaho, who worked at
the Ministry of Education Regional Office and lived in Bolga, was able to
mobilize support behind his ideas and the chief had to renounce a formal
fee for the land allocation. His strong position in the village nevertheless
enabled him to receive token gratuities by most plot holders.

Soon after, however, another opportunity emerged as two entrepreneurs-
cum-farmers from Bolga approached the chief in order to get land by the
dam site for the cultivation of tomatoes and onions. The two entrepreneurs,
John Guinness and Serkin Ali, asked for large tracts of land, and as they
disposed of diesel pumps and hoses, they would be able to irrigate land
that would not otherwise be reached through gravitational irrigation. The
chief agreed, and an area larger than the existing sixty plots combined was
marked out for the two stranger-farmers. The land had not previously been
cultivated, and although no one contested the right of the chief to allocate
the land as such, the problem lay in the fact that, thanks to their diesel
pumps, the area was now irrigable, and such lands were not to be given to
outsiders. The farmers and the Pongo Youth Association gathered at the
dam site to discuss the situation, and it was agreed to approach the chief to
get him to "sack" the two strangers. Land should be reserved for the natives
of the village; this was even stated in the bylaws.

The chief responded with a three-tier argument. First, it was his right to
allocate land to whomever he chose regardless of any bylaws. Second, John
Guinness and Serkin Ali had already planted their seedlings, and it would

9 Interviews with the chief of Pongo, the Chairman of the Pongo Youth Association, and different
groups of farmers, 12, 13, and 18 March 2002; 31 October 2002; 1, 4, and 7 November 2002).

be unfair to let their investment go to waste. Third, these stranger-farmers had paid 150,000 cedis per acre as an allocation fee of which the chief would transfer 50,000 cedis to the dam accounts. Now, if anyone would insist on denying these farmers access, he should also be prepared to compensate the chief and the dam account accordingly. Nobody was now willing or able to pay off the two farmers, and despite villagers' disgruntlement, the two were allowed to farm their huge plots for one year. When John Guinness and Serkin Ali returned the following year to resume their work, the members of Pongo Youth first wanted to throw the two farmers off the land – violently, if need be – but Philip Anaho proposed a different avenue. The chairman of Pongo Youth Association took matters to the police and wrote a letter as one of the community's opinion leaders. "Following a discussion with the chief . . . after community meeting with him . . . I wish to bring to your notice a possible conflict within the Pongo native and stranger farmers. . . . The said strangers are going to course more harm than good in our community."[10]

Soon after Philip Anaho had sent his letter, the police commander invited him, the chief, the Water Users' Association, and the two stranger-farmers to the police station. First, Philip Anaho was allowed to argue that the village bylaws had been violated by the chief. However, instead of letting the chief speak for himself, the police commander began to tell off the chairman of Pongo Youth. First of all, it was argued, "we are all Ghanaian, and no rules should preclude honest citizens from working anywhere in Ghana. After all, Accra is full of strangers."[11] Second, the police commander challenged Philip Anaho's legitimacy. The letter to the police was signed "opinion leader," and as the police commander dismissively argued, "one can decide to call oneself Asuma Nelson,[12] that does not change matters."[13] None of the other members of Pongo Youth came to Philip Anaho's support, and the matter was closed by the police with no written records.

During the following season, John Guinness and Serkin Ali managed to cultivate a large area again. They employed villagers for weeding and harvesting, and as one of the canals proved not to function correctly, the two strangers helped out by using their diesel pumps and hoses to irrigate the concerned plots, so as to prevent the crop from going to waste. More importantly, they offered to pump water past their own plots so that other

---

[10] Letter to District Commander of Police, Bolgatanga from Pongo Youth (Philip Anaho), "A Possible Conflict in Pongo, a Village near Bolgatanga," dated 18 September 2002. Material in private possession.

[11] This quotation is reconstructed based on independent interviews with the chief and Philip Anaho.

[12] Asuma Nelson is a Ghanaian boxer (featherweight).

[13] This quotation is reconstructed based on independent interviews with the chief and Philip Anaho.

villagers even further afield would be able to benefit from the dam. Finally, their large production and business experience allowed them to make sure that wholesalers from Kumase would fetch the harvest at Pongo. All this benefited other smaller producers, and it made it difficult for villagers without plots and for the Pongo Youth Association to sustain a campaign against the two strangers. Thus, although land was to be allocated by the committee, and allocated to the villagers only, on a temporary basis, the local political negotiations produced a system with long-term indefinite landholding of very unequal size plots. While the mobilization of Pongo Youth was instrumental in securing long-term rights of the land users, the divide-and-rule tactics of the chief and the skillful helpfulness of John Guinness and Serkin Ali secured for the large-scale stranger-farmers continued access to the land in Pongo. The following case equally involved a youth organization, but it also had more conspicuous connections to the political establishment in Bolgatanga.

Giving Up Private Lands for the Public Good

Zorobogo is a village some twelve miles outside Bolgatanga. The village had a small dugout from 1960, but in 1999 the local district assemblyman and the area's member of Parliament, who was from Zorobogo itself, decided to put their weight behind the construction of a proper dam with a large capacity in the center of their constituency. As members of NDC (National Democratic Congress), then in power, it was not very difficult to have Zorobogo's name put on the list with the Ministry of Agriculture. Thus, when pegging for the new dam was undertaken in 2000, there were great expectations among most villagers. However, some few families soon discovered that their land was "on the wrong side of the pegs" and that their fields would soon be in the reservoir for the dam. This marked the starting point for a series of meetings. The first meeting between the villagers and the two politicians was held in early November 2000. The result was all but peaceful. Mr. Mata, whose lands were the most affected by the plans, protested loudly. Not only would his family graves be affected, but a small grove of mango trees would be destroyed, and most of the land to which he had a hereditary claim would be affected.

At first, the chief of Zorobogo offered the concerned families to be settled elsewhere and to provide alternative sites for the graves, but this was flatly refused. The thought of exhuming the buried bodies and relocating the shrines was humiliating and disgraceful. Moreover, Mr. Mata was of the belief that he would never be able to obtain rights to land allocated to him equivalent to the rights he held to land he had inherited and which was his patrimony. At one point, however, the member of Parliament dismissed his objections, arguing that the *particular* interests of Mr. Mata and the other concerned families would have to yield for the greater common good.[14]

Mr. Mata repeatedly tried to convene another meeting by inviting the district chief executive – known to be of a different party color than the member of Parliament and the assemblyman, namely NPP – but despite promises, no meetings were held until Mr. Mata issued a press release in September 2001. Mr. Mata was a teacher and his son, John Mata, a student of political science at the University of Legon in Accra. Thus, unlike most of their fellow villagers, the Matas were men of letters. The press release displays the bitterness of the conflict in all but bucolic prose:

The supreme spiritual leaders and land owners of [Zoroboro] and the [Mata] family has been hit with a growing threat of a revolutionary iconoclasm (i.e. total destruction of our religious shrines) all in an effort to construct a dam for the development of [Zoroboro] and its environs. Indications are that the dam will be constructed by either fair or foul means. Meetings have been convened to discuss the matter on hand since the construction of the dam pose a serious threat to the religious and social survival of the affected people. It is worthy of note that these meetings the supreme spiritual leaders and the [Mata] family remain largely unyielding to such a development. . . .

Position of the proponents of the development as against supposedly anti-development advocates:

They seem to be espousing a utilitarian ethos. All appeals to let the matter have a peaceful settlement seem to be a failure. Rumours are ripe in the grapevine that come the dry season some people's religious rights and land will be encroached upon for the benefit of the wider society. Meetings are now being organized behind closed doors minus the landowners, a clear violation of our rights and a sure recipe for social disagreement. There is even a boom in employment at the area since those going to help in the construction of the dam have their names written down speedily. They are poised for the construction of the dam and compensation packages are mentioned in the air, a package the Tindanas and the [Mata] family disregard as a mismatch to our religion.

Position of the Tindanas and the [Mata] family as regards development:

. . . [T]he moves by the proponents of the construction of the dam [are] entirely arbitrary and doesn't encourage peace, the very trust and fruit of development. We believe that for development to be total and beneficial to the people it must be all embracing and not selective. The purpose for which the dam is going to be constructed to our mind is even bogus and fraudulent and not worth trying.

[14] Interviews with Mr. Mata, 7 and 9 November 2002; with John Mata (son of Mr. Mata), 4 November 2002 and 11 March 2004; with the member of Parliament, 11 November 2002, and the chief and elders of Zorobogo, 7 November 2002.

Conclusion: Finally, we consider the possible construction of the dam as the most inhuman event in Nabdam history and thus should not be allowed to take root and be used as a blueprint for future similar events. Consequently, we humbly appeal to the District Chief Executive (Bolgatanga), chiefs within the area and all pressure groups within and without Nabdam to intervene to help avert a seemingly simmering Palestinian intifada. Between peace, unity, development and internecine feud, we, that is the Tindanas and the [Mata] family pledge our unifying support for the former.[15]

After this press release Mr. Mata wrote a letter to the district chief executive, and a new meeting was scheduled for February 2002. On 4 February the assemblyman, the district chief executive, and the district director of agriculture gathered in a meeting at Zorobogo with the villagers. The district chief executive implored the village chief to find alternative sites for a possible dam. The chef and the assemblyman refused to negotiate and remained determined.

During the recent national elections, however, NDC had lost out to NPP, and not only did the results affect the district chief executive, but the local member of Parliament from Zorobogo had lost his seat to an NPP candidate from a different village in the electoral area. It would seem that the tide would turn in favor of Mr. Mata and the other concerned families. He was particularly encouraged when the district chief executive and the newly appointed regional minister came to the area for a rally on 17 February to thank the population for having voted the NPP into office. The other villagers of Zorobogo were similarly discouraged by the fact that the village no longer had "its own" member of Parliament.

For a good while nothing seemed to happen, and the villagers began to expect that the project was abandoned, after the transition of government. However, in August 2002, the district agricultural officer came to Zorobogo to announce that the work of the dam would resume. A week later, the contractor known to be affiliated with NPP arrived and began to work with the grader to level the area.

Mr. Mata and his son now mobilized the Zorobogo Electoral Area Students' Union, of which Mata the younger was a member. The Students' Union made a petition to the district chief executive urging the authorities to reconsider the placement of the dam.

In addition, Mr. Mata again wrote to the authorities, this time to the Regional Security Council and in a more belligerent tone.

We wish to remind your good offices that the battle lines are drawn between the feuding parties. Though the matter has not yet been resolved by any honest broker,

---

[15] Press Release, "Proposed Construction of a Dam at [Zorobogo] and the Issues That Arise Thereupon," 21 September 2001. Material in private possession.

there is physical evidence, demonstrably shown by the presence of a tractor to commence business. We humbly wish to re-echo our position clearly that our family dignity, family gods and future lives of the people of the area would not be compromised on the altar of some vague notion of development. Consequently, the willing and ready youth of the area and beyond are being mobilised in an unprecedented fashion for the war effort. Following this development we are respectfully calling on your good offices to intervene to avert a possible humanitarian disaster. We count on your prompt action.[16]

Neither the Students' Union nor Mr. Mata received any written response, and when Mr. Mata approached the district agricultural officer, he was merely told that the planning of public infrastructure did not depend on the colors of the government and that the contract with the contractor had been signed and part of the money already transferred to his account.[17] Mr. Mata and the Students' Union then made a new move; they organized a public demonstration for 19 October and invited the press. The Students' Union managed to mobilize around 100 youths and other villagers, and with journalists from *Ghanaian Times* and from the local radio, the demonstration made the national news. Mr. Mata addressed the crowd:

It is worthy of note that these problems were brought to the attention of the Hon. District Chief Executive. He quickly convened a meeting of the feuding parties and stressed that minority views should not be sidelined. However, the matter was not resolved there and then. Immediately following the meeting was the Hon. Regional Minister thanksgiving rounds to the place when he intimated that there was a real problem at [Zorobogo] and that the feuding parties will be called at his convenience for a discussion on the matter.... [C]onstruction is steadily growing. Four trees have been levelled and farmlands, un-harvested totally destroyed.... We cannot reconcile government position . . . about the return of the vested land to their owners with this growing threat of land seizure.... Having made use of the constitutional outlet in the form of demonstration, we still humbly wish to appeal to the powers that be that they intervene to avert a looming bloodbath.... We are also appealing to His Excellency the Vice President through the Regional Minister to intervene and help matters out. This appeal is necessary because we have heard that it is his construction firm that is carrying out the construction.[18]

The speech was repeated in the press, and copies were circulated to the regional minister, the district chief executive, the district director of agriculture, the assemblyman, and the police commander in Bolgatanga.

[16] Letter to the Regional Security Council from [Mr. Mata], 27 September 2002. Material in private possession.

[17] Interviews with Mr. Mata, 9 September 2002, and John Mata, 11 March 2004.

[18] Statement by [Mr. Mata] and the Tindana during a public demonstration against the Construction of a Dam at [Zorobogo], 19 October 2002. Material in private possession.

When Mr. Mata had first announced the public demonstration to the police, they had asked the local assemblyman to oversee it and report back to them. However, the villagers who were in favor of the construction saw this as if the assemblyman had "crossed the carpet" and now sided with Mr. Mata, his clan, and the district chief executive. As a consequence, they threatened to initiate a legal process against him.

The [Zorobogo] community was shocked to see our Hon Assembly Member ... leading a mob of demonstrators who are said to be kicking against the construction of a dam. ... It is ... highly surprising for the Hon Member of the community who is to lead in developmental projects is trying to thwart the efforts of the dam construction. ... We the undersigned wish to draw your attention that for the unhonorable behaviour we will initiate the legal processes of withdrawing you as an assembly member.[19]

Following the events of the demonstration, a meeting was organized in the Regional Coordinating Council between the regional coordinating director, the agricultural officers, the assemblyman, Mr. Mata, the village chief, and the earthpriest. It was agreed that a meeting at the village should be organized in order to look for alternative sites for the dam. The meeting was held in mid January 2003, led by the police commander. During the meeting, he asked the tindana whether the concerned land belonged to Mr. Mata as an individual or to the earthpriest as the custodian of the land, as caretaker of the shrines, and as the medium for the gods. The earthpriest could confirm only his own ownership, and the police commander quickly concluded the meeting by declaring that not only would public interest be served by the construction of the dam, but the man who claimed ownership and reverence for tradition and spirituality, Mr. Mata, was irreverent in not respecting the earthpriest's ownership.[20]

Mr. Mata and the other concerned families finally conceded at the meeting, and within a couple of days, machines had uprooted all the mango trees in what was to become the reservoir. However, he sent yet another letter to the district director of agriculture threatening to obstruct the work.

A BIG PROBLEM AT YOUR HANDS. You are informed that your intransigence at constructing a dam at [Zorobogo] will be met with the fiercest resistance. You are to inform the drivers at the place to stop coming or face severe beating anytime they appear. ... We tried moving there this morning but were told that the machines are broken down. You are noted for treating our messages with disdain. Don't try

---

[19] Letter to the assemblyman, "Unacceptable Behaviour of Hon ... an Assembly Member for [Zorobogo] Electoral Area," 1 November 2002. Signed by village chief and chiefs of two neighboring hamlets. Material in private possession.

[20] Interviews with John Mata, 11 March 2004, and the assemblyman, 29 November 2004).

doing so to this message. The frequent breakdown of the machines is a strong clue to your secret moves.[21]

This seems to mark the end of the open confrontation at Zorobogo, because soon after, the contractor pulled out his machines. Trees had been uprooted, some leveling had been done, but the construction of the dam had not been initiated. Mr. Mata's property had largely been destroyed, but no benefits had come to the community. Cynics in Bolga argued that the contract was awarded to the vice president's company, but the contractor was told to do "a shoddy job," so that the former NDC member of Parliament would not be able to boast about "his" achievements for Zorobogo.[22]

The most remarkable feature of this case is probably the high-risk nature of drawing on support from the outside. Although it seemed an obvious avenue to pursue for the Matas, outside support comes at a price. Disputes between individual members of politically opposed groups may be transformed, so the confrontation is absorbed into the broader political competition between the larger players who have more overarching agendas. The smaller conflict may become a vehicle for a large one, so to speak. In that case, any settlement has more far-reaching implications, and the course of conflict is strongly influenced by relations and events outside the disputes. The case also gives a hint about the actual importance the administration attaches to the earthpriests and to the divestiture of land from government. Obviously, Mr. Mata's ownership of his land was inconvenient to politics and planning, and it would appear that the earthpriest was invoked only to deprive him of his rights. This harks back to the days of the colonial administration, when administrative expediency seemed to be the overarching priority (see Chapter 2).

Conclusion

For the farmers in the villages engaged in small-scale irrigation, complying with or circumventing the law is part of a pragmatic adjustment to circumstance and opportunity. Landowners, tenants, beneficiaries of government allocation, and stranger-farmers alike engage in a host of small-scale negotiations, thus adjusting and transforming property relations and the significance of legislation. As Moore (1998: 37) notes, such activities "are not mobilisations of collective political action, but they can undo the plans of a government as effectively as if they had been." In villages with

---

[21] Handwritten letter to District Director of Agriculture from [Mr. Mata], 17 February 2003). Material in private possession.

[22] This version was actually repeated to me by a variety of sources independent of each other in and around Bolga. While this does not guarantee the veracity of the collusion, it shows that standard explanations can circulate between people in Bolgatanga.

small dams in the Upper East Region, public and private interests have competed in various ways, and with rising land values the competition to institutionalize opposing interests appears to intensify. In practical terms, the private and public nature of the land affected by the small dam schemes has changed over the past forty years, but it is often at variance with legislation. Moreover, little seems to confirm any evolutionary direction in the forms of ownership. Nor is it easy to be very categorical about the public or private nature of any particular piece of landed property; rather, a more equivocal picture emerges.

Before 1979 land was privately owned but controlled by – vested in – the government. Government development policies made it render private lands effectively public to the detriment of the owners, but the new beneficiaries in practice soon reprivatized it to their own benefit. The government's control over land was strong enough in the public eye to suspend private landholders' rights and dispense with procedure for public acquisition. In practice, however, landowners and in particular the new beneficiaries of the land allocation generally managed to undo plot rotation, which was the government's key instrument to assure the actual public ownership and control of land and infrastructure.

During the second round of building infrastructure for irrigation in the 1990s, efforts were made by the Ministry of Agriculture to "do it correctly." However, government's meticulous efforts to secure the public nature of its infrastructure were undermined by the political expediency of "getting started" and the general perception that land had since 1979 been returned to its owners. Thus, landowners managed to capture a sizable portion of the improvements, which was not the intention of government, but it would appear that landowners also found it necessary to relinquish parts of their property rights to the Water Users' Association – turning their private property public, at least temporarily. In practice, a deal developed whereby some of the private land was placed in the public realm of the WUA in exchange for private long-term access to the new public infrastructure.

Government policies are not implemented unscathed by local political negotiations, and the categories of public and private are corrupted as a consequence. Policies and politics "work through" social relations, and as property is dynamic, composite, and essentially contingent, quite unintended outcomes result. This is not to suggest that land policies and categories do not matter. While policies may not always deliver the outcome they propose, what they propose seems always to be part of the production of the eventual outcome. People take account of policies, even if effective implementation is less than accomplished. Thus, the small-dam policies occasioned a renegotiation of land rights, and the restitution of land with the 1979 Constitution provided a change in context for these negotiations.

The significant rise in the value of property imbued the renegotiation with a considerable degree of urgency.

Laws, rules, and, as in Pongo, bylaws were referred to as important markers, but structural powers and contingent events also fashioned the local political struggles over the rights and control over resources. Landowners seem in general better able to take advantage of contingencies and the "open moments" provided by policy. Thus, social stratification along the lines of property and control over land seem to result in landowners profiting from the increase in value of the land while particular "stranger" tenants are placed in a situation of increasing vulnerability. However, powerful entrepreneurs or tenants with family ties to owners can also build up some form of longer-term land holding, but landowners whose rights do not enjoy the recognition and protection of their fellow villagers are quite vulnerable.

Most land tenure systems in Africa are characterized by a coexistence of multiple rights that are often held by different persons or institutions. Government regulation intended to replace norms in the name of clarity seems rather to add to a growing repertoire of regulations and defeats its purpose. This richness of norms affords considerable room for competing arguments in a dispute, and when new government regulation is introduced, new opportunities for rearrangement arise. With the Constitution of 1979, landowners were dealt a good hand.

9

Conclusion

> "This history of mine," Herodotus says, "has from the beginning sought out the supplementary to the main argument." What you find in him are *cul-de-sacs* within the sweep of history – how people betray each other for the sake of nations, how people fall in love.
>
> Michael Ondaatje, *The English Patient*

Over the past decade or so, the interest in African land tenure has reemerged, with the international organizations and the World Bank as the most prominent actors (World Bank, 2003). In contrast to an earlier fine focus on market imperfections and the absence of private property, the ambit of concerns is now broadened to include historical evolution of property, political institutions, and customary rules among others. These are no longer seen as inherent obstacles to growth and tenure security, but as elements to take seriously in the institutional tinkering and engineering. The more comprehensive approach no doubt captures the complexity of property more adequately. However, this thinking privileges a perspective where institutions of public authority issue and enforce rules, and where rules condition behavior. My argument has been that it works both ways; behavior and rules also validate and recognize institutions.

Property and public authority are mutually constitutive and contingent. As a consequence, where land tenure is fluid and the range of public authorities considerable, landed property as well as political institutions become highly negotiable and the object of local politics. Individuals, groups, and institutions struggle to gain access to land, hold on to it, or reduce their loss of it. They maneuver to secure their right to and control over property and effect processes of consolidation and exclusion with institutional consequences as well. By focusing on how public authority feeds on the confusion over land rights, this book has attempted to "normalize" land issues in local politics. Land issues are thus not something to be "sorted out" in order for more mundane topics to enter the political agenda; land and property issues to a large extent *determine* the agenda and the institutional configuration in the local political arena and constitute the lens through which other issues are interpreted. Moreover, in societies where property is a central and controversial issue, the constitution of property is in essence a process of state formation solidifying or undermining institutions of public authority.

"The difficulties of seeing trends 'in process' are enormous and the dangers of prediction even greater" (Peters, 2002: 61). Peters's observation serves as a warning against either wishful thinking or simple extrapolation of current happenings. Bearing these words of caution in mind, it is nonetheless possible to point out some patterns in the dynamics of property and its institutional configuration. Moreover, as Peters argues, specific historical developments may well resonate with examples from different contexts, which may point out structural developments and conflicts.

Land has been the object of policy in Ghana since colonial times, though with varying intensity (Berry, 2002b; Firmin-Sellers, 1996). Government policies for northern Ghana such as the Land and Native Rights Ordinance from the 1930s and the 1979 Constitution have had dramatic and far-reaching effects in the powers and interests they unleashed. However, the outcome seemed to have been less in the hands of government and more a question of endless instances of governance in many local public spheres, with powers and interests difficult to harness to any particular institution. Although some of these opportunities were created at least partially through the mobilization of local political forces, the outcomes were hardly controllable by any single group. Governments in Ghana have through time proved a strong capacity to create opportunities for the renegotiation of land rights, but with a much more limited control over how opportunities were actually seized locally. The tension between the state power to engender changes, and state incapacity to direct them, is not restricted to land matters or to African governance in general, but the story of the Upper East provides a particularly vivid illustration of this paradox.

Structural Patterns

Like other tenure reforms in Africa,[1] the reform embedded in the 1979 Constitution reconfigured the possibilities of recognizing property and allocating land; it provoked a redefinition of benefits and control of tenure. It has been particularly dynamic because it opened up space for the redefinition of the institutional structures controlling and guaranteeing rights and allocating land. When compensations were paid out following the watershed court cases, the term "allodial titleholder" thus became very important in two ways.

---

[1] See, for example, Le Roy (1985) for Senegal, Lund (1998, 2002) for Niger and Burina Faso; Le Meur (2002) for Benin; Fisiy (1992) for Cameroon; Chauveau (2000) for Côte d'Ivoire; and Cousins (2002) for South Africa.

First, the need to define the allodial owner emerged. The cases over compensation and the "customary share" of the value of land transactions changed the authority structure in customary land matters. Henceforth, it was made economically very attractive to be recognized as *the* customary authority and allodial titleholder, holding the original title from which other rights derive. In the prevailing context of legal and institutional pluralism, and rising competition over land, the constitutional reversal of land tenure that took place in 1979 brought to life potential conflicts over land claims *and* over competing claims to authority to address those conflicts. The "rediscovery" of the earthpriest meant that land conflicts became political conflicts over traditional authority and its role in modern governance.

In parallel, precision about the powers entailed in that title vis-à-vis other rights to the same land also became an issue. While the customary authority used to sanction transfers of use rights – sometimes hereditary use rights – where little or no money changed hands, increased monetary value attached to land raised the question of who should reap the benefits of lease arrangements. In Bolga town, the relatives or the clan of earthpriests saw an opportunity to have allodial rights encompass the economic benefits of land transfers. Similarly, in the irrigable areas – be it in the forest reserves or in connection to small dams – chiefs claiming allodial title attempted to make sure that the economic benefits of land transactions went their way and not in the direction of owners with customary freehold. For ordinary people, the high value of the past puts newcomers at a disadvantage. While government policies may have intended to help certain land users to acquire permanent land rights, processes of exclusion tend to work to the advantage of people who can claim land rights with reference to belonging in a broad sense.

As a consequence of increased competition, exclusion seems to be on the rise as a general process for land users as well as between institutions. Before the constitutional reforms, ambiguity and overlap in authority between chiefs and earthpriests were not a very political issue. With the divestiture, however, the economic implications became consequential, and the interests in clarity (i.e., advantageous clarity) became more explicit. The constitutional change also provided the policy-discursive background for owners of irrigable land to extend their command over the resources and to drive a hard bargain against tenants. The trend toward greater exclusivity also concerns the "vertical" relationship between "ordinary" and allodial landowners. When land was of limited commercial value, little income had to be distributed from land transactions. Now, however, it is in the balance how it will evolve. If landowners manage to secure more control over land – that is, deciding on transactions without the consent, let alone payment, of the earthpriest as the public authority and allodial owner – the question of who guarantees and validates property becomes acute. Owners may eventually have more exclusive yet less certain land rights.

The political struggles over land in the Upper East Region are therefore imbued with two paradoxes. First, the important currencies in debates are history and tradition, while the negotiation and argument follow paths laid out by contemporary concerns, institutions, and opportunities. The past is generally used to justify competing designs for the future recast – by selectively justifying claims through reference either to particular events of the past or to an unbroken seamless continuation of it. The Bawku skin affair amply demonstrates the potential longevity of conflicts. As the constitutions of 1979 and 1992 expressly endowed customary authorities with allodial land rights, and the economic benefits that flow from it, they furthermore put a state-sponsored premium on tradition and history. And although the past is not infinitely malleable, there is sufficient scope in it to allow for several competing understandings to make sense locally. Enshrined in the constitution, the past is solidly confirmed as an important terrain in land issues. A much more open question is who commands it.

This leads to the second paradox. The increasing importance of customary authorities has not consolidated the chieftaincy institution as such but resurrected a competitor, the earthpriest. Early theories on property rights argued that as land became more valuable, narrower definitions of property would emerge and clearer rights would ensue (Demsetz, 1967; see also Firmin-Sellers, 1996, 2000; Platteau, 1996). Although scarcity may indeed promote exclusivity, the evidence from Ghana shows that when there are many institutions competing for the right to authorize claims to land, the result of an effort to unify and clarify the law (as happened in 1979) is to intensify competition among them and weaken their legitimacy. This is a key to understanding the dynamic of property and authority. Thus, as the opportunities arise with reform, strong interests in having rights recognized, and in having the authority to recognize them defined, are voiced and acted out. The consequences are greater than the gradually more exclusive allocation of land rights; the future fault lines of *property* are at stake, and the consequences impinge on the very constitution of public authority in society.

One of the most policy-influential books on property and land in recent years is *The Mystery of Capital* by de Soto (2000). The author drives a very forceful argument that the state should secure and guarantee formalized private property for the small in society in order to enable them to produce, have, and control capital. De Soto's work has incurred praise as well as criticism for its simplicity.[2] The evidence from the present study points to one

---

[2] De Soto is indebted to a large body of work, spanning the latter half of the twentieth century, devoted to hypothesizing, testing, or insisting on the superiority of freehold tenure and the necessity of title deeds to land. See, for example, Ault and Rutman (1979); Demsetz (1967); Feder and Noronha (1987); Simpson (1954); World Bank (1974). For comprehensive critique of this school of thought for Africa, see Platteau (1996) and Shipton (1989). For critique of de Soto's work, see Bromley (forthcoming), Fitzpatrick (2006), T. Mitchell (2005), and F. von Benda-Beckman (2003).

particular issue: De Soto's idea works with the confident assumption that the state exists – that is, that it exists as a set of congruent and hegemonic institutions capable of enforcing one particular interpretation of property. The history of property in the Upper East Region suggests that such confidence is misplaced. Incongruence and competition between institutions that form the governance structure explain why property rights are not merely consolidating and formalizing. As Firmin-Sellers (1996: 144) concludes in her historical work on land in the Gold Coast, "[s]tate actors cannot simply impose their preferred property rights systems upon their subjects; neither can subjects enforce property rights at a local level without the state's support." However, if the state is fragmented, made up by institutions that move in and out of a capacity to exercise public authority, chances are that property rights will be challenged. In Boone's (2003) comparison of Ghana and Côte d'Ivoire, the successful central state imposition in Côte d'Ivoire accounts for the relative institutional stability in relations between central and local political powers. The much fiercer political competition between government and powerful institutions in Ghana would account for more fragmented state formation and hence, I argue, in less consolidated and less certain property rights. The fact that more recent political upheavals in Côte d'Ivoire have disrupted property relations (Chauveau, 2007) only underscores the point and serves as a reminder of the inherently political and precarious nature of property.

Processual Patterns

Patterns are not restricted to structural outcomes in terms of institutions, ownership, or exclusion, however. Patterns can equally be identified in the processual dynamics of property, that is, how and where struggles take place, and what the implications are for the central concepts and ideas.

Power, wealth, and meaning (Shipton and Goheen, 1992) are semantic as well as sociopolitical "construction sites" where people's efforts to order and institutionalize are relentless, and challenges to such efforts endless. However, the story of the Upper East Region tells us that the "construction sites" are not equally active at all times. Long periods were characterized by modest government interference and the reproduction of certain conditions where only incremental changes in positions and property resulted. As Boone points out, "[s]ome zones were governed intensively, through tight, top-down control, while others were left to their own devices, granted extensive autonomy, or simply neglected and not incorporated into the national space" (Boone, 2003: 8; see also Ladouceur, 1979). The Upper East definitely belonged to the latter category most of the time.

At certain moments, however, opportunities for the renegotiation of the situation materialized in more dramatic ways. For example, the policy of indirect rule and the Land and Native Rights Ordinance from 1931 provided an opportunity for chiefs in the Northern Territories to assert and confirm a position of control over land. The situation established during the 1930s was in general reproduced over the years but was disrupted, not with Independence, but only with the Constitution of 1979. The Constitution's declaration that land held in trust by government was henceforth to be handed back to its "original owners" created an opportunity to reverse an order that had developed since the 1930s. Similar opportunities for settling old scores and pressing new and old claims have occurred over the decades in the Upper East. The mere changes of government thus provided a series of opportunities to pursue interests in the Bawku skin affair. Here, old claims of the defeated party in the chieftaincy conflict were brought out, as the opportunity materialized for overturning past decisions with the arrival of a new government into office. Also, the decision to create a new district in the Tallensi-Nabdam area in 2002 was equally seen as a particularly propitious moment for renegotiating the meaning of the past, of space, and of the ensuing rights to resources.

The evidence from bigger and smaller conflicts in northern Ghana demonstrates that claims to land and property are not necessarily extinct merely because the rights are. In her book on chiefs and property in Asante, Berry argues that negotiations over property appear to be inconclusive (Berry, 2001: 198; see also Firmin-Sellers, 1996). This picture fits very well for the North also. The inconclusiveness can best be understood in a historical perspective where no single institution has been able to enforce and sustain hegemony over rule making. The ambiguous policies by the colonial government and the political rent seeking of later governments undoing previous policies have engendered expectations of future gratification of presently denied claims.

Hence, people's capacity for "opportunism" has proved decisive. Vigilance, improvisation, and alliance making are rewarded, and the ability to select fora and means of articulation of interests are crucial for seizing the opportunities successfully. Obviously, economic and other resources, alliances and acumen are not equally distributed in society, but the events after 1979 demonstrated that chiefs' firm grip on allodial titles could indeed be challenged and undone. Land claims have an extended shelf life and store well, however. It seems that for every opportunity occurring there is an ample stock of pent up competing claims to be put forth. No one should expect the last words to have been uttered yet.

If we take a broader look, there has in recent years been a change in the official attitude toward customary tenure. Agencies such as the World Bank now recognize that customary systems of land tenure are often more flexible and adapted to local circumstances than centralized and uniform systems. Examples from Niger (Lund, 1998), Burkina Faso (Lund, 2002), and Côte d'Ivoire (Chauveau, 2007) are obvious examples from the region, but it seems to be a general trend in Africa (Fitzpatrick, 2005). Introduction of customary elements in policy does no doubt reflect recognition of the problems in denying their existence. It is in all likelihood easier to make policies work if they somehow resonate with existing conditions. Still, privileging customary law seems inevitably to politicize customary authority and the competition over it.

Organization and Terminology

The study also contributes to an understanding of the importance of the organization of interests for change. Legislation, government policies, and administrative culture all contribute to the opportunities for action and change. Organization was what made change happen – either because of the numbers organized or because of their skills and qualities. The competing arguments and interests in the Upper East Region were expressed in many ways and many fora. No single domain, be it political, legal, social, or cultural, was in itself decisive, and most "negotiations" or conflicts were marred by violence or the threat of it. Violence or physical intimidation was never reserved for government alone, although most governments over time have made ample use of it. Angry claims have often been protested by individuals and groups accompanied by physical violence – sometimes even to provoke police or military intervention. Those who have mastered successful control over land in the Upper East have juggled legal, economic, and political strategies and have timed them to take advantage of opportunities presented by national legislation and political circumstance.

Interestingly, it was rather straightforward claims for compensation for the loss of land to government by local owners in the 1990s that unleashed a dramatic political mobilization, as the court settlement entailed the recognition of the local earthpriests. At this point, the numbers of people organized were not the crucial factor. It was the political ambition of a few informed people returning from the South and the legal ingenuity of a couple of lawyers that made the difference. The subsequent creation of the Association of Tindambas of Bolgatanga provided earthpriests' interests with a new political vehicle. The resulting struggles were not restricted to the court system. Earthpriests were organized in a union, chiefs relied on the Regional House of Chiefs, petitions were written and diffused in various ways, and the Land Commission was solicited. Moreover, a broad array of tensions over land surfaced on this occasion. The access to forest reserves and landowners' control over irrigation infrastructure suddenly became issues to be renegotiated in different public fora and by change of practice. While some of this negotiation included violence – sometimes even organized violence – and while some of the wheeling and dealing in these conflicts was definitely not intended for all to see, there was a distinct public character about it. The outcomes of the rekindled controversies soon got to be known by the public, and, as knowledge spread, others pressed similar claims with reference to them. Hence, outcomes had implications well beyond the immediate protagonists themselves.

The institutions such as the Forestry Department, the Ministry of Agriculture, the police, the Town and Country Planning, and the Land Commission were more than just technical bureaucratic institutions when conflicts emerged from the 1990s; they were theaters where conflicts were debated and outcomes had far-reaching effects. They were not Viennese coffeehouses (*pace* Habermas), but the open-ended character of administrative procedure and the widespread knowledge about outcomes imbued these institutions with a dimension of a public sphere (see Whitfield, 2003). The legal and institutional plurality of society in the Upper East, as in Ghana in general, is a significant context for the public sphere, that is, the public spaces where different interests are transacted. Its fragmented nature is demonstrated in the case studies throughout the book.

This picture, however, is contrasted by the image and notion of a state as an institution with power and authority to define, recognize, and sanction claims as rights. The Bawku skin affair demonstrates that while governance institutions and their legitimacy were at the heart of the matter, the state as a superior institution was never called into question. Rather, it was called upon in the guise of the court system, the national government and its ministers, and even the army to settle the conflict. Similarly, in the other chapters the constitutional changes of 1979 and 1992 were not called into question, but only the different interpretations of them. Thus, the idea of a central state with a legitimate will seemed generally accepted. The government set out the framework for action and credited the "state" as the ultimate reference point for legality and legitimacy – a sort of imaginary "gold standard" of public authority – in matters of land or chieftaincy, or for assessing the significance of the past in the present.

Abrams (1988) reminds us of the difficulties of studying the state. He points out its double nature as an idea and an apparatus. Whereas the former is characterized by concerns for the common good, the latter is populated with groups with more or less vested interests (see also Bates, 1983). However, the "state" is not the only duplicitous concept at work in local politics and land struggles. Public, private, government, and state are concepts upon which much theoretical literature feeds. These concepts and ideas about political systems and processes not only inform the analysis. Imperialism, modernization, and globalization have meant a decisive trafficking in ideas and values between the many worlds of the world. As a consequence, we find that concepts are actively employed and interpreted by people in their attempts to enact different political projects and interests. Concepts and ideas of different origin enter local arenas and become "idiomatized." They are not merely instruments of analysis but are equally their object. Thus, in addition to competition over land claims and claims over authority, the many conflicts have also engendered an ongoing (re)definition of some of the concepts we might otherwise tend to see as fixed. For example, it is quite clear that what is considered legitimate property is historically contingent. What constitutes a good claim at one moment may be less rewarding at another and not resonate with what is generally or politically accepted. Although arguments are often carried forth with reference to precedent and the past, the right moment for pressing a particular claim depends on the contemporary political constellation of institutions that can recognize claims as valid. Similarly, what is perceived as legal or illegal may well change over time without any change in legislation. Government policies, statements, and practices can effectively outlaw certain legal practices and nullify established rights. The effective forestry policies are an example. Also, government may effectively turn private property into public land, and farmers' inventive opportunism may secure them private rights to public infrastructure, quite contrary to the legislation in place.

The local politics in the Upper East Region in Ghana displays many instances where the meaning of public, private, government, legitimacy, ownership, and similar concepts are effectively debated. When a national policy or a constitution – such as the Constitution of 1979 restoring land rights – is resisted, embraced, or diverted, the negotiation is propelled by double-barreled concepts as central reference points in political debate. They *appear* stable. At the same time, however, in the larger claims for a livelihood and a position in life, people struggle over the local, idiomatic *meaning* of these concepts. But despite the inadequacy of the concepts in describing the real situation, it is important to see these ideal concepts as integral parts of the political struggle. When various forms of indigenous land tenure are translated into one-dimensional *ownership* in such discussions and debates, it bespeaks a deliberate simplification of a complex composite tenure system. The cases throughout this book demonstrate the importance of having a command of the terminology.

> Vladimir: That passed the time.
> Estragon: It would have passed in any case.
> Vladimir: Yes, but not so rapidly.
>> Samuel Beckett, *Waiting for Godot*

References

Primary Sources

Archives

Department of Rural Housing, Bolgatanga
    Correspondence files
District Forest Office, Bolgatanga
    Correspondence files
Ghana National Archives, Accra
Public Record Office, London
Public Records and Archives Administration Department, Regional Office, Tamale
    NRG 8/1 Series: Land
    NRG 8/2 Series: Chieftaincy and Native Affairs
    NRG 8/4 Series: Confidential Diaries
    NRG 8/11 Series: Forestry
    NRG 9/4 Series: Agriculture
Regional House of Chiefs, Bolgatanga
    Record of Proceedings in the Matter of Appeal (1/AJ/80)
Regional Lands Commission, Bolgatanga
    Correspondence files

Official Publications

Ghana Gazette
Local Government Bulletin

Selected Court Cases

High Court, Bolgatanga

Newspapers

Daily Graphic (Accra)
Ghanaian Chronicle (Accra)
Ghanaian Times (Accra)
Northern Advocate (Tamale)

Unofficial Sources

Many people have kept copies of letters, reports, newspaper clippings, petitions, and minutes of meetings, and I have encountered only trust and generosity as people let me make copies of their "private archives." Such sources are not indexed with archival reference numbers, but I have specified the nature of the documents in the footnotes and noted "material in private possession."

Secondary Sources

Abraham, A., and Platteau, J.-P. 2001. "Participatory development in the presence of endogenous community imperfections." Paper presented at a symposium "Managing Common Resources – What Is the Solution?" Lund University, Lund, 10–11 September.

Abrams, P. 1988. "Notes on the difficulty of studying the state." *Journal of Historical Sociology* 1, no. 1: 58–89.

Agbosu, L. K. 1980. "Land administration in northern Ghana." *Review of Ghana Law* 12: 104–33.

Agbosu, L. K. 1983. "The origins of forest law and policy in Ghana during the colonial period." *Journal of African Law* 27, no. 2: 169–87.

Akwetey, E. 1996. "Ghana: Violent ethno-political conflicts and the democratic challenge." In A. O. Olukoshi and L. Laakso (eds.), *Challenges to the Nation-State in Africa*. Uppsala: Nordic African Institute. Pp. 102–35.

Alhassan, R. I. 1996. "Traditional land tenure system in the Northern, Upper East and Upper West Regions – Similarities, differences and modern trends." In Konrad Adenauer Foundation, *Decentralisation, Land Tenure and Land Administration in Northern Ghana*. Report on a seminar held at Bolgatanga, Accra, 28–30 May. Pp. 41–43.

Allman, J., and J. Parker, 2005. *Tongnaab: The History of a West African God*. Bloomington: Indiana University Press.

Allot, A. 1960. *Essays on African Law with Special Reference to the Law of Ghana*. London: Butterworth.

Amanor, K. 1999. *Global Restructuring and Land Rights in Ghana: Forest Food Chains, Timber and Rural Livelihoods*. Uppsala: Nordic Africa Institute.

Anafu, M. 1973. "The impact of colonial rule on Tallensi political institutions, 1898–1967." *Transactions of the Historical Society of Ghana* 14, no. 1: 17–37.

Andanye, J. E. 1995. "Revised list of dams and dugouts in the Upper East Region – Ghana." Mimeo, Irrigation Development Authority, Bolgatanga.

Anon. 1950. *The Colonial Territories (1949–50)*. Cmd. 8243. London: HMSO.

Appadurai, A. 1981. "The past as a scarce resource." *Man*, n.s., 16, no. 2: 201–19.

Appiah-Kubi, K. 2001. "State-owned enterprises and privatisation in Ghana." *Journal of Modern African Studies* 39, no. 2: 197–229.

Apter, A. 1999. "The subvention of tradition: A genealogy of the Nigerian Durbar." In G. Steinmetz (ed.), *State/Culture: State Formation after the Cultural Turn*. Ithaca: Cornell University Press. Pp. 213–52.

Apter, D. 1968. *Ghana in Transition*. New York: Athneum.

Arhin, K. (ed.). 1974. *The Papers of George Ekem Ferguson. A Fanti Official of the Government of the Gold Coast, 1890–1897*. Leiden: Africa Studies Centre.

Asare, O. E. 1993. *Investigation Report on the Illegal Farming in Tankwidi East Forest Reserve (incl 22 statements)*. Bolgatanga: District Forest Office.

Ault, G., and D. Rutman. 1979. "The development of individual rights to property in tribal Africa." *Journal of Law and Economics* 22, no. 1: 163–82.

Austin, D. 1970. *Politics in Ghana, 1946–1960*. Oxford: Oxford University Press.

Ayee, J. 1994. *An Anatomy of Public Policy Implementation: The Case of Decentralization Policies in Ghana*. Aldershot: Avebury.

Ayee, J. 2000. "Sub-district structures and popular participation. A preliminary assessment." In W. Thomi, P. W. K. Yankson, and S. Y. M. Zanu (eds.), *A Decade of Decentralisation and Local Government Reform in Ghana: Retrospect and Prospects*. Accra: Ministry of Local Government and Rural Development. Pp. 127–56.

Basset, T. J., and D. E. Crummey (eds.). 1993. *Land in African Agrarian Systems*. Madison: University of Wisconsin Press.

Bates, R. 1983. *Essays on the Political Economy of Rural Africa*. Berkeley: University of California Press.

Bawku Peace Initiative. 2001. "Bawku East Consultations on Peace and Development." Report prepared by J. A. Mohammed for Bawku Peace Initiative. Mimeo.

Bayart, J.-F. 1989. *L'État en Afrique. La politique du ventre*. Paris: Fayard.

Bayart, J.-F., P. Geschiere, and F. Nyamnjoh. 2001. "Autochtonie, démocratie et citoyenneté en Afrique." *Critique Internationale*, no. 10: 177–94.

Beckman, B. 1981. "Ghana, 1951–78: The agrarian basis of the post-colonial state." In J. Heyer, P. Roberts, and G. Williams (eds.), *Rural Development in Tropical Africa*. London: Macmillan. Pp. 143–67.

Bendix, R. 1984. *Force, Fate and Freedom*. Berkeley: University of California Press.

Bening, R. B. 1973. "Indigenous concepts of boundaries and significance of administrative stations and boundaries in northern Ghana." *Bulletin of the Ghana Geographical Association* 15: 7–20.

Bening, R. B. 1974a. "Location of regional and provincial capitals in northern Ghana, 1897–1960." *Bulletin of the Ghana Geographical Association* 16: 54–66.

Bening, R. B. 1974b. "The development of education in northern Ghana, 1908–1957." *Ghana Social Science Journal* 1, no. 2: 21–42.

Bening, R. B. 1975a. "Colonial development policy in northern Ghana, 1898–1950." *Bulletin of the Ghana Geographical Association* 17: 65–79.

Bening, R. B. 1975b. "Foundations of the modern native states of northern Ghana." *Universitas* 5, no. 1: 116–38.

Bening, R. B. 1977. "Administration and development in northern Ghana, 1898–1931." *Ghana Social Science Journal* 4, no. 2: 58–76.

Bening, R. B. 1990. *A History of Education in Northern Ghana: 1907–1976*. Accra: Ghana University Press.

Bening, R. B. 1995. "Land policy and administration in northern Ghana." *Transactions of the Historical Society of Ghana* 16, no. 2 (n.s., no. 1): 227–66.

Bening, R. B. 1996. "Land ownership, divestiture and beneficiary rights in northern Ghana." In Konrad Adenauer Foundation, *Decentralisation, Land Tenure and Land Administration in Northern Ghana*. Report on a seminar held at Bolgatanga, Accra, 28–30 May. Pp. 20–40.

Bening, R. B. 1999. *Ghana: Regional Boundaries and National Integration*. Accra: Ghana University Press.

Berry, S. 1985. *Fathers Work for Their Sons – Accumulation, Mobility and Class Formation in an Extended Yoruba Community*. Berkeley: University of California Press.

Berry, S. 1988. "Concentration without privatization? Some consequences of changing patterns of rural land control in Africa." In R. E. Downs and S. P. Reyna (eds.), *Land and Society in Contemporary Africa*. Hanover, N.H.: University Press of New England. Pp. 53–75.

Berry, S. 1993. *No Condition Is Permanent – the Social Dynamics of Agrarian Change in sub-Saharan Africa*. Madison: University of Wisconsin Press.

Berry, S. 1997. "Tomatoes, land and hearsay. Property and history in Asante in the time of structural adjustment." *World Development* 25, no. 8: 1225–41.

Berry, S. 2001. *Chiefs Know Their Boundaries: Essays on Property, Power, and the Past in Asante, 1896–1996*. Portsmouth and Oxford: Heinemann and James Currey.

Berry, S. 2002a. "The everyday politics of rent-seeking. Land allocation on the outskirts of Kumase, Ghana." In K. Juul and C. Lund (eds.), *Negotiating Property in Africa*. Portsmouth: Heinemann. Pp. 107–33

Berry, S. 2002b. "Debating the land questions." *Comparative Studies in Society and History* 44, no. 4: 638–68.

Berry, S. 2004. "Questions of precedence: Land, authority and the politics of knowledge in Ghana." Paper presented at the Centre of African Studies, Copenhagen, 30 April.

Bierschenk, T., J.-P. Chauveau, and J.-P. Olivier de Sardan. 2000. "Les courtiers entre développement et État." In T. Bierschenk, J.-P. Chauveau, and J.-P. Olivier de Sardan (eds.), *Courtiers en développement. Les villages africains en quête de projets*. Paris: Karthala. Pp. 5–42.

Bierschenk, T., and J.-P. Olivier de Sardan. 1997. "Local powers and a distant state in rural Central African Republic." *Journal of Modern African Studies* 35, no. 3: 441–68.

Bierschenk, T., and J.-P. Olivier de Sardan. 1998. "Les arènes locales face à la décentralisation et à la démocratisation." In T. Bierschenk and J.-P. Olivier de Sardan (eds.), *Les pouvoirs au village. Le Bénin rural entre démocratisation et décentralisation*. Paris: Karthala. Pp. 11–51.

Bierschenk, T., and J.-P. Olivier de Sardan. 2003. "Powers in the village. Rural Benin between democratisation and decentralisation." *Africa* 73, no. 2: 145–73.

Bloch, Maurice. 1977. "The past and the present in the present." *Man*, n.s., 12: 278–92.

Blundo, G., and J.-P. Olivier de Sardan. 2001a. "La corruption quotidienne an Afrique de l'Ouest." *Politique Africaine*, no. 83: 8–37.

Blundo, G., and J.-P. Olivier de Sardan. 2001b. "Sémiologie populaire de la corruption." *Politique Africaine*, no. 83: 98–114.

Boahen, A. A. 2000 [1975]. *Ghana: Evolution and Change in the Nineteenth and Twentieth Centuries*. Accra: Sankofa.

Bohannan, P. 1963. "'Land,' 'tenure' and land-tenure." In D. Biebuyck (ed.), *African Agrarian Systems*. Oxford: Oxford University Press. Pp. 101–15.

Boone, C. 1998. "State building in the African countryside: Structure and politics at the grassroots." *Journal of Development Studies* 34, no. 4: 1–31.

Boone, C. 2003. *Political Topographies of the African State: Territorial Authority and Institutional Choice*. Cambridge: Cambridge University Press.

Bourdieu, P. 1994. *Raisons pratiques. Sur la théorie d'action*. Paris: Seuil.

Bourret, F. M. 1949. *The Gold Coast: A Survey of the Gold Coast and British Togoland, 1919–1946*. Hoover Library on War, Revolution, and Peace Publication no. 23. Stanford: Stanford University Press. Pp. 87–108.

Briggs, P. 2001. *The Bradt Travel Guide to Ghana*. 2nd ed. Bucks: Bradt Travel Guides.

Bromley, D. (Forthcoming). "Formalising property relations in the developing world. The wrong prescription for the wrong malady." *Land Use Policy*.

Brooks, R. L. 1947. *Empire Forests and the War*. Accra: Government Printer, Gold Coast Colony.

Bruce, J. 1986. *Land Tenure Issues in Project Design and Strategies for Agricultural Development in Sub-Saharan Africa*. Paper no. 128. Madison: Land Tenure Center, University of Wisconsin.

Bruce, J. 1993. "Do indigenous tenure systems constrain agricultural development?" In T. J. Basset and D. E. Crummey (eds.), *Land in African Agrarian Systems*. Madison: University of Wisconsin Press. Pp. 35–56.

Bruce, J., and S. E. Migot-Adholla (eds.). 1994. *Searching for Land Tenure Security in Africa*. Dubuque: Kendall/Hunt Publishers.

Brukum, N. J. K. 2000. "Ethnic conflict in northern Ghana." *Transactions of the Historical Society of Ghana New Series*, nos. 4–5: 131–47.

Brukum, N. J. K. 2001. *The Guinea Fowl, Mango and Pito Wars: Episodes in the History of Northern Ghana, 1980–1999*. Legon: Ghana University Press.

Cell, J. W. 1989. "Lord Hailey and the making of the African Survey." *African Affairs* 88, no. 353: 481–505.

Chabal, P., and J.-P. Daloz. 1999. *Africa Works: Disorder as Political Instrument*. Oxford and Bloomington: James Currey, International African Institute, and Indiana University Press.

Chalfin, B. 2000. "Risky business. Economic uncertainty, market reforms and female livelihoods in northeast Ghana." *Development and Change* 31, no. 4: 987–1008.

Chalfin, B. 2001. "Border zone trade and the economic boundaries of the state in north-East Ghana." *Africa* 71, no. 2: 202–24.

Chanock, M. 1991a. "A peculiar sharpness – an essay on property in the history of customary law in colonial Africa." *Journal of African History* 32, no. 1: 65–88.

Chanock, M. 1991b. "Paradigms, policies and property. A review of the customary law of land tenure." In K. Mann and R. Roberts (eds.), *Law in Colonial Africa*. Portsmouth: Heinemann. Pp. 61–84.

Chanock, M. 1998. *Law, Custom and Social Order. The Colonial Experience in Malawi and Zambia*. Portsmouth: Heinemann.

Chauveau, J.-P. 2000. "Question foncière et construction nationale en Côte d'Ivoire." *Politique Africaine*, no. 78: 94–125.

Chauveau, J.-P. 2007. *La loi de 1998 sur les droits fonciers coutumiers dans l'histoire des politiques foncières en Côte d'Ivoire*. Working Paper. Montpellier: IRD/INRA.

Chazan, N. 1983. *An Anatomy of Ghanaian Politics: Managing Political Recession, 1969–1982*. Boulder: Westview.

Chazan, N. 1991. "The political transformation of Ghana under the PNDC." In D. Rothchild (ed.), *Ghana: The Political Economy of Recovery*. Boulder: Lynne Rienner Publishers. Pp. 21–47.

Comaroff, J. 2002. "Governmentality, materiality, legality, modernity. On the colonial state in Africa." In J.-G. Deutsch, P. Probst, and H. Schmidt (eds.), *African Modernities: Entangled Meanings in Current Debate*. Portsmouth: Heinemann. Pp. 107–34.

Comaroff, J., and S. Roberts. 1981. *Rules and Processes – the Cultural Logic of Dispute in an African Context*. Chicago: University of Chicago Press.

Cooper, F. 1997. "Modernizing bureaucrats, backward Africans and the development concept." In F. Cooper and R. Packard (eds.), *International Development and the Social Sciences: Essays on the History and Politics of Knowledge*. Berkeley: University of California Press. Pp. 64–92.

Cousins, B. 2002. "Legislating negotiability. Tenure reform in post-apartheid South Africa." In K. Juul and C. Lund (eds.), *Negotiating Property in Africa*. Portsmouth: Heinemann. Pp. 67–106.

Cox, A. J. 1943. *Forest Policy in the Northern Territories*. Manuscript, 16 November. NRG 8/11/4. Public Records and Administration Department, Tamale.

Crook, R. 1987. "Legitimacy, authority and the transfer of power in Ghana." *Political Studies* 35: 552–72

Crook, R. 1994. "Four years of the Ghana District Assemblies in operation. Decentralization, democratization and administrative performance." *Public Administration and Development* 14: 339–64.

Crook, R., and J. Manor. 1998. *Democracy and Decentralisation in South Asia and West Africa: Participation, Accountability and Performance*. Cambridge: Cambridge University Press.

Cruise O'Brien, D. B. 2003. *Symbolic Confrontations: Muslims Imagining the State in Africa*. London: Hurst & Company.

Daanaa, H. S. 1996. "Interest in land in northern Ghana – a historical review of legal issues." In Konrad Adenauer Foundation, *Decentralisation, Land Tenure and Land Administration in Northern Ghana*. Report on a seminar held at Bolgatanga, Accra, 28–30 May. Pp. 44–52.

Das, V., and D. Poole. 2004. "State and its margins. Comparative ethnographies." In V. Das and D. Poole (eds.), *Anthropology in the Margins of the State*. Santa Fe and Oxford: School of American Research Press and James Currey. Pp. 3–33.

Demsetz, H. 1967. "Toward a theory of property rights." *American Economic Review* 57, no. 2: 347–59.

Der, B. G. 1975. "Colonial land policy in the Northern Territories of the Gold Coast, 1900–1957." *Universitas* 4, no. 2: 129–42.

Dery, A. 1998. "The legal empowerment of water user's associations." Mimeo, Consultancy report, Bolgatanga.

de Soto, H. 2000. *The Mystery of Capital: Why Capitalism Triumphs in the West and Fails Everywhere Else*. New York: Basic Books.

Downs, R. E., and P. Reyna (eds.). 1988. *Land and Society in Contemporary Africa*. Hanover, N.H.: University Press of New England.

Drucker-Brown, S. 1981. "The structure of the Mamprusi Kingdom and the cult of the *Naam*." In H. J. M. Claessen and P. Skalník. (eds.), *The Study of the State*. The Hague: Mouton. Pp. 117–31.

Drucker-Brown, S. 1988. "Local wars in northern Ghana." *Cambridge Anthropology* 13, no. 2: 86–106.

Drucker-Brown, S. 1994. "Communal violence in northern Ghana: An accepted warfare." In R. Hinde and H. Watson (eds.), *Warfare a Cruel Necessity?* London: I. B. Tauris. Pp. 37–53.

Dubois, O. 1997. *Rights and Wrongs of Rights to Land and Forest Resources in Sub-Saharan Africa: Bridging the Gap between Customary and Formal Rules*. Forest Participation Series no. 10. International Institute for Environment and Development (IIED). London: IIED.

Dunn, J., and A. F. Robertson. 1973. *Dependence and Opportunity: Political Change in Ahafo*. Cambridge: Cambridge University Press.

Eades, J. S. 1994. *Strangers and Traders: Yoruba Migrants, Markets and the State in Northern Ghana*. Trenton, N.J.: Africa World Press.

Edsman, B. M. 1979. *Lawyers in Gold Coast Politics, c. 1900–1945: From Mensah Sarbah to J. B. Danquah*. Uppsala: Acta Universitatis Upsaliensis.

Elias, N. 1994 [1939]. *The Civilizing Process*. London: Blackwell.

Elbow, K., and A. Rochegude. 1990. *A Layperson's Guide to the Forest Codes of Mali, Niger and Senegal*. LTC Paper 139. Madison: Land Tenure Center, University of Wisconsin.

Eriksen, S. S., J. Naustdalslid, and R. Schou (eds.). 1999. *Decentralisation from Above: A Study of Local Government in Botswana, Ghana, Tanzania and Zimbabwe*. NIBR's PLUSS Series 4-99. Oslo.

Fairhead, J., and M. Leach. 1996. *Misreading the African Landscape: Society and Ecology in a Forest-Savanna Mosaic*. Cambridge: Cambridge University Press.

Fairhead, J., and M. Leach. 1998. *Reframing Deforestation: Global Analysis and Local Realities; Studies in West Africa*. London: Routledge.

Feder, G., and R. Noronha. 1987. "Land rights systems and agricultural development in Sub-Saharan Africa." *World Bank Research Observer*, no. 2: 143–69.

Ferguson, J. 1990. *The Anti-Politics Machine: "Development," Depoliticization and Bureaucratic Power in Lesotho*. Minneapolis: University of Minnesota Press.

Ferguson, J. 1999. *Expectations of Modernity: Myths and Meanings of Urban Life on the Zambian Copperbelt*. Berkeley: University of California Press.

Ferguson, P., and I. Wilks. 1970. "Chiefs, constitutions and the British in northern Ghana." In M. Crowder and O. Ikime (eds.), *West African Chiefs: Their Changing Status under Colonial Rule and Independence*. New York and Ile Ife: Africana Publishing Corporation and University of Ife Press. Pp. 326–69.

Firmin-Sellers, K. 1996. *The Transformation of Property Rights in the Gold Coast*. Cambridge: Cambridge University Press.

Firmin-Selers, K. 2000. "Custom, capitalism, and the state. The origins of insecure land tenure in West Africa." *Journal of Theoretical and Institutional Economics* 156: 513–30.

Fisiy, C. 1992. "Power and privilege in the administration of law – land law reform and social differentiation in Cameroon." Ph.D. dissertation, African Studies Centre, Leiden.

Fitzpatrick, D. 2005. "'Best Practice' options for the legal recognition of customary tenure." *Development and Change* 36, no. 3: 449–75.

Fitzpatrick, D. 2006. "Evolution and chaos in property rights systems. The Third World tragedy of contested access." *Yale Law Journal* 115, no. 5: 996–1048.

Forestry Commission. 2001. *Report on Forest Management Options and Constraints in the Three Northern Regions.* Accra: Forestry Commission.

Forestry Department. 1947. *Minutes and Resolutions of the North Mamprusi Forestry Conference, 12–14 November 1947, Navrongo.* Tamale: Public Records Administration and Archives Department (PRAAD).

Forestry Department. 1951. *Statement Presented to the British Commonwealth Forestry Conference in Canada, 1952.* Accra: Government Printer.

Forestry Department. 1957. *Ghana Forest Policy with Details of Execution up to 1957.* Accra: Government Printer.

Forestry Department. 1997. *Rates for Non-Timber Forest Produce. Chief Conservator of Forests Ref: G.222.V.2/113.* Accra: Forestry Department.

Forest Services Division. 1998. *Manual of Procedures: Forest Resource Management Planning in the HFZ; Section A: Strategic Planning.* Accra: Forest Services Division.

Fortes, M. 1936. "Culture contact as a dynamic process. An investigation in the Northern Territories of the Gold Coast." *Africa* 9, no. 1: 24–55.

Fortes, M. 1940. "The political system of the Tallensi of the Northern Territories of the Gold Coast." In M. Fortes and E. E. Evans-Pritchard (eds.), *African Political Systems.* London: International African Institute and Oxford University Press. Pp. 238–71.

Fortes, M. 1945. *The Dynamics of the Clanship among the Tallensi: Being the First Part of an Analysis of the Social Structure of the Trans-Volta Tribe.* London: International African Institute and Oxford University Press.

Fortmann, L. 1995. "Talking claims. Discursive strategies in contesting property." *World Development* 23, no. 6: 1053–63.

Geisler, C. 2000. "Property pluralism." In C. Geisler and G. Daneker (eds.), *Property and Values: Alternatives to Public and Private Ownership.* Washington, D.C.: Island Press. Pp. 65–86.

Gilbert, M. 1994. "Aesthetic strategies. The politics of a royal ritual." *Africa* 64, no. 1: 99–125.

Gluckman, M. 1958. *Analysis of a Social Situation in Modern Zululand.* Manchester: Rhodes-Livingstone Institute and Manchester University Press.

Gluckman, M. 1961. "Ethnographic data in British social anthropology." *Sociological Review* 9, no. 1: 5–17.

Gluckman, M. 1968 [1943]. *Essays on Lozi Land and Royal Property.* Manchester: Rhodes-Livingstone Institute and Manchester University Press.

Gluckman, M. 1973. "Limitations of the case method in the study of tribal law." *Law & Society Review* 7, no. 4: 611–41.

Gold Coast Colony. 1902. *Northern Territories Order in Council. Gold Coast Gazette, 1 January 1902.* Accra: National Archives of Ghana.

Gold Coast Colony. 1928. *Forest Settlement: A Summary of Principles of Forest Law in Their Application to Settlement Procedure. M.P. 15497/27.* Accra: Government Printer.

Gold Coast Colony. 1933. *Statement Presented to the Empire Forestry Conference 1933.* Accra: Government Printer.

Gold Coast Colony. 1951. *Local Government Ordinance* (no. 29). Accra: Government Printer.

Goody, J. 1980. "Rice-burning and the green revolution in northern Ghana." *Journal of Development Studies* 16, no. 2: 136–55.

Gough, K., and P. W. K. Yankson. 2000. "Land markets in African cities: The case of peri-urban Accra, Ghana." *Urban Studies* 37, no. 13: 2485–2500.

Government of Ghana. 1962a. *Administration of Lands Act*, 1962 (Act 123).

Government of Ghana. 1962b. *State Lands Act*, 1962 (Act 125).

Government of Ghana. 1966. *Chieftaincy (Amendment) Decree 1966* (NLCD 112).

Government of Ghana. 1974. *Forest Protection Decree* (NRCD 243).

Government of Ghana. 1978. "Report of the Committee on Ownership of Lands and Position of Tenants in the Northern and Upper Regions" (Committee chaired by R. I. Alhassan).

Government of Ghana. 1983a. *Control of Bushfires Law* (PNDCL 46).

Government of Ghana. 1983b. *Chieftaincy (Restoration of Status of Chiefs) Law, 1983* (PNDCL 75).

Government of Ghana. 1984a. *Prohibited Organisations (Bawku District) Law, 1984* (PNDCL 98).

Government of Ghana. 1984b. *Bawku Lands (Vesting) Law, 1984* (PNDCL 99).

Government of Ghana. 1985. "Report of the Committee to Investigate the Bawku Lands Dispute 1984" (Committee chaired by G. Minyilla).

Government of Ghana. 1986a. *Forest Protection (Amendment) Law* (PNDCL 142).

Government of Ghana. 1986b. *Land Title Registration Law, 1986* (PNDCL 152).

Government of Ghana. 1988. *Local Government Law, 1988* (PNDCL 207).

Government of Ghana. 1990. *Control and Prevention of Bushfires Law* (PNDCL 229).

Government of Ghana. 1994. *Forest and Wildlife Policy*. Accra: Ministry of Lands and Forestry.

Greenwood, A. F. 1962. "Ten years of Local Government in Ghana." *Journal of Local Administration Overseas* 1, no. 1: 23–28.

Grindle, M. S. 1997. "Divergent cultures? When public organisations perform well in developing countries." *World Development* 25, no. 4: 481–95.

Hailey, W. M. 1938. *An African Survey: A Study of Problems Arising in Africa South of the Sahara*. Oxford: Oxford University Press.

Hailey, W. M. 1951. *Native Administration in the British African Territories, Part III, West Africa: Nigeria, Gold Coast, Sierra Leone, Gambia*. London: HMSO.

Hansen, E., and P. Collins. 1980. "The army, the state and the 'Rawlings Revolution' in Ghana." *African Affairs* 79, no. 314: 3–23.

Hansen, T. B., and F. Stepputat. 2001. "States of imagination. Introduction." In T. Blom Hansen and F. Stepputat (eds.), *States of Imagination: Ethnographic Explorations of the Post-colonial State*. Durham: Duke University Press. Pp. 1–38.

Harris, D. 1983. "Central power and local reform: Ghana during the 1970s." In P. Mawhood (ed.), *Local Government in the Third World*. Chichester: John Wiley & Sons. Pp. 201–23.

Harvey, W. B. 1966. *Law and Social Change in Ghana*. Princeton: Princeton University Press.

Hawkins, S. 2002. *Writing and Colonialism in Northern Ghana: The Encounter between the LoDagaa and the "World on Paper."* Toronto: University of Toronto Press.

Hayford, J. C. 1913. *The Truth about the West African Land Question*. London: C. M. Philips.

Haynes, J. 1991. "The PNDC and political decentralisation in Ghana, 1981–91." *Journal of Commonwealth and Comparative Politics* 29, no. 3: 283–307.

Hecht, D., and M. Simone. 1994. *Invisible Governance: The Art of African Micropolitics*. New York: Autonomedia.

Hunter, J. M. 1966. "River blindness in Nangodi, northern Ghana. A hypothesis of cyclical advance and retreat." *Geographical Review* 56: 389–416.

Juul, K., and C. Lund (eds.). 2002. *Negotiating Property in Africa*. Portsmouth: Heinemann.

Kasanga, K. 1988. *Land Tenure and the Development Dialogue: The Myth Concerning Communal Landholding in Ghana*. Cambridge: Department of Land Economy, University of Cambridge, and Granta Editions.

Kasanga, K. 1992. *Agricultural Land Administration and Social Differentiation: A Case Study of the Tono, Vea, and Fumbisi Belts of North-Eastern Ghana*. Working Paper no. 10. New York: Joint Committee on African Studies, Social Science Research Council, and American Council of Learned Societies.

Kasanga, K. 1996. *The Role of Chiefs in Land Administration in Northern Ghana*. London: Royal Institution of Chartered Surveyors ("Our Common Estate" – Programme).

Kasanga, K., and N. A. Kotey. 2001. *Land Management in Ghana: Building on Tradition and Modernity*. London: International Institute for Environment and Development.

Kintz, D. 1990. "L'amant blessé ou une discussion peule sur le pluralisme juridique." *Politique Africaine*, no. 40: 42–50.

Konings, P. 1986. *The State and Rural Class Formation in Ghana: A Comparative Analyses*. London: Routledge/Kegan Paul.

Kotey, N. A., F. François, J. G. K. Owusu, R. Yeboah, K. Amanor, and L. Antiwi. 1998. *Falling into Place: Policy That Works for Forests and People*. Ghana Country Study No. 4. London: International Institute for Environment and Development.

Kunbuor, B. 1996. "Decentralisation and land administration in northern Ghana – a legal perspective." In Konrad Adenauer Foundation, *Decentralisation, Land Tenure and Land Administration in Northern Ghana*. Report on a seminar held at Bolgatanga, Accra, 28–30 May. Pp. 83–91.

Ladouceur, P. A. 1979. *Chiefs and Politicians: The Politics of Regionalism in Northern Ghana*. London: Longman.

Lemarchand, R. 1992. "Uncivil states and civil societies. How illusion became reality." *Journal of Modern African Studies* 30, no. 2: 177–91.

Le Meur, P.-Y. 2002. "Trajectories for the politicisation of land issues. Case studies from Benin." In K. Juul and C. Lund (eds.), *Negotiating Property in Africa*. Portsmouth: Heinemann. Pp. 135–56.

Lentz, C. 1995. "'Unity for development.' Youth associations in North-Western Ghana." *Africa* 65, no. 3: 395–429.

Lentz, C. 1998a. *Die Konstrucktion von Ethnizität. Eine Politische Geschichte Nord-West Ghanas, 1870–1990*. Cologne: Köppe Verlag.

Lentz, C. 1998b. "The chief, the mine captain and the politician: Legitimating power in northern Ghana." *Africa* 68, no. 1: 46–65.

Lentz, C. 1999. "Colonial ethnography and political reform. The works of A. C. Duncan-Johnstone, R. S. Rattray, J. Eyre-Smith and J. Guiness on northern Ghana." *Ghana Studies*, no. 2: 119–69.

Lentz, C. 2000a. "Contested identities: The history of ethnicity in Northwestern Ghana." In C. Lentz and P. Nugent (eds.), *Ethnicity in Ghana: The Limits of Invention*. London: Macmillan Press. Pp. 137–61.

Lentz, C. 2000b. "Of hunters, goats and earth-shrines: Settlement histories and the politics of oral tradition in northern Ghana." *History in Africa* 27: 193–214.

Lentz, C. 2001. "Local culture in the national arena: The politics of cultural festivals in Ghana." *African Studies Review* 44, no. 3: 47–72.

Lentz, C. 2002. "'The time when politics came': Ghana's decolonisation from the perspective of a rural periphery." *Journal of Contemporary African Studies* 20, no. 2: 245–74.

Lentz, C. 2006a. *Ethnicity and the Making of History in Northern Ghana*. Edinburgh: Edinburgh University Press.

Lentz, C. 2006b. "Decentralization, the state and conflicts over local boundaries in northern Ghana." *Development and Change* 37, no. 4: 901–19.

Lentz, C. 2006c. "Land rights and the politics of belonging in Africa." In R. Kuba and C. Lentz (eds.), *Land and the Politics of Belonging in West Africa*. Leiden: Brill. Pp. 1–34.

Lentz, C., and P. Nugent. 2000. "Ethnicity in Ghana: A comparative perspective." In C. Lentz and P. Nugent (eds.), *Ethnicity in Ghana: The Limits of Invention*. London: Macmillan Press. Pp. 1–28.

Le Roy, É. 1985. "La loi sur le domaine national a vingt ans: Joyeux anniversaire?" *Monde en Développement* 13, no. 52: 667–85.

Le Roy, É., A. Karsenty, and A. Bertrand. 1995. *La sécurisation foncière en Afrique. Pour une gestion viable des ressources renouvellables*. Paris: Karthala.

Lugard, Lord. 1965 [1929]. *The Dual Mandate in British Tropical Africa*. London: Frank Cass.

Lund, C. 1998. *Law, Power and Politics in Niger – Land Struggles and the Rural Code*. Hamburg: LIT Verlag.

Lund, C. 2002. "Negotiating property institutions. On the symbiosis of property and authority in Africa." In K. Juul and C. Lund (eds.), *Negotiating Property in Africa*. Portsmouth: Heinemann. Pp. 11–44.

Lund, C. 2003. "'Bawku is still volatile!': Ethno-political conflict and state recognition in northern Ghana." *Journal of Modern African Studies* 41, no. 4: 587–610.

Lund, C. 2006. "Twilight institutions. Public authority and local politics in Africa." *Development and Change* 37, no. 4: 685–705.

MacPherson, C. B. 1978. *Property – Mainstream and Critical Positions*. Oxford: Basil Blackwell.

Mamdani, M. 1996. *Citizen and Subject: Contemporary Africa and the Legacy of Late Colonialism*. London: James Currey.

Mann, K., and R. Roberts. 1991. "Law in colonial Africa." In Kristin Mann and Richard Roberts (eds.), *Law in Colonial Africa*. Portsmouth and London: Heinemann and James Currey. Pp. 3–58.

Manoukian, M. 1952. *Tribes of the Northern Territories of the Gold Coast*. London: International African Institute.

Marshall, R. C. 1945. *Forestry in the Northern Territories of the Gold Coast*. Accra: Gold Coast Colony Government Printing Department.

Mbembe, A. 2001. *On the Postcolony*. Berkeley: University of California Press.

McCaskie, T. C. 2000. *Asante Identitie: History and Modernity in an African Village, 1850–1950*. Edinburgh and Bloomington: Edinburgh University Press and Indiana University Press.

McLeod, N. C. 1922. "Report on a tour of inspection in the Northern Territories." In *General Tour and Inspection Reports by Local Officers on the Northern Territories. Case No. 01611*. Kumasi: Gold Coast Colony Forest Department.

Meek, C. K. 1946. *Land Law and Custom in the Colonies*. London: Oxford University Press.

Metcalfe, G. E. 1994. *Great Britain and Ghana: Documents of History, 1807–1957*. London: S Gregg Revivals.

Mettle, M. A. 1972. "Compulsory acquisition of land." *Review of Ghana Law* 4: 129–37.

Mitchell, J. C. 1983. "Case and situation analysis." *Sociological Review* 31, no. 2: 187–211.

Mitchell, J. C. 1987. *Cities, Society, and Social Perception – a Central African Perspective*. Oxford: Clarendon Press.

Mitchell, T. 1991. "The limits of the state: Beyond statist approaches and their critics." *American Political Science Review* 85, no. 1: 77–96.

Mitchell, T. 2005. "The property of markets. Informal housing and capitalism's mystery." *Cultural and Political Economy Working Paper Series* no. 2. Institute for Advanced Studies in Social and Management Sciences, University of Lancaster.

Moor, H. W. 1935. "Preliminary report on the forest requirements of the Northern Territories." In *General Tour and Inspection Reports by Local Officers on the Northern Territories. Case No. 01611*. Kumasi: Gold Coast Colony Forest Department.

Moore, S. F. 1978. *Law as Process*. London: Routledge & Kegan Paul.

Moore, S. F. 1986. *Social Facts and Fabrications – "Customary" Law on Kilimanjaro, 1880–1980*. Cambridge: Cambridge University Press.

Moore, S. F. 1992. "Treating law as knowledge. Telling colonial officers what to say to Africans about running 'their own' native courts." *Law & Society Review* 26, no. 1: 11–46.

Moore, S. F. 1994. "The ethnography of the present and the analysis of process." In R. Borofsky (ed.), *Assessing Cultural Anthropology*. New York: McGraw Hill. Pp. 362–74.

Moore, S. F. 1998. "Changing African land tenure. Reflections on the incapacities of the state." *European Journal of Development Research* 10, no. 2: 33–49.

Moore, S. F. 2001. "Certainties undone. Fifty turbulent years of legal anthropology, 1949–1999." *Journal of the Royal Anthropological Institute* 7: 95–116.

Mortimore, M. 1999. "History and evolution of land tenure and administration in West Africa." *IIED Issue Paper* no. 71. London: International Institute for Environment and Development.

Mosse, D. 1997. "The symbolic making of a common property resource. History, ecology and locality in a tank-irrigated landscape in South India." *Development and Change* 28, no. 3: 467–504.

Mosse, D. 2004. "Is good policy unimplementable? Reflections on the ethnography of aid policy and practice." *Development and Change* 35, no. 4: 639–71.

Ninsin, K. 1989. "The land question since the 1950s." In E. Hansen and K. Ninsin (eds.), *The State, Development and Politics in Ghana*. London: CODESRIA. Pp. 165–83.

Nugent, P. 1995. *Big Men, Small Boys and Politics in Ghana: Power, Ideology and the Burden of History, 1982–1994*. London: Pinter.

Nugent, P. 2001. "Winners, losers and also rans: Money, moral authority and voting patterns in the Ghana 2000 elections." *African Affairs* no. 100: 405–28.

Nyari, B. S. 1995. "Interface of the traditional and the modern land tenure systems in the urban land market and its effects on the urban development process: a study of the land reform process in Ghana." Master's thesis, ISS, The Hague.

Nyari, B. S. 2002. "Colonial land policy in northern Ghana: Its shortcomings and influences on the current national land policy." Paper presented at the National Workshop organized by LandNet Ghana, Bolgatanga, 13–15 March.

Olivier de Sardan, J.-P. 1999a. "L'Éspace public introuvable. Chefs et projets dans les villages nigériens." *Revue Tiers Monde* 40, no. 157: 139–67.

Olivier de Sardan, J.-P. 1999b. "A moral economy of corruption in Africa?" *Journal of Modern African Studies* 37, no. 1: 25–52.

Olivier de Sardan, J.-P. 2005. *Anthropology and Development: Understanding Contemporary Social Change*. London: Zed Books.

Onibon, A. 2000. "From participation to 'responsibleness.'" *Forests, Trees and People*, no. 42: 4–10.

Osborn, P. G. 1964. *A Concise Law Dictionary*. 5th ed. London: Sweet & Maxwell.

Ostrom, E. 1990. *Governing the Commons – the Evolution of Institutions for Collective Action*. Cambridge: Cambridge University Press.

Peel, J. D. Y. 1983. *Ijeshas and Nigerians: The Incorporation of a Yourouba Kingdom, 1890s–1970s*. Cambridge: Cambridge University Press.

Peters, P. 1994. *Dividing the Commons: Politics, Policy and Culture in Botswana*. Charlottesville: University Press of Virginia.

Peters, P. 2002. "The limits of negotiability: security, equity and class formation in Africa's land systems." In K. Juuland and C. Lund (eds.), *Negotiating Property in Africa*. Portsmouth: Heinemann. Pp. 45–66

Peters, P. 2004. "Inequality and social conflict over land in Africa." *Journal of Agrarian Change* 4, no. 3: 269–314.

Platteau, J.-P. 1996. "The evolutionary theory of land rights as applied to Sub-Saharan Africa: A critical assessment." *Development and Change* 27: 29–86.

Pogucki, R. J. H. 1951. *Report on Land Tenure in Native Customary Law of the Protectorate of the Northern Territories of the Gold Coast.* Part II. Accra: Lands Department.

Pogucki, R. J. H. 1955. *Gold Coast and Land Tenure.* Vol. 1, *A Survey of Land Tenure in Customary Law of the Protectorate of the Northern Territories.* Accra: Lands Department.

Pratten, D., and C. Gore. 2002. "The Politics of Plunder. The Rhetorics of Order and Disorder in Southern Nigeria." *African Affairs* 102: 211–40.

Ramsay, J. M. 1957. "Land planning in the Northern Territories." *Gold Coast Teacher's Journal* 29: 20–26.

Rathbone, R. 2000. *Nkrumah and the Chiefs: The Politics of Chieftaincy in Ghana, 1951–60.* Accra, Athens (Ohio), and Oxford: Reimmer, Ohio University Press, and James Currey.

Rattray, R. S. 1932. *The Tribes of the Ashanti Hinterland.* 2 vols. Oxford: Clarendon Press.

Ray, D. 1996. "Divided sovereignty. Traditional authority and the state in Ghana." *Journal of Legal Pluralism,* nos. 37–38: 181–202.

Ray, D. 1999. "Chief-state relations in Ghana. Divided sovereignty and legitimacy." In E. A. B. van Rouveroy van Nieuwaal and W. Zips (eds.), *Sovereignty, Legitimacy, and Power in West African Societies: Perspectives from Legal Anthropology.* Hamburg: LIT Verlag. Pp. 48–69.

Republic of Ghana. 1979. *Constitution of the Republic of Ghana, 1979.* Tema: Ghana Publishing Corporation.

Republic of Ghana. 1992. *Constitution of the Republic of Ghana, 1992.* Tema: Ghana Publishing Corporation.

Ribot, J. C. 1995. "From exclusion to participation. Turning Senegal's forestry policy around?" *World Development* 23, no. 9: 1587–99.

Ribot, J. C. 1999. "Decentralisation, participation and accountability in Sahelian forestry: Legal instruments of political-administrative control." *Africa* 69, no. 1: 23–65.

Ribot, J. C. 2001. *Science, Use Rights, and Exclusion: A History of Forestry in Francophone West Africa.* Issue paper no. 104. London: Drylands Programme, International Institute for Environment and Development.

Ribot, J. C., A. Agrawal, and A. M. Larson. 2006. "Recentralizing while decentralizing. How national governments reappropriate forest resources." *World Development* 34, no. 11: 1864–86.

Rocha, B. J., and C. H. K. Lodoh. 1995. *Ghana Land Law and Conveyancing.* Accra: Anaseem Publications.

Roe, E. 1999. *Except Africa: Remaking Development, Rethinking Power.* New Brunswick: Transaction Publishers.

Roncoli, M. C. 1994. "Managing on the margins: Agricultural production and household reproduction in northeastern Ghana." Ph.D. dissertation, State University of New York, Binghamton.

Rose, C. 1994. *Property and Persuasion – Essays on the History, Theory and Rhetoric of Ownership.* Boulder: Westview.

Rose, C. 1998. "Canons of property talk; or, Blackstone's anxiety." *Yale Law Journal* 108, no. 3: 601–32.

Rothchild, D. 1991. "Ghana and structural adjustment: An overview." In D. Rothchild (ed.), *Ghana: The Political Economy of Recovery.* Boulder Lynne Rienner Publishers. Pp. 3–17.

Rural Forestry Division. 1992. *A Guide to the Management of Savanna Forest Reserves in the Upper-East Region.* Accra: Rural Forestry Division, Forestry Department.

Saaka, Y. 1978. *Local Government and Political Change in Northern Ghana.* Washington, D.C.: University Press of America.

Saaka, Y. (ed.). 2001. *Regionalism and Public Policy in Northern Ghana*. New York: Peter Lang.

Sack, R. D. 1986. *Human Territoriality: Its Theory and History*. Cambridge: Cambridge University Press.

Saul, M. 1993. "Land custom in Bare. Agnatic cooperation and rural capitalism in Western Burkina." In T. Basset and D. Crummey (eds.), *Land in African Agrarian Systems*. Madison: University of Wisconsin Press. Pp. 75–100.

Schlotner, M. 2000. "'We stay, others come and go.' Identity among the Mamprusi in northern Ghana." In C. Lentz and P. Nugent (eds.), *Ethnicity in Ghana: The Limits of Invention*. London: Macmillan Press. Pp. 49–67.

Scott, J. C. 1985. *Weapons of the Weak: Everyday Forms of Peasant Resistance*. New Haven: Yale University Press.

Scott, J. C. 1998. *Seeing Like a State: How Certain Schemes to Improve the Human Condition Have Failed*. New Haven: Yale University Press.

Shepherd, A. 1981. "Agrarian change in northern Ghana: Public investment, capitalist farming and famine." In J. Heyer, P. Roberts, and G. Williams (eds.), *Rural Development in Tropical Africa*. London: Macmillan. Pp. 168–92.

Shipton, P. 1989. *How Private Property Emerges in Africa – Directed and Undirected Land Tenure Reforms in Densely Settled Areas South of the Sahara*. Boston: Harvard University (HIID and Dept. of Anthropology).

Shipton, P. 1994. "Land and culture in tropical Africa. Soils, symbols, and the metaphysics of the mundane." *Annual Review of Anthropology* 23: 347–77.

Shipton, P., and M. Goheen. 1992. "Understanding African land-holding. Power, wealth, and meaning." *Africa* 63, no. 3: 307–25.

Simpson, S. R. 1954. "Land tenure: Some explanations and definitions." *Journal of African Administration*, no. 6: 50–64.

Skalník, P. 2002. "The state and local ethno-political identities: The case of community conflicts in northern Ghana." *Nouveaux Mondes* 10: 141–66.

Spear, T. 2003. "Neo-traditionalism and the limits of invention in British Colonial Africa." *Journal of African History* 44: 3–27.

Staniland, M. 1975. *The Lions of Dagbon: Political Change in Northern Ghana*. Cambridge: Cambridge University Press.

Steinmetz, G. 1999. "Culture and the state." In G. Steinmetz (ed.), *State/Culture: State Formation after the Cultural Turn*. Durham: Duke University Press. Pp. 1–49.

Stopford, J. G. B. 1903. "English governor and African chiefs." *Journal of the Royal African Society* 2, no. 7: 308–11.

Swartz, M. J. 1968. Introduction to M. J. Swartz (ed.), *Local-Level Politics*. Chicago: Aldine. Pp. 1–46.

Tait, D. 1952. Review of *Land Tenure in Native Customary Law of the Protectorate of the Northern Territories of the Gold Coast*, by J. H. Pogucki. *Africa* 22, no. 4: 380–82.

Temple, L., and P. Moustier. 2003. "L'Agriculture périurbaine en Afrique tropical. Caractéristiques, functions, contraintes et opportunités à partir des études de cas." In S. Lund, K. Juul, C. Lund, and R. Harpøth (eds.), *Proceedings of the 15th Danish Sahel Workshop*. SEREIN Occasional Papers no. 15. Pp. 39–59.

Thomas, R. 1983. "The 1916 Bongo 'riots' and their background. Aspects of colonial administration and African response in Eastern Upper Ghana." *Journal of African History* 24: 57–75.

Thompson, E. P. 1975. *Whigs and Hunters*. New York: Pantheon Books.

Thompson, E. P. 1991. *Customs in Common*. New York: New Press.

Tilley, H. 2003. "African Environments and Environmental Sciences." In W. Beinart and J. McGregor (eds.), *Social History and African Environments*. Oxford: James Currey. Pp. 109–30.

Tilly, C. 1985. "War making and state making as organized crime." In P. Evans, D. Rueschemeyer, and T. Skocpol (eds.), *Bringing the State Back In*. Cambridge: Cambridge University Press. Pp. 169–91.

Toulmin, C., and J. Quan. 2000. *Evolving Land Rights, Policy and Tenure in Africa*. London: IIED/Natural Resources Institute.

van der Linde, A., and R. Naylor. 1999. *Building Sustainable Peace: Conflict, Conciliation, and Civil Society in Northern Ghana*. Oxfam Working Papers. Oxford: Oxfam.

van Rouveroy van Nieurwaal, E. A. B. 1999. "Chieftaincy in Africa: Three facets of a hybrid role." In E. A. B van Rouveroy van Nieurwaal and R. van Dijk (eds.), *African Chieftaincy in a New Socio-Political Landscape*. Hamburg: LIT Verlag. Pp. 21–48.

van Velsen, J. 1967. "The extended-case method and situational analysis." In A. L. Epstein (ed.), *The Craft of Social Anthropology*. London: Tavistock Publications. Pp. 129–49.

Vigne, C. 1935. "Forestry problems in the Northern Territories." In *General Tour and Inspection Reports by Local Officers on the Northern Territories. Case No. 01611*. Kumasi: Gold Coast Colony Forest Department. Vol. 26, nos. 1–2: 13–31; vol. 31, no. 2: 187–211.

von Benda-Beckmann, F. 2003. "Mysteries of capital or mystifications of legal property?" *Focaal*, no. 41: 187–91.

von Benda-Beckmann, F., K. von Benda-Beckmann, and M. Wiber (eds.). 2006. *Changing Properties of Property*. Oxford: Berghan Books.

von Benda-Beckmann, K. 1981. "Forum shopping and shopping forums, dispute processing in a Minangkabau village in West Sumatra." *Journal of Legal Pluralism*, no. 19: 117–62.

Walker, P., and P. Peters. 2001. "Maps, metaphors, and meanings: Boundary struggles and village forest use on private and state land in Malawi." *Society and Natural Resources*, no. 14: 411–24.

Wardell, D. A. 2002. "Historical review of the development of forest policy in the Northern Territories of the Gold Coast Colony 1901–1957." In A. Reenberg (ed.), *SEREIN Working Paper 41: 2002*. Copenhagen: Institute of Geography, University of Copenhagen. Pp. 102–61.

Wardell, D. A., and C. Lund. 2006. "Governing access to forests in northern Ghana. Micropolitics and the rent on non-enforcement." *World Development* 34, no. 11: 1887–1906.

Wardell, D. A., A. Reenberg, and C. Tøttrup. 2003. "Historical footprints in contemporary land use systems: Forest cover changes in savanna woodland in the Sudano-Sahelian zone." *Global Environmental Change*, no. 13: 235–54.

Webber, P. 1996. "Agrarian change in Kusasi, north east Ghana." *Africa* 66, no. 3: 437–57.

Whitfield, L. 2003. "Civil society as an idea and civil society as process. The case of Ghana." *Oxford Development Studies* 31, no. 3: 379–400.

Wolf, E. 1990. "Facing power; old insights, new questions." *American Anthropologist* 92, no. 3: 586–96.

Woodman, G. R. 1996. *Customary Land Law in Ghanaian Courts*. Accra: Ghana University Press.

Worby, E. 1998. "Tyranny, parody, and ethnic polarity: Ritual engagements with the state in Northwestern Zimbabwe." *Journal of Southern African Studies* 24, no. 3: 561–78.

World Bank. 1974. *Land Reform*. Washington, D.C.: World Bank.

World Bank. 1988. *Ghana Forest Resource Management Project. Staff Appraisal Report No. 7295-GH*. Washington, D.C.: Africa Department, Agriculture Operations Division, World Bank.

World Bank. 1996. *Towards Environmentally Sustainable Development*. Washington D.C.: World Bank.

World Bank. 2001. *Ghana Northern Savannah Biodiversity Conservation Project. Project Appraisal Document. Report No. 21847-GH*. Washington, D.C.: Africa Regional Office, World Bank.

World Bank. 2003. *Land Policies for Growth and Poverty Reduction*. Washington, D.C.: World Bank.

Index

Made in the USA
Lexington, KY
23 July 2018